Fodor's

Nova Scotia, New Brunswick, Prince Edward Island

"When it comes to information on regional history, what to see and do, and shopping, these guides are exhaustive."

—*USAir Magazine*

"Usable, sophisticated restaurant coverage, with an emphasis on good value."
—Andy Birsh, *Gourmet Magazine* columnist

"Valuable because of their comprehensiveness."
—*Minneapolis Star-Tribune*

"Fodor's always delivers high quality...thoughtfully presented...thorough."

—*Houston Post*

"An excellent choice for those who want everything under one cover."

—*Washington Post*

Reprinted from Fodor's Canada.

Fodor's Travel Publications, Inc.
New York • Toronto • London • Sydney • Auckland

Fodor's Nova Scotia, New Brunswick, Prince Edward Island

Editor: Nancy van Itallie

Editorial Contributors: Steven K. Amsterdam, Robert Andrews, Susan Brown, Silver Don Cameron, Tracy Patruno, Linda K. Schmidt, Mary Ellen Schultz, M.T. Schwartzman (Gold Guide editor), Dinah Spritzer, Julie Watson, Ana Watts

Creative Director: Fabrizio La Rocca

Cartographer: David Lindroth

Cover Photograph: Bob Krist

Text Design: Between the Covers

Copyright

Copyright © 1995 by Fodor's Travel Publications, Inc.

Fodor's is a registered trademark of Fodor's Travel Publications, Inc.

All rights reserved under International and Pan-American Copyright Conventions. Published in the United States by Fodor's Travel Publications, Inc., a subsidiary of Random House, Inc., New York, and simultaneously in Canada by Random House of Canada Limited, Toronto. Distributed by Random House, Inc., New York.

No maps, illustrations, or other portions of this book may be reproduced in any form without written permission from the publishers.

Third Edition

ISBN 0–679–03056–5

Special Sales

Fodor's Travel Publications are available at special discounts for bulk purchases for sales promotions or premiums. Special editions, including personalized covers, excerpts of existing guides, and corporate imprints, can be created in large quantities for special needs. For more information, contact your local bookseller or write to Special Markets, Fodor's Travel Publications, 201 East 50th Street, New York, NY 10022. Inquiries from Canada should be directed to your local Canadian bookseller or sent to Random House of Canada, Ltd., Marketing Department, 1265 Aerowood Drive, Mississauga, Ontario L4W 1B9. Inquiries from the United Kingdom should be sent to Fodor's Travel Publications, 20 Vauxhall Bridge Road, London, England SW1V 2SA.

PRINTED IN THE UNITED STATES OF AMERICA

10 9 8 7 6 5 4 3 2 1

CONTENTS

ON THE ROAD WITH FODOR'S

A GOOD TRAVEL GUIDE is like a wonderful traveling companion. It's charming, it's brimming with sound recommendations and solid ideas, it pulls no punches in describing lodging and dining establishments, and it's consistently full of fascinating facts that make you view what you've traveled to see in a rich new light. In the creation of *Fodor's Nova Scotia, New Brunswick, Prince Edward Island,* we have gone to great lengths to provide you with the very best of all possible traveling companions—and to make your trip the best of all possible vacations.

About Our Writers

The information in these pages is a collaboration of a whole roster of extraordinary writers.

Novelist, playwright, and sailor **Silver Donald Cameron,** who wrote the chapter on Nova Scotia, is one of Canada's most versatile authors. His books *Wind, Whales and Whisky: A Cape Breton Voyage* and *Sun, Sand and Strawberries: An Acadian Voyage* record cruises with his wife and son in *Silversark,* a 27-foot sailboat, which they built themselves. Award-winning Fredericton columnist **Ana Watts** updated the chapter on her province, New Brunswick, and the one on Newfoundland and Labrador. Food and travel writer **Julie Watson,** who updated Nova Scotia and Prince Edward Island for this edition, lives on Prince Edward Island and tours the region researching articles and books such as her latest: *Ship Wrecks and Seafaring Tales* and *A Fine Catch Seafood Cookbook.*

We'd also like to thank the Canadian Consulate General office in New York; the Nova Scotia Department of Tourism; the New Brunswick Department of Tourism; Carol Horne of Enterprise Prince Edward Island; and the Government of Newfoundland and Labrador Department of Development.

What's New

A New Design

If this is not the first Fodor's guide you've purchased, you'll immediately notice our new look. More readable and easier to use than ever? We think so—and we hope you do, too.

Travel Updates

Just before your trip, you may want to order a Fodor's Worldview Travel Update. From local publications all over Nova Scotia, New Brunswick, Prince Edward Island, and Newfoundland, the lively, cosmopolitan editors at Worldview gather information on concerts, plays, opera, dance performances, gallery and museum shows, sports competitions, and other special events that coincide with your visit. See the order blank at the back of this book, call 800/799–9609, or fax 800/799–9619.

And in the Maritime Provinces

NEW BRUNSWICK➤ About 11 miles west of Fredericton, the Malicete Indian Band has built the modern Best Western **Mactaquac Inn** with government assistance as compensation for surrender of traditional salmon net-fishing rights. New Brunswick's recently introduced Scenic Drives are well marked and take you to the heart of the province. Use maps available at tourist information centers to find the **Discovery By-Way** network.

PRINCE EDWARD ISLAND➤ Travelers coming to PEI aboard the Borden–New Brunswick Ferry can see the Island's newest attraction: the construction of the longest continuous multi-span bridge in the world, linking the Island with New Brunswick.

NEWFOUNDLAND AND LABRADOR➤ Newfoundland and Labrador continue to prepare for 1997's year-long celebration with festivals and arts events marking the 500th anniversary of John Cabot's voyage from England that launched the European exploration and settlement of North America.

How To Use This Book

Organization

Up front is the **Gold Guide,** comprising two sections on gold paper that are chock-full of information about traveling within your destination and traveling in general. Both are in alphabetical order by topic.

Important Contacts A to Z gives addresses and telephone numbers of organizations and companies that offer destination-related services and detailed information or publications. Here's where you'll find information about how to get to Eastern Canada from wherever you are. **Smart Travel Tips A to Z,** the Gold Guide's second section, gives specific tips on how to get the most out of your travels, as well as information on how to accomplish what you need to in the area. Here you'll also find suggestions for pretrip reading, both fiction and nonfiction to get you in the mood for your travels.

Each chapter covers exploring, shopping, sports, dining, lodging, and arts and nightlife, and ends with a section called Essentials, which tells you how to get there and get around and gives you important local addresses and telephone numbers.

Stars

Stars in the margin are used to denote highly recommended sights, attractions, hotels, and restaurants.

Currency

Throughout this guide, unless otherwise stated, prices are quoted in Canadian dollars.

Restaurant and Hotel Criteria and Price Categories

Restaurants and lodging places are chosen with a view to giving you the cream of the crop in each location and in each price range. In all restaurant price charts, costs are per person, excluding drinks, tip, and tax. In hotel price charts, rates are for standard double rooms, excluding taxes.

Hotel Facilities

Note that in general you incur charges when you use many hotel facilities. We wanted to let you know what facilities a hotel has to offer, but we don't always specify whether or not there's a charge, so when you're planning a vacation that entails a stay of several days, it's wise to ask what's included in the rate.

Hotel Meal Plans

Assume that hotels operate on the **European Plan** (EP, with no meals) unless we note that they use the **American Plan** (AP, with all meals), the **Modified American Plan** (MAP, with breakfast and dinner daily), or the **Continental Plan** (CP, with a Continental breakfast daily).

Dress Code in Restaurants

The **What to Wear** section at the beginning of individual chapters' dining sections tells you what's most common in that area. In general, we note a dress code only when men are required to wear a jacket or a jacket and tie.

Credit Cards

The following abbreviations are used: **AE,** American Express; **DC,** Diners Club; **MC,** MasterCard; and **V,** Visa. Discover is not accepted outside the United States.

Please Write to Us

Everyone who has contributed to *Fodor's Nova Scotia, New Brunswick, Prince Edward Island* has worked hard to make the text accurate. All prices and opening times are based on information supplied to us at press time, and Fodor's cannot accept responsibility for any errors that may have occurred. The passage of time will bring changes, so it's always a good idea to call ahead and confirm information when it matters—particularly if you're making a detour to visit specific sights or attractions. When making reservations at a hotel or inn, be sure to speak up if you have a disability or are traveling with children, if you prefer a private bath or a certain type of bed, or if you have specific dietary needs or any other concerns.

Were the restaurants we recommended as described? Did our hotel picks exceed your expectations? Did you find a museum we recommended a waste of time? We would love your feedback, positive and negative. If you have complaints, we'll look into them and revise our entries when the facts warrant it. If you've happened upon a special place that we haven't included, we'll pass the information along to the writers so they can check it out. So please send us a letter or postcard (we're at 201 East 50th Street, New York, New York 10022). We look forward to hearing from you. And in the meantime, have a wonderful trip!

Karen Cure

Karen Cure
Editorial Director

Canada

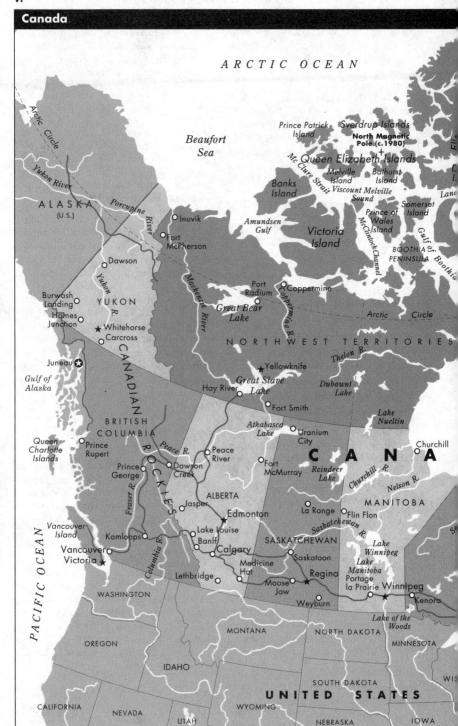

ARCTIC OCEAN

Beaufort
Sea

Prince Patrick
Island

Sverdrup Islands

**North Magnetic
Pole (c.1980)**
+

Mc Clure Strait Queen Elizabeth Islands

Melville
Island   Bathurst
Island

Banks
Island   Viscount Melville
Sound

Prince of
Wales
Island

Somerset
Island

McClintock Channel

BOOTHIA
PENINSULA

Gulf of Boothia

Arctic Circle

Yukon River

ALASKA
(U.S.)

Porcupine

Inuvik

Amundsen
Gulf

Victoria
Island

River

Fort
McPherson

Dawson

Port
Radium

Coppermine

Mackenzie River

Great Bear
Lake

Coppermine R.

Arctic   Circle

Burwash
Landing

YUKON

Yukon R.

Haines
Junction

★ Whitehorse
Carcross

Juneau ⊕

NORTHWEST TERRITORIES

Thelon R.

★ Yellowknife

Great Slave
Lake

Dubawnt
Lake

Lake
Nueltin

Gulf of
Alaska

CANADIAN

Hay River

Fort Smith

BRITISH
COLUMBIA

Athabasca
Lake   Uranium
City

C A N A

Churchill

Queen
Charlotte
Islands

Prince
Rupert

Peace R.

Fort
McMurray

Reindeer
Lake

Churchill R.

Nelson R.

ROCKIES

Prince
George

Dawson
Creek

Peace
River

Fraser R.

Jasper

ALBERTA

La Ronge   Flin Flon

MANITOBA

Vancouver
Island

Kamloops

Lake Louise
Banff

Edmonton

Saskatchewan R.

Lake
Winnipeg

Vancouver
Victoria ★

Columbia R.

Calgary

SASKATCHEWAN

Saskatoon

Lake
Manitoba

Portage
la Prairie

Winnipeg

Medicine
Hat

Regina ★

Lethbridge

Moose
Jaw

Weyburn

Kenora

WASHINGTON

Lake of the
Woods

PACIFIC OCEAN

MONTANA

NORTH DAKOTA

MINNESOTA

OREGON

IDAHO

SOUTH DAKOTA

WIS

CALIFORNIA

NEVADA

UTAH

WYOMING

UNITED   STATES

NEBRASKA

IOWA

VIII

World Time Zones

Numbers below vertical bands relate each zone to Greenwich Mean Time (0 hrs.).
Local times frequently differ from these general indications,
as indicated by light-face numbers on map.

Algiers, **29**
Anchorage, **3**
Athens, **41**
Auckland, **1**
Baghdad, **46**
Bangkok, **50**
Beijing, **54**

Berlin, **34**
Bogotá, **19**
Budapest, **37**
Buenos Aires, **24**
Caracas, **22**
Chicago, **9**
Copenhagen, **33**
Dallas, **10**

Delhi, **48**
Denver, **8**
Djakarta, **53**
Dublin, **26**
Edmonton, **7**
Hong Kong, **56**
Honolulu, **2**

Istanbul, **40**
Jerusalem, **42**
Johannesburg, **44**
Lima, **20**
Lisbon, **28**
London
(Greenwich), **27**
Los Angeles, **6**
Madrid, **38**
Manila, **57**

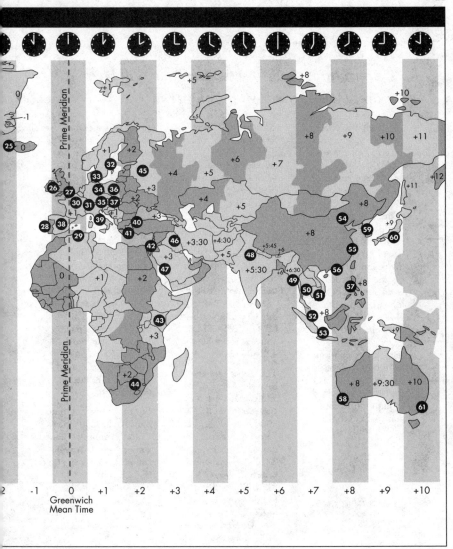

IMPORTANT CONTACTS A TO Z

An Alphabetical Listing of Publications, Organizations, and Companies That Will Help You Before, During, and After Your Trip

No single travel resource can give you every detail about every topic that might interest or concern you at the various stages of your journey—when you're planning your trip, while you're on the road, and after you get back home. The following organizations, books, and brochures will supplement the information in *Fodor's Nova Scotia, New Brunswick, Prince Edward Island.* For related information, including both basic tips on visiting Eastern Canada and background information on many of the topics below, study Smart Travel Tips A to Z, the section that follows Important Contacts A to Z.

A

AIR TRAVEL

The major international hubs to Canada are Montréal, Toronto, and Vancouver, but international flights also fly into Halifax, Ottawa, Calgary, and Edmonton. *See* individual chapters for specific airports in the maritime provinces.

Flying time to **Halifax, Nova Scotia** is 2 hours fron New York, 5¾ hours from Chicago, 7 hours from Los Angeles. To **Sydney, Nova Scotia:** 3½ hours from

New York, 7 hours from Chicago, 9 hours from Los Angeles. To **St. John's, Newfoundland:** 4½ hours from New York, 6½ hours from Chicago, 10 hours from Los Angeles.

CARRIERS

Carriers serving Canada include **American** (☎ 800/433–7300), **Continental** (☎ 800/525–0280), **Delta** (800/221–1212), **Northwest** (☎ 800/225–2525), and **USAir** (tel 800/428–4322).

The major carriers between Great Britain and Canada are **Air Canada** (☎ 800/776–3000 in the U.S., 0181/759–2636 in the London area, or 0345/222111 elsewhere), **British Airways** (☎ 0181/897–4000 in the London area or 0345/616767 in all other areas), and **Canadian Airlines International** (☎ 800/426–7000 in the U.S., 0181/577–7722 in the London area or 0345/616767 elsewhere). Air Canada has the most flights and serves, among other cities, St. John's from Heathrow and Halifax from Prestwick (Glasgow).

COMPLAINTS

To register complaints about charter and scheduled airlines, contact the U.S. Department of Transporta-

tion's **Office of Consumer Affairs** (400 7th St. NW, Washington, DC 20590, ☎ 202/366–2220 or 800/322–7873).

PUBLICATIONS

For general information about charter carriers, ask for the Office of Consumer Affairs' brochure **"Plane Talk: Public Charter Flights."** The Department of Transportation also publishes a 58-page booklet, **"Fly Rights"** ($1.75; Consumer Information Center, Dept. 133-B, Pueblo, CO 81009).

For other tips and hints, consult the Consumers Union's monthly **"Consumer Reports Travel Letter"** ($39 a year; Box 53629, Boulder CO 80322, ☎ 800/234–1970) and the newsletter **"Travel Smart"** ($37 a year; 40 Beechdale Rd., Dobbs Ferry, NY 10522, ☎ 800/327–3633); *The Official Frequent Flyer Guidebook,* by Randy Petersen ($14.99 plus $3 shipping; 4715-C Town Center Dr., Colorado Springs, CO 80916, ☎ 719/597–8899 or 800/487–8893); *Airfare Secrets Exposed,* by Sharon Tyler and Matthew Wonder (Universal Information Publishing; $16.95 plus $3.75 shipping from Sandcastle Publishing, Box 3070-A, South

Pasadena, CA 91031, ☎ 213/255–3616 or 800/655–0053); and *202 Tips Even the Best Business Travelers May Not Know,* by Christopher McGinnis ($10 plus $3.00 shipping; Irwin Professional Publishing, Box 52927, Atlanta, GA 30355, ☎ 708/789–4000 or 800/634–3966).

WITHIN CANADA

Air Canada (☎ 800/776–3000) operates in every province. The other major domestic carrier is **Canadian Airlines International** (☎ 800/426–7000). Regularly scheduled flights to every major city and to most smaller cities are available on Air Canada or Canadian Airlines International or the domestic carriers associated with them: **Air Atlantic** (☎ 902/427–5500) and **Air Nova** (☎ 902/429–7111) serve Atlantic Canada. These airlines can also be contacted at local numbers within each of the many cities they serve. Check with the regional tourist agencies for charter companies and with the District Controller of Air Services in the territorial (and provincial) capitals for the locations of air bases that allow private flights and for regulations.

B

BETTER BUSINESS BUREAU

For local contacts in the home town of a tour operator you may be considering, consult the **Council of Better Business Bureaus** (4200 Wilson Blvd., Arlington, VA 22203, ☎ 703/276–0100).

BUS TRAVEL

Greyhound (☎ 800/231–2222) has the most widespread bus service to Canada, and you can get from almost any point in the United States to any point in Canada on its extensive network.

WITHIN CANADA

The bus is an essential form of transportation in Canada, especially if you want to visit out-of-the-way towns that do not have airports or rail lines. Two major bus companies, **Greyhound** (222 1st Ave. SW, Calgary, AB, T2P 0A6, ☎ 403/265–9111) and **Voyageur** (505 E Boulevard Maisonneuve H2L 1Y4, Montréal, ☎ 514/843–4231), offer interprovincial service. In the United Kingdom, contact **Greyhound World Travel Ltd.,** Sussex House, London Road, E. Grinstead, West Surrey, RHI9 1LD (☎ 01342/317317).

C

CAR RENTAL

Major car-rental companies represented in Canada include **Avis** (☎ 800/331–1084, 800/879–2847 in Canada), **Budget** (☎ 800/527–0700, 0800/181–181 in the U.K.), and **Hertz** (☎ 800/654–3001, 800/263–0600 in Canada, 0181/679–1799 in the U.K.).

CAR TRAVEL FROM THE U.S.

The U.S. Interstate Highway System leads directly into eastern Canada: I–95 from Maine to New Brunswick.

CHILDREN AND TRAVEL

FLYING

Look into **"Flying With Baby"** ($5.95 plus $1 shipping; Third Street Press, Box 261250, Littleton, CO 80126, ☎ 303/595–5959), cowritten by a flight attendant. **"Kids and Teens in Flight,"** free from the U.S. Department of Transportation's Office of Consumer Affairs, offers tips for children flying alone. Every two years the February issue of *Family Travel Times* (*see* Know-How, *below*) details children's services on three dozen airlines.

KNOW-HOW

Family Travel Times, published 10 times a year by Travel With Your Children (TWYCH, 45 W. 18th St., New York, NY 10011, ☎ 212/206–0688; annual subscription $55), covers destinations, types of vacations, and modes of travel.

The *Family Travel Guides* catalogue ($1 postage; ☎ 510/527–5849) lists about 200 books and articles on family travel. *Traveling with Children—And Enjoying It,* by Arlene K. Butler ($11.95 plus $3 shipping; Globe Pequot Press, Box 833, 6 Business Park Rd., Old Saybrook, CT 06475, ☎ 203/395–0440 or 800/243–0495, 800/962–0973 in CT) helps plan your trip with children, from toddlers to teens. Also check *Take Your Baby and Go! A Guide for Traveling with Babies, Toddlers and Young Children,* by Sheri Andrews, Judy Bordeaux, and Vivian Vasquez ($5.95 plus $1.50 shipping; Bear Creek Publications, 2507 Minor Ave., Seattle, WA 98102, ☎ 206/322–7604 or 800/326–6566). Also from Globe Pequot are *Recommended Family Resorts in the United States, Canada, and the Caribbean,* by Jane Wilford with Janet Tice ($12.95), and *Recommended Family Inns of America* ($12.95).

CUSTOMS

U.S. CITIZENS

The **U.S. Customs Service** (Box 7407, Washington, DC 20044, ☎ 202/927–6724) can answer questions on duty-free limits and publishes a helpful brochure, "Know Before You Go." For information on registering foreign-made articles, call 202/927–0540.

U.K. CITIZENS

HM Customs and Excise (Dorset House, Stamford St., London SE1 9NG, ☎ 0171/202–4227) can answer questions about U.K. customs regulations and publishes "A Guide for Travellers," detailing standard procedures and import rules.

D
FOR TRAVELERS WITH DISABILITIES

COMPLAINTS

To register complaints under the provisions of the Americans with Disabilities Act, contact the U.S. Department of Justice's **Public Access Section** (Box 66738, Washington, D.C. 20035, ☎ 202/514–0301, TDD 202/514–0383, FAX 202/307–1198).

ORGANIZATIONS

The **Canadian Paraplegic Association National Office** (520 Sutherland Dr., Toronto, Ont., M4G 3U9, ☎ 416/422–5640) provides information about touring in Canada.

In the United Kingdom, contact the **Royal Association for Disability and Rehabilitation** (RADAR, 12 City Forum, 250 City Rd., London EC1V 8AF, ☎ 0171/250–3222) or **Mobility International** (Rue de Manchester 25, B–1070 Brussels, Belgium, ☎ 00–322–410–6297), an international clearinghouse of travel information for people with disabilities.

FOR TRAVELERS WITH HEARING IMPAIRMENTS> Contact the **American Academy of Otolaryngology** (1 Prince St., Alexandria, VA 22314, ☎ 703/836–4444, FAX 703/683–5100, TTY 703/519–1585).

FOR TRAVELERS WITH MOBILITY PROBLEMS> Contact the **Information Center for Individuals with Disabilities** (Fort Point Pl., 27–43 Wormwood St., Boston, MA 02210, ☎ 617/727–5540, 800/462–5015 in MA, TTY 617/345–9743); **Mobility International USA** (Box 10767,

Eugene, OR 97440, ☎ and TTY 503/343–1284; FAX 503/343–6812), the U.S. branch of an international organization based in Belgium (*see above*) that has affiliates in 30 countries; **MossRehab Hospital Travel Information Service** (1200 W. Tabor Rd., Philadelphia, PA 19141, ☎ 215/456–9603, TTY 215/456–9602); the **Society for the Advancement of Travel for the Handicapped** (347 5th Ave., Suite 610, New York, NY 10016, ☎ 212/447–7284, FAX 212/725–8253); the **Travel Industry and Disabled Exchange** (TIDE, 5435 Donna Ave., Tarzana, CA 91356, ☎ 818/344–3640, FAX 818/344–0078); and **Travelin' Talk** (Box 3534, Clarksville, TN 37043, ☎ 615/552–6670, FAX 615/552–1182).

FOR TRAVELERS WITH VISION IMPAIRMENTS> Contact the **American Council of the Blind** (1155 15th St. NW, Suite 720, Washington, DC 20005, ☎ 202/467–5081, FAX 202/467–5085) or the **American Foundation for the Blind** (15 W. 16th St., New York, NY 10011, ☎ 212/620–2000, TTY 212/620–2158).

PUBLICATIONS

Several publications are available from the **Consumer Information Center** (Box 100, Pueblo, CO 81009, ☎ 719/948–3334). Call or write for a free catalogue of current titles.

The 500-page *Travelin' Talk Directory* ($35; ☎ 615/552–6670) lists people and organizations who help travelers with disabilities. For specialist travel agents worldwide, consult the *Directory of Travel Agencies for the Disabled* ($19.95 plus $2 shipping; Twin Peaks Press, Box 129, Vancouver, WA 98666, ☎ 206/694–2462 or 800/637–2256) and the *Directory of Travel Agencies for the Disabled,* by Helen Hecker ($19.95 plus $3.50 handling; Disability Bookshop, Box 129, Vancouver, WA, 98666; ☎ 206/694-2462).

TRAVEL AGENCIES, TOUR OPERATORS

The Americans with Disabilities Act requires that travel firms serve the needs of all travelers. However, some agencies and operators specialize in making group and individual arrangements for travelers with disabilities, among them **Access Adventures** (206 Chestnut Ridge Rd., Rochester, NY 14624, ☎ 716/889–9096), run by a former physical-rehab counselor. In addition, many of the operators and agencies listed below (*see* Tour Operators) can also arrange vacations for travelers with disabilities.

FOR TRAVELERS WITH MOBILITY PROBLEMS➤ A number of operators specialize in working with travelers with mobility impairments: **Hinsdale Travel Service** (201 E. Ogden Ave., Suite 100, Hinsdale, IL 60521, ☎ 708/325–1335), a travel agency that will give you access to the services of

wheelchair traveler Janice Perkins; and **Wheelchair Journeys** (16979 Redmond Way, Redmond, WA 98052, ☎ 206/885–2210), which can handle arrangements worldwide.

FOR TRAVELERS WITH DEVELOPMENTAL DISABILITIES➤ Contact the nonprofit **New Directions** (5276 Hollister Ave., Suite 207, Santa Barbara, CA 93111, ☎ 805/967–2841), for travelers with developmental disabilities and their families as well as the general-interest operations above.

DISCOUNT CLUBS

Options include **Privilege Card** ($74.95 annually; 3391 Peachtree Rd. NE, Suite 110, Atlanta GA 30326, ☎ 404/262–0222 or 800/236-9732) and **Travelers Advantage** ($49 annually, single or family; CUC Travel Service, 49 Music Sq. W, Nashville, TN 37203, ☎ 800/548–1116 or 800/648–4037).

DRIVING

AUTO CLUBS

Members of the Automobile Association of America (AAA) can contact the **Canadian Automobile Association** (1775 Courtwood Crescent, Ottawa, Ont. K2C 3J2, ☎ 613/226–7631; emergency road service, ☎ 800/336–4357). Members of the Automobile Association of Great Britain, the Royal Automobile Club, the Royal Scottish Automobile Club, the Royal Irish Automobile Club and the automobile clubs of the Al-

liance Internationale de Tourisme (AIT) and Fédération Internationale de l'Automobile (FIA) are entitled to all the services of the CAA on presentation of a membership card.

F

FERRIES

Car ferries provide essential transportation on the east coast of Canada. **Marine Atlantic** (Box 250, North Sydney, NS B2A 3M3, ☎ 902/794–5700 or 800/341–7981 in the U.S. only) operates ferries between Nova Scotia and Newfoundland; New Brunswick and Prince Edward Island; New Brunswick and Nova Scotia; and also between Portland, Maine, and Nova Scotia.

G

GAY AND

LESBIAN TRAVEL

ORGANIZATIONS

The **International Gay Travel Association** (Box 4974, Key West, FL 33041, ☎ 800/448–8550), a consortium of 800 businesses, can supply names of travel agents and tour operators.

PUBLICATIONS

The premier international travel magazine for gays and lesbians is *Our World* ($35 for 10 issues; 1104 N. Nova Rd., Suite 251, Daytona Beach, FL 32117, ☎ 904/441–5367). The 16-page monthly *"Out & About"* ($49 for 10 issues; ☎ 203/789–8518 or 800/929–2268), covers gay-friendly resorts,

THE GOLD GUIDE / IMPORTANT CONTACTS

hotels, cruise lines, and airlines.

TOUR OPERATORS

Cruises and resort vacations are handled by **R.S.V.P. Travel Productions** (2800 University Ave. SE, Minneapolis, MN 55414, ☎ 800/328–RSVP) for gay travelers.

TRAVEL AGENCIES

The largest agencies serving gay travelers are **Advance Travel** (10700 Northwest Freeway, Suite 160, Houston, TX 77092, ☎ 713/682–2002 or 800/695–0880), **Islanders/Kennedy Travel** (183 W. 10th St., New York, NY 10014, ☎ 212/242–3222 or 800/988–1181), **Now Voyager** (4406 18th St., San Francisco, CA 94114, ☎ 415/626–1169 or 800/255–6951), and **Yellowbrick Road** (1500 W. Balmoral Ave., Chicago, IL 60640, ☎ 312/561–1800 or 800/642–2488). **Skylink Women's Travel** (746 Ashland Ave., Santa Monica, CA 90405, ☎ 310/452–0506 or 800/225–5759) works with lesbians.

I

INSURANCE

Travel insurance covering baggage, health, and trip cancellation or interruptions is available from **Access America** (Box 90315, Richmond, VA 23286, ☎ 804/285–3300 or 800/284–8300), **Carefree Travel Insurance** (Box 9366, 100 Garden City Plaza, Garden City, NY 11530, ☎ 516/294–0220 or 800/323–

3149), **Near Services** (Box 1339, Calumet City, IL 60409, ☎ 708/868–6700 or 800/654–6700), **Tele-Trip** (Mutual of Omaha Plaza, Box 31716, Omaha, NE 68131, ☎ 800/228–9792), **Travel Insured International** (Box 280568, East Hartford, CT 06128-0568, ☎ 203/528–7663 or 800/243–3174), **Travel Guard International** (1145 Clark St., Stevens Point, WI 54481, ☎ 715/345–0505 or 800/826–1300), and **Wallach & Company** (107 W. Federal St., Box 480, Middleburg, VA 22117, ☎ 703/687–3166 or 800/237–6615).

IN THE U.K.

The **Association of British Insurers** (51 Gresham St., London EC2V 7HQ, ☎ 0171/600–3333; 30 Gordon St., Glasgow G1 3PU, ☎ 0141/226–3905; Scottish Provident Bldg., Donegall Sq. W, Belfast BT1 6JE, ☎ 01232/249176; and other locations) gives advice by phone and publishes the free **"Holiday Insurance,"** which sets out typical policy provisions and costs.

L

LODGING

APARTMENT AND VILLA RENTALS

Contact **Property Rentals International** (1 Park West Circle, Suite 108, Midlothian, VA 23113, ☎ 804/378–6054 or 800/220–3332).

FARM HOLIDAYS

For more information about farm vacations,

contact the **Canadian Country Vacations Association** (525 Kylemore Ave., Winnipeg, Manitoba R3L 1B5, ☎ 204/475-6624).

HOME EXCHANGE

Principal clearinghouses include **Home-Link International/Vacation Exchange Club** ($60 annually; Box 650, Key West, FL 33041, ☎ 305/294–1448 or 800/638–3841), which gives members four annual directories, with a listing in one, plus updates; and **Intervac International** ($65 annually; Box 590504, San Francisco, CA 94159, ☎ 415/435–3497), which has three annual directories.

HOTELS

The major hotel chains in Canada include **Best Western International** (☎ 800/528–1234, in the U.K., 0181/541–0033), **CP (Canadian Pacific) Hotels & Resorts** (☎ 800/828–7447, in the U.K., 0800/898852), **Choice Hotels International** (☎ 800/424–6423, in the U.K. 0800/444–4444), **Days Inns** (☎ 800/325–2525, in the U.K. 01483/440470), **Delta Hotels** (☎ 800/877–1133, in the U.K., 0171/937–8033), **Holiday Inns** (☎ 800/465–4329, in the U.K., 0800/897121), **Ramada** (☎ 800/228–2828, in the U.K., 0181/688–1418), **Sheraton** (☎ 800/325–3535, in the U.K., 0800/353535), and **Travelodge** (☎ 800/255–3050, in the U.K., 0345/404040).

M
MONEY MATTERS

ATMS

For specific **Cirrus** locations in the United States and Canada, call 800/424–7787. For **Plus** locations in both countries, call 800/843–7587.

CURRENCY EXCHANGE

If your bank doesn't exchange currency, contact **Thomas Cook Currency Services** (41 E. 42nd St., New York, NY 10017, or 511 Madison Ave., New York, NY 10022, ☎ 212/757–6915 or 800/223–7373 for locations) or **Ruesch International** (☎ 800/424–2923 for locations).

WIRING FUNDS

Funds can be wired via **American Express MoneyGram℠** (☎ 800/926–9400 from the U.S. and Canada for locations and information) or **Western Union** (☎ 800/325–6000 for agent locations or to send using Mastercard or Visa, 800/321–2923 in Canada).

P
PASSPORTS
AND VISAS

U.S. CITIZENS

For fees, documentation requirements, and other information, call the **Office of Passport Services** information line (☎ 202/647–0518).

U.K. CITIZENS

For fees, documentation requirements, and to get an emergency passport, call the **London Passport**

Office (☎ 0171/271–3000).

PHONE MATTERS

For local access numbers in Canada, contact **AT&T** USADirect (☎ 800/874–4000), **MCI** Call USA (☎ 800/444–4444), or **Sprint** Express (☎ 800/793–1153).

PHOTO HELP

The **Kodak Information Center** (☎ 800/242–2424) answers consumer questions about film and photography.

R
RAIL TRAVEL

Amtrak (☎ 800/872–7245) currently has service from New York to Montréal, New York and Buffalo to Toronto, Chicago to Toronto, and Seattle to Vancouver, providing connections between Amtrak's U.S.-wide network and VIA Rail's Canadian routes.

Transcontinental rail service is provided by **VIA Rail Canada** (☎ 800/665–0200). In the United Kingdom, **Long-Haul Leisurail** (Box 113, Peterborough, PE3 8HY, ☎ 01733/335599) represents VIA Rail.

DISCOUNT PASSES

The **Canrailpass** allows 12 days of coach-class travel within a 30-day period; sleeping cars are available, but they sell out very early and must be reserved at least a month in advance during the high season (June 1–Sept. 30) when the pass is C$510 for adults age 25–60, C$460 for travelers under 25 or over 60.

Low season rates (Oct. 1–Dec. 14 and Jan. 6–May 31) are C$349 for adults and C$319 for youth and senior citizens. The pass is not valid during the Christmas period (Dec. 15–Jan. 5). The Canrailpass must be purchased prior to arrival in Canada; for more information and reservations, contact VIA Rail in the U.S. or **Long-Haul Leisurail** in the U.K.

S
SENIOR CITIZENS

EDUCATIONAL TRAVEL

The nonprofit **Elderhostel** (75 Federal St., 3rd Floor, Boston, MA 02110, ☎ 617/426–7788), for people 60 and older, has offered inexpensive study programs since 1975. The nearly 2,000 courses cover everything from marine science to Greek myths and cowboy poetry. Fees for programs in the United States and Canada, which usually last one week, run about $300, not including transportation.

ORGANIZATIONS

Contact the **American Association of Retired Persons** (AARP, 601 E St. NW, Washington, DC 20049, ☎ 202/434–2277; $8 per person or couple annually). Its Purchase Privilege Program gets members discounts on lodging, car rentals, and sightseeing, and the AARP Motoring Plan furnishes domestic trip-routing information and emergency road-service aid for an annual fee of $39.95 per person or couple ($59.95 for a premium version).

For other discounts on lodgings, car rentals, and other travel products, along with magazines and newsletters, contact the **National Council of Senior Citizens** (membership $12 annually; 1331 F St. NW, Washington, DC 20004, ☎ 202/347–8800) and **Mature Outlook** (subscription $9.95 annually; Box 10448, Des Moines, IA 50306, ☎ 800/336–6330).

PUBLICATIONS

The 50+ Traveler's Guidebook: Where to Go, Where to Stay, What to Do, by Anita Williams and Merrimac Dillon ($12.95; St. Martin's Press, 175 5th Ave., New York, NY 10010, ☎ 212/674–5151 or 800/288–2131), offers many useful tips. **"The Mature Traveler"** ($29.95; Box 50820, Reno, NV 89513), a monthly newsletter, covers travel deals.

STUDENTS

HOSTELING

Contact **Hostelling International–American Youth Hostels** (733 15th St. NW, Suite 840, Washington, DC 20005, ☎ 202/783–6161) in the United States, **Hostelling International–Canada** (205 Catherine St., Suite 400, Ottawa, Ontario K2P 1C3, ☎ 613/748–5638) in Canada, and the **Youth Hostel Association of England and Wales** (Trevelyan House, 8 St. Stephen's

Hill, St. Albans, Hertfordshire AL1 2DY, ☎ 01727/855215 and 01727/845047) in the United Kingdom. Membership ($25 in the U.S., C$26.75 in Canada, and £9 in the U.K.) gets you access to 5,000 hostels worldwide that charge $7–$20 nightly per person.

I.D. CARDS

To be eligible for discounts on transportation and admissions, get the **International Student Identity Card** (ISIC) if you're a bona fide student or the **International Youth Card** (IYC) if you're under 26. In the United States, the ISIC and IYC cards cost $18 each and include basic travel-accident and illness coverage, plus a toll-free travel hot line. Apply through the Council on International Educational Exchange (*see* Organizations, *below*). Cards are available for $18 each in Canada from Travel Cuts (*see* Organizations, *below*) and in the United Kingdom for £5 each at student unions and student travel companies.

ORGANIZATIONS

A major contact is the **Council on International Educational Exchange** (CIEE, 205 E. 42nd St., 16th Floor, New York, NY 10017, ☎ 212/661–1450) with locations in Boston (729 Boylston St., 02116, ☎ 617/266–1926), Miami (9100 S. Dadeland Blvd., 33156, ☎ 305/670–9261), Los Angeles (10904 Lindbrook Dr., 90024, ☎ 310/208–3551), 43 college towns nationwide, and

the United Kingdom (28A Poland St., London W1V 3DB, ☎ 0171/437–7767). Twice a year, it publishes *Student Travels* magazine. The CIEE's Council Travel Service is the exclusive U.S. agent for several student-discount cards.

Campus Connections (325 Chestnut St., Suite 1101, Philadelphia, PA 19106, ☎ 215/625–8585 or 800/428–3235) specializes in discounted accommodations and airfares for students. The **Educational Travel Centre** (438 N. Frances St., Madison, WI 53703, ☎ 608/256–5551) offers rail passes and low-cost airline tickets, mostly for flights departing from Chicago.

In Canada, also contact **Travel Cuts** (187 College St., Toronto, Ontario M5T 1P7, ☎ 416/979–2406 or 800/667–2887).

T

TOUR OPERATORS

Among the companies selling tours and packages to Canada, the following have a proven reputation, are nationally known, and offer plenty of options.

GROUP TOURS

For deluxe escorted tours to Canada, contact **Maupintour** (Box 807, Lawrence KS 66044, ☎ 913/843–1211 or 800/255–4266) and **Tauck Tours** (276 Post Rd. W, Westport, CT 06880, ☎ 203/226–6911 or 800/468–2825). Another operator falling between deluxe and first-class is **Globus** (5301 South Federal Circle, Littleton, CO 80123-2980, ☎ 303/797-2800 or 800/221–0090). In the first-class and tourist range, look into **Collette Tours** (162 Middle Street, Pawtucket, RI 02860, ☎ 401/728-3805 or 800/832–4656) and **Mayflower Tours** (1225 Warren Ave., Downers Grove, IL 60515, ☎ 708/960–3430 or 800/323–7604). For budget and tourist class programs, try Cosmos (*see* Globus, above).

PACKAGES

Independent vacation packages are available from major tour operators and airlines. **Funjet Vacations** based in Milwaukee, Wisconsin, and **Gogo Tours,** based in Ramsey, New Jersey, sell Canada packages only through travel agents.

FROM THE U.K.

Travel agencies that offer cheap fares to Canada include **Trailfinders** (42–50 Earl's Court Rd., London W8 6FT, ☎ 0171/937–5400), **Travel Cuts** (295a Regent St., London W1R 7YA, ☎ 0171/637–3161; *see* Students, *above*), and **Flightfile** (49 Tottenham Court Rd., London W1P 9RE, ☎ 0171/700–7000).

THEME TRIPS

ADVENTURE➤ **All Adventure Travel** (5589 Arapahoe #208, Boulder, CO 80303, ☎ 800/537–4025), which represents more than 80 adventure operators, can satisfy virtually any

thirst for adventure in Canada.

BICYCLING➤ **Backroads** (1516 5th St., Suite A550, Berkeley, CA 94710, ☎ 510/527–1555 or 800/462–2848) has trips throughout Canada. **Bike Riders** (Box 254, Boston, MA 02113, ☎ 617/723–2354 or 800/473–7040) focuses on Prince Edward Island, Iles de-la-Madeleine, and Nova Scotia. For biking, walking, and kayaking in Nova Scotia, try **Butterfield & Robinson** (70 Bond St., Toronto, Ontario, Canada M5B 1X3, ☎ 416/864–1354 or 800/678–1147).

DOGSLEDDING➤ Contact **American Wilderness Experience** (Box 1486, Boulder, CO 80306, ☎ 800/444–0099, FAX 303/444–3999) has dogsledding programs.

FISHING➤ For fishing throughout Canada, contact **Anglers Travel Connections** (1280 Terminal Way, Suite 30, Reno, NV 89502, ☎ 702/324–0580 or 800/624–8429), **Cutting Loose Expeditions** (Box 447, Winter Park, FL 32790-0447, ☎ 407/629–4700, FAX 407/644–9944), and **Fishing International** (Box 2132, Santa Rosa, CA 95405, ☎ 800/950–4242, FAX 707/539–1320).

HEALTH➤ **Spa-Finders** (91 Fifth Ave., New York, NY 10003, ☎ 212/924–6800 or 800/255–7727) represents several spas in Canada.

LEARNING VACATIONS➤ The **Smithsonian Na-**

tional Associate Program (1100 Jefferson Dr. SW, Room 3045, Washington, DC 20560, ☎ 202/357–4700) and the **National Wildlife Federation** (1400 S. 16th St., NW, Washington, DC 20036, ☎ 703/790–4363 or 800/245–5484) operate natural history programs led by specialists in a variety of scientific fields.

ORGANIZATIONS

The **National Tour Association** (546 E. Main St., Lexington, KY 40508, ☎ 606/226–4444 or 800/682–8886) and **United States Tour Operators Association** (USTOA, 211 E. 51st St., Suite 12B, New York, NY 10022, ☎ 212/750–7371) can provide lists of member operators and information on booking tours.

PUBLICATIONS

Consult the brochure **On Tour** and ask for a current list of member operators from the National Tour Association (*see above*). Also get a copy of the **"Worldwide Tour & Vacation Package Finder"** from the USTOA (*see above*) and the Better Business Bureau's **"Tips on Travel Packages"** (publication No. 24-195, $2; 4200 Wilson Blvd., Arlington, VA 22203).

For names of reputable agencies in your area, contact the **American Society of Travel Agents** (1101 King St., Suite 200, Alexandria, VA

THE GOLD GUIDE / IMPORTANT CONTACTS

22314, ☎ 703/739–2782).

V
VAT REFUNDS

Apply through **Revenue Canada** (Visitor's Rebate Program, Ottawa, Ont. K1A 1J5, ☎ 800/668–4748 in Canada).

VISITOR
INFORMATION

Contact the tourism department of the province or territory you plan to visit: **Nova Scotia Dept. of Tourism and Culture** (Box 456, Halifax, NS B3J 2R5, ☎ 800/341–6096), **Tourism New Brunswick** (Box 12345, Fredericton, NB E3B 5C3, ☎ 800/561–0123), **Prince Edward Island Dept. of Tourism, Parks and Recreation,** (Visitors Services Division, Box 940, Charlottetown, PEI C1A 7M5, ☎ 800/565–0267), **Newfoundland and Labrador Dept. of Tourism and Culture,** Box 8370, St. John's, NF A1B 4K2, ☎ 800/563–6353).

In the U.K., contact the **Visit Canada Center** (62-65 Trafalgar Square, London, WC2 5DT, ☎ 0171/839–2299).

U.S. GOVERNMENT TRAVEL BRIEFINGS

The U.S. Department of State's Overseas Citizens Emergency Center (Room 4811, Washington, DC 20520; enclose SASE) issues **Consular Information Sheets,** which cover crime, security, political climate, and health risks as well as embassy locations, entry requirements, currency regulations, and other routine matters. For the latest information, stop in at any U.S. passport office, consulate, or embassy; call the interactive hot line (☎ 202/647–5225, FAX 202/647–3000); or, with your PC's modem, tap into the Bureau of Consular Affairs' computer bulletin board (☎ 202/647–9225).

W
WEATHER

For current conditions and forecasts, plus the local time and helpful travel tips, call the **Weather Channel Connection** (☎ 900/932–8437; 95¢ per minute) from a touch-tone phone.

SMART TRAVEL TIPS A TO Z

Basic Information on Traveling in Eastern Canada and Savvy Tips to Make Your Trip a Breeze

The more you travel, the more you know about how to make trips run like clockwork. To help make your travels hassle-free, Fodor's editors have rounded up dozens of tips from our contributors and travel experts all over the world, as well as basic information on visiting Canada. For names of organizations to contact and publications that can give you more information, *see* Important Contacts A to Z, *above.*

A

AIR TRAVEL

If time is an issue, **always look for nonstop flights,** which require no change of plane. If possible, **avoid connecting flights,** which stop at least once and can involve a change of plane, although the flight number remains the same; if the first leg is late, the second waits.

CUTTING COSTS

The Sunday travel section of most newspapers is a good source of deals.

MAJOR AIRLINES➤ The least-expensive airfares from the major airlines are priced for round-trip travel and are subject to restrictions. You must usually **book in advance and buy the ticket within 24 hours** to get cheaper fares, and you may have to **stay over a Saturday night.**

The lowest fare is subject to availability, and only a small percentage of the plane's total seats are sold at that price. It's good to **call a number of airlines, and when you are quoted a good price, book it on the spot**—the same fare on the same flight may not be available the next day. Airlines generally allow you to change your return date for a $25 to $50 fee, but most low-fare tickets are nonrefundable. However, if you don't use it, you can apply the cost toward the purchase price of a new ticket, again for a small charge.

CONSOLIDATORS➤ Consolidators, who buy tickets at reduced rates from scheduled airlines, sell them at prices below the lowest available from the airlines directly—usually without advance restrictions. Sometimes you can even get your money back if you need to return the ticket. Carefully read the fine print detailing penalties for changes and cancellations. If you doubt the reliability of a consolidator, **confirm your reservation with the airline.**

ALOFT

AIRLINE FOOD➤ If you hate airline food, **ask for special meals when booking.** These can be vegetarian, low-choles-terol, or kosher, for example; commonly prepared to order in smaller quantities than standard catered fare, they can be tastier.

SMOKING➤ Smoking is banned on all flights within the U.S. of less than six hours' duration and on all Canadian flights; the ban also applies to domestic segments of international flights aboard U.S. and foreign carriers. Delta has banned smoking system-wide.

B

BACKGROUND READING

Canada North is by Farley Mowat, as is *Never Cry Wolf,* his humorous account of a naturalist who goes to a remote part of Canada to commune with wolves. Andrew Malcolm gives a cultural and historical overview of the country in *The Canadians.* Stephen Brook's *The Maple Leaf Rag* is a collection of idiosyncratic travel essays. *Why We Act Like Canadians: A Personal Exploration of Our National Character,* by Pierre Burton, is one his many popular nonfiction books focusing on Canada's history and culture. *Short History of Canada,* by Desmond Morton, is a recent historical account of the country. *Local Colour—Writers Discovering Canada,* edited

THE GOLD GUIDE / SMART TRAVEL TIPS

by Carol Marin, is a series of articles about Canadian places by leading travel writers.

BUSINESS HOURS

Stores, shops, and supermarkets are usually open Monday through Saturday from 9 to 6—although.in major cities, supermarkets are often open from 7:30 AM until 9 PM. Blue laws are in effect in much of Canada, but a growing number of provinces have stores with limited Sunday hours, usually from noon to 5 (shops in areas highly frequented by tourists are usually open on Sunday). Retail stores are generally open on Thursday and Friday evenings, most shopping malls until 9 PM. Most **banks** in Canada are open Monday through Thursday from 10 to 3, and from 10 to 5 or 6 on Friday. Some banks are open longer hours and are also open on Saturday morning; all banks are closed on national holidays. **Drugstores** in major cities are often open until 11 PM, and **convenience stores** are often open 24 hours a day, seven days a week.

NATIONAL HOLIDAYS

National holidays for 1996 are: New Year's Day (January 1), Good Friday (April 5), Easter Monday (April 8), Victoria Day (May 20), Canada Day (July 1), Labor Day (September 2), Thanksgiving (October 14), Remembrance Day (November 11), Christmas (December 25), and Boxing Day (December 26).

PROVINCIAL HOLIDAYS

Nova Scotia: Civic Holiday (August 5); **New Brunswick:** New Brunswick Day (August 5); **Prince Edward Island:** Civic Holiday (August 5); **Newfoundland and Labrador:** Commonwealth Day (March 11), St. Patrick's Day (March 18), St. George's Day (April 29), Discover Day (July 1), Memorial Day (July 8), and Orangeman's Day (July 15).

C

CAMERAS, CAMCORDERS, AND COMPUTERS

LAPTOPS

Before you depart, **check your portable computer's battery,** because you may be asked at security to turn on the computer to prove that it is what it appears to be. At the airport, you may prefer to **request a manual inspection,** although security X-rays do not harm hard-disk or floppy-disk storage; metal detectors, being magnetic, do harm disk storage. Also, **register your foreign-made laptop with U.S. Customs.** If your laptop is U.S.-made, call the consulate of the country you'll be visiting to find out whether or not it should be registered with local customs upon arrival. You may want to **find out about repair facilities at your destination** in case you need them.

PHOTOGRAPHY

If your camera is new or if you haven't used it

for a while, **shoot and develop a few rolls of film** before you leave. Always **store film in a cool, dry place**—never in the car's glove compartment or on the shelf under the rear window.

Every pass of film through an X-ray machine increases the chance of clouding. To protect it, carry it in a clear plastic bag and **ask for hand inspection at security.** Such requests are virtually always honored at U.S. airports, and usually are accommodated abroad. Don't depend on a lead-lined bag to protect film in checked luggage—the airline may increase the radiation to see what's inside.

VIDEO

Before your trip, **test your camcorder, invest in a skylight filter to protect the lens, and charge the batteries.** (Airport security personnel may ask you to turn on the camcorder to prove that it's what it appears to be).

Videotape is not damaged by X-rays, but it may be harmed by the magnetic field of a walk-through metal detector, so **ask that videotapes be hand-checked.**

CHILDREN AND TRAVEL

BABY-SITTING

For recommended local sitters, **check with your hotel desk.**

DRIVING

If you are renting a car, **arrange for a car seat when you reserve.** Sometimes they're free.

FLYING

Always **ask about discounted children's fares.** On international flights, the fare for infants under age 2 not occupying a seat is generally either free or 10% of the accompanying adult's fare; children ages 2 through 11 usually pay half to two-thirds of the adult fare. On domestic flights, children under 2 not occupying a seat travel free, and older children currently travel on the lowest applicable adult fare.

BAGGAGE➤ In general, the adult baggage allowance applies for children paying half or more of the adult fare. Before departure, **ask about carry-on allowances,** if you are traveling with an infant. In general, those paying 10% of the adult fare are allowed one carry-on bag, not to exceed 70 pounds or 45 inches (length + width + height) and a collapsible stroller; you may be allowed less if the flight is full.

SAFETY SEATS➤ According to the FAA, it's a good idea to **use safety seats aloft.** Airline policy varies. U.S. carriers allow FAA-approved models, but airlines usually require that you buy a ticket, even if your child would otherwise ride free, because the seats must be strapped into regular passenger seats. Foreign carriers may not allow infant seats, may charge the child's rather than the infant's fare for their use, or may require you to hold your baby during takeoff and landing, thus defeating the seat's purpose.

FACILITIES➤ When making your reservation, **ask for children's meals or freestanding bassinets** if you need them; the latter are available only to those with seats at the bulkhead, where there's enough legroom. If you don't need a bassinet, **think twice before requesting bulkhead seats**—the only storage for in-flight necessities is in the inconveniently distant overhead bins.

LODGING

Most hotels allow children under a certain age to stay in their parents' room at no extra charge, while others charge them as extra adults; be sure to **ask about the cut-off age.** In addition, priority for connecting rooms is often given to families. Inquire about programs and discounts when you make your reservation.

CUSTOMS AND DUTIES

IN CANADA

American and British visitors may bring in the following items duty-free: 200 cigarettes, 50 cigars, and two pounds of tobacco; 1 bottle (1.1 liters or 40 imperial ounces) of liquor or wine, or 24 355-milliliter (12-ounce) bottles or cans of beer for personal consumption; gifts up to the value of $60 per gift. A deposit is sometimes required for trailers (refunded upon return).

Cats and dogs must have a certificate issued by a licensed veterinarian that clearly identifies the animal and certifies that it has been vaccinated against rabies during the preceding 36 months. Plant material must be declared and inspected. With certain restrictions (some fruits and vegetables), visitors may bring food with them for their own use, providing the quantity is consistent with the duration of the visit.

Canada's firearms laws are significantly stricter than the U.S.'s. All handguns, semi-automatic, and fully automatic weapons are prohibited and cannot be brought into the country. Sporting rifles and shotguns may be imported provided they are to be used for sporting, hunting, or competition while in Canada. All firearms must be declared to Canada Customs at the first point of entry. Failure to declare firearms will result in their seizure, and criminal charges may be made. (New legislation has just been introduced in Parliament to further tighten Canada's gun laws).

BACK HOME

IN THE U.S.➤ You may bring home $400 worth of foreign goods duty-free if you've been out of the country for at least 48 hours and haven't already used the $400 exemption, or any part of it, in the past 30 days.

Travelers 21 or older may bring back one

liter of alcohol duty-free, provided the beverage laws of the state through which they reenter the United States allow it. In addition, 100 non-Cuban cigars and 200 cigarettes are allowed, regardless of your age. Antiques and works of art more than 100 years old are duty-free.

Duty-free, travelers may mail packages valued at up to $200 to themselves and up to $100 to others, with a limit of one parcel per addressee per day (and no alcohol or tobacco products or perfume valued at more than $5); outside, identify the package as being for personal use or an unsolicited gift, specifying the contents and their retail value. Mailed items do not count as part of your exemption.

IN THE U.K.➤ From countries outside the EU, including Canada, you may import duty-free 200 cigarettes, 100 cigarillos, 50 cigars or 250 grams of tobacco; 1 liter of spirits or 2 liters of fortified or sparkling wine; 2 liters of still table wine; 60 milliliters of perfume; 250 milliliters of toilet water; plus £136 worth of other goods, including gifts and souvenirs.

D

FOR TRAVELERS WITH DISABILITIES

When discussing accessibility with an operator or reservationist, **ask hard questions.** Are there any stairs, inside *or* out? Are there grab bars next to the toilet *and* in the shower/tub? How wide is the doorway to the room? To the bathroom? For the most extensive facilities, meeting the latest legal specifications, **opt for newer accommodations,** which more often have been designed with access in mind. Older properties or ships must usually be retrofitted and may offer more limited facilities as a result. Be sure to **discuss your needs before booking.**

DISCOUNT CLUBS

Travel clubs offer members unsold space on airplanes, cruise ships, and package tours at as much as 50% below regular prices. Membership may include a regular bulletin or access to a toll-free hot line giving details of available trips departing from three or four days to several months in the future. Most also offer 50% discounts off hotel rack rates. Before booking with a club, **make sure the hotel or other supplier isn't offering a better deal.**

DRIVING

Canada's highway system is excellent. It includes the Trans-Canada Highway, the longest highway in the world, which runs about 5,000 miles from Victoria, British Columbia, to St. John's, Newfoundland, using ferries to bridge coastal waters at each end.

By law, you are required to **wear seat belts** (and use infant seats). Some provinces have a statutory requirement to drive with vehicle headlights on for extended periods after dawn and before sunset. **Speed limits** vary from province to province, but they are usually within the 90–100 kph (50–60 mph) range outside the cities. The price of gasoline varies more than the speed limit, from 40¢ to 72¢ a liter. (There are 3.8 liters in a U.S. gallon, 4.5 liters in a Canadian Imperial gallon.) Distances are now always shown in kilometers, and gasoline is always sold in liters. The Imperial gallon is seldom used.

FROM THE U.S.

Drivers must have proper owner registration and proof of insurance coverage, which is compulsory in Canada. The Canadian Non-Resident Inter-Provincial Motor Vehicle Liability Insurance Card, available from any U.S. insurance company, is accepted as evidence of financial responsibility anywhere in Canada. Minimum insurance requirement in the maritime provinces is $200,000. For more information, contact the Insurance Bureau of Canada (181 University Ave., Toronto, Ont., M5H 3M7, ☎ 416/362–2301). If you are driving a car that is not registered in your name, carry a letter from the owner that authorizes your use of the vehicle.

I

INSURANCE

Travel insurance can protect your investment, replace your luggage and its contents, or provide for medical coverage should you fall ill during your trip. Most tour operators, travel agents, and insurance agents sell specialized health-and-accident, flight, trip-cancellation, and luggage insurance as well as comprehensive policies with some or all of these features. Before you make any purchase, **review your existing health and homeowner's policies** to find out whether they cover expenses incurred while traveling.

BAGGAGE

Airline liability for your baggage is limited by the terms of your ticket (*see* Packing for the Maritime Provinces, *below*). Insurance for losses exceeding the terms of your airline ticket can be bought directly from the airline at check-in for about $10 per $1,000 of coverage; note that it excludes a rather extensive list of items, shown on your airline ticket.

FLIGHT

You should **think twice before buying flight insurance.** Often purchased as a last-minute impulse at the airport, it pays a lump sum when a plane crashes, either to a beneficiary if the insured dies or sometimes to a surviving passenger who loses eyesight or a limb. Supplementing the airlines' coverage described in the limits-of-liability paragraphs on your ticket, it's expensive and basically unnecessary. Charging

an airline ticket to a major credit card often automatically entitles you to coverage and may also embrace travel by bus, train, and ship.

HEALTH

If your own health insurance policy does not cover you outside the U.S., **consider buying supplemental medical coverage.** It can cover from $1,000 to $150,000 worth of medical and/or dental expenses incurred as a result of an accident or illness during a trip. These policies also may include a personal-accident, or death-and-dismemberment, provision, which pays a lump sum ranging from $15,000 to $500,000 to your beneficiaries if you die or to you if you lose one or more limbs or your eyesight, and a medical-assistance provision, which may either reimburse you for the cost of referrals, evacuation, or repatriation and other services, or may automatically enroll you as a member of a particular medical-assistance company.

FOR U.K. TRAVELERS➤ You can buy an annual travel-insurance policy valid for most vacations during the year in which it's purchased. If you go this route, make sure it covers you if you have a preexisting medical condition or are pregnant.

TRIP

Without insurance, you will lose all or most of your money if you must cancel your trip due to illness or any other reason. Especially if

your airline ticket, cruise, or package tour is nonrefundable and cannot be changed, it's essential that you **buy trip-cancellation-and-interruption insurance.** When considering how much coverage you need, look for a policy that will cover the cost of your trip plus the nondiscounted price of a one-way airline ticket should you need to return home early. Read the fine print carefully, especially sections defining "family member" and "preexisting medical conditions." Also **consider default or bankruptcy insurance,** which protects you against a supplier's failure to deliver. However, such policies often do not cover default by a travel agency, tour operator, airline, or cruise line if you bought your tour and the coverage directly from the firm in question.

L
LANGUAGE

Canada's two official languages are English and French. Though English is widely spoken, **learn a few French phrases** for the French Canadian communities in Nova Scotia, New Brunswick, and Prince Edward Island.

LODGING

Canada's range of accommodations more closely resembles that of the United States than Europe. In the cities you'll have a choice of luxury hotels, moderately priced modern properties, and smaller older hotels with perhaps fewer conveniences but a bit more charm. Options in smaller towns and in the country include large, full-service resorts; small, privately owned hotels; roadside motels; and bed-and-breakfast establishments. Canada's answer to the small European family-run hotel is the mom-and-pop motel, but even though Canada is as attuned to automobile travel as the United States, you won't find these motels as frequently. Even here you'll need to make reservations at least on the day on which you're planning to pull into town.

Expect accommodations to cost more in summer than in the off-season. When making reservations, **ask about special deals** and packages when reserving. Big city hotels that cater to business travelers often offer weekend packages, and many city hotels offer rooms at up to 50% off in winter. If you're planning to visit a major city or resort area in high season, **book well in advance.** Also be aware of any special events or festivals that may coincide with your visit and block every room for miles around.

APARTMENT AND VILLA RENTALS

If you want a home base that's roomy enough for a family and comes with cooking facilities, **consider a furnished rental.** It's generally cost-wise, too, although not always—some rentals are luxury properties (economical

only when your party is large). Home-exchange directories do list rentals—often second homes owned by prospective house swappers—and some services search for a house or apartment for you (even a castle if that's your fancy) and handle the paperwork. Some send an illustrated catalogue and others send photographs of specific properties, sometimes at a charge; up-front registration fees may apply.

B&BS

One way to save on lodging and spend some time with a native Canadian is to stay at a bed-and-breakfast. They can be found in both the country and the cities. Every provincial tourist board either has a listing of B&Bs or can refer you to an association that will help you secure reservations. Rates range from $20 to upwards of $70 a night and include a Continental or a full breakfast. Because most bed-and-breakfasts are in private homes, you might not have your own bathroom. Some B&B hosts lock up early; be sure to ask. Room quality varies from house to house as well, so don't be bashful about asking to see a room before making a choice. Fodor's *Canada's Great Country Inns* lists places to stay from coast to coast—from unpretentious houses with something special to the elegant Relais & Châteaux (*see* Hotels *in* Lodging, *above*). You can buy it in most

bookstores or ask to have it ordered.

DORMS AND HOSTELS

There are a few alternatives to camping if - you're on a budget. Among them are hostels, which are open to young and old, families and singles (*see* Students on the Road, *below*), and university campuses, which open their dorms to travelers for overnight stays from May through August.

HOME EXCHANGE

If you would like to find a house, an apartment, or other vacation property to exchange for your own while on vacation, **become a member of a home-exchange organization,** which will send you its annual directories listing available exchanges and will include your own listing in at least one of them. Arrangements for the actual exchange are made by the two parties to it, not by the organization.

M
MAIL

In Canada you can buy stamps at the post office or from automatic vending machines in most hotel lobbies, railway stations, airports, bus terminals, many retail outlets, and some newsstands. Within Canada, postcards and letters up to 30 grams cost 46¢; between 30 grams and a kilogram, the cost is $3.75. Letters and postcards to the United States cost 52¢ for up to 30 grams, and $3.40

for up to 250 grams. Prices include GST.

International mail and postcards run 92¢ for up to 30 grams, and $2.10 for up to 100 grams.

Telepost is a fast "next day or sooner" service that combines the CN/CP Telecommunications network with letter-carrier delivery service. Messages may be telephoned to the nearest CN/CP Public Message Centre for delivery anywhere in Canada or the United States. Telepost service is available 24 hours a day, seven days a week, and billing arrangements may be made at the time the message is called in. Intelpost allows you to send documents or photographs via satellite to many Canadian, American, and European destinations. This service is available at main postal facilities in Canada, and is paid for in cash.

RECEIVING MAIL

Visitors may have mail sent to them c/o General Delivery in the town they are visiting, for pickup in person within 15 days, after which it will be returned to the sender.

MONEY AND EXPENSES

American money is accepted in much of Canada (especially in communities near the border). However, visitors are encouraged to exchange at least some of their money into Canadian funds at a bank or other finan-

cial institution in order to get the most favorable exchange rate. Traveler's checks (some are available in Canadian dollars) and major U.S. credit cards are accepted in most areas.

The units of currency in Canada are the Canadian dollar (C$) and the cent, in almost the same denominations as U.S. currency—the $1 bill is no longer used; instead it has been replaced by a $1 coin ($2, $5, $10, $20, 1¢, 5¢, 10¢, 25¢, etc.). The use of $2 paper currency is common here although rare in the United States. At press time the exchange rate was C$1.38 to US$1 and C$2.15 to £1.

ATMS

Chances are that you can **use your bank card at ATMs** to withdraw money from an account and get cash advances on a credit-card account if your card has been programmed with a personal identification number, or PIN. Before leaving home, **check in on frequency limits** for withdrawals and cash advances.

On cash advances you are charged interest from the day you receive the money, whether from a teller or an ATM. Although transaction fees for ATM withdrawals abroad may be higher than fees for withdrawals at home, Cirrus and Plus exchange rates are excellent because they are based on wholesale rates only offered by major banks.

EXCHANGING CURRENCY

For the most favorable rates, **change money at banks.** You won't do as well at exchange booths in airports, rail, and bus stations, nor in hotels, restaurants, and stores, although you may find their hours more convenient. To avoid lines at airport exchange booths, **get a small amount of currency before you leave home.**

TAXES

A goods and services tax of 7% (GST) applies on virtually every transaction in Canada except for the purchase of basic groceries.

HOTEL➤ New Brunswick charges 11% tax on hotel rooms.

SALES➤ In addition to the GST, all maritime provinces levy a sales tax from 4% to 12% on most items purchased in shops, on restaurant meals, and sometimes on hotel rooms. Nova Scotia and Newfoundland offer a sales-tax rebate system similar to the federal one; call the provincial toll-free information lines for details (*see* Important Contacts A to Z, *above*). Most provinces do not tax goods shipped directly by the vendor to the visitor's home address.

VAT➤ **You can get a full GST refund** on any purchase taken out of the country and on short-term accommodations (but not on food, drink, tobacco, car or motorhome rentals, or transportation); rebate forms, which must be submitted within 60 days of leaving Canada, may be obtained from certain retailers, duty-free shops, customs officials or from Revenue Canada (*see* VAT Refunds *in* Important Contacts A to Z). Instant rebates are provided by some duty-free shops when leaving Canada, and most provinces do not tax goods that are shipped directly by the vendor to the purchaser's home. You'll need your receipts.

TRAVELER'S CHECKS

Whether or not to buy traveler's checks depends on where you are headed; **take cash to rural areas and small towns, traveler's checks to cities.** The most widely recognized are American Express, Citicorp, Thomas Cook, and Visa, which are sold by major commercial banks for 1% to 3% of the checks' face value—it pays to **shop around.** Both American Express and Thomas Cook issue checks that can be counter-signed and used by you or your traveling companion, and they both provide checks, at no extra charge, denominated in Canadian dollars. You can cash them in banks without paying a fee (which can be as much as 20%) and use them as readily as cash in many hotels, restaurants, and shops. So you won't be left with excess foreign currency, **buy a few checks in small denominations** to cash toward the end of your trip. Record the numbers of the checks,

cross them off as you spend them, and keep this information separate from your checks.

WIRING MONEY

You don't have to be a cardholder to send or receive funds through MoneyGram℠ from American Express. Just go to a MoneyGram agent, located in retail and convenience stores and in American Express Travel Offices. Pay up to $1,000 with cash or a credit card, anything over that in cash. The money can be picked up within 10 minutes in the form of U.S. dollar traveler's checks or local currency at the nearest MoneyGram agent, or, abroad, the nearest American Express Travel Office. There's no limit, and the recipient need only present photo identification. The cost runs from 3% to 10%, depending on the amount sent, the destination, and how you pay.

You can also send money using Western Union. Money sent from the United States will be available for pickup at agent locations in 100 countries within 15 minutes. Once the money is in the system, it can be picked up at any one of 25,000 locations. Fees range from 4% to 10%, depending on the amount you send.

P
PACKAGES
AND TOURS

A package or tour to eastern Canada can make your vacation less

expensive and more convenient. Firms that sell tours and packages purchase airline seats, hotel rooms, and rental cars in bulk and pass some of the savings on to you. In addition, the best operators have local representatives to help you out at your destination.

A GOOD DEAL?

The more your package or tour includes, the better you can predict the ultimate cost of your vacation. Make sure you know exactly what is included, and **beware of hidden costs.** Are taxes, tips, and service charges included? Transfers and baggage handling? Entertainment and excursions? These can add up.

Most packages and tours are rated deluxe, first-class superior, first class, tourist, and budget. The key difference is usually accommodations. If the package or tour you are considering is priced lower than in your wildest dreams, **be skeptical.** Also, **make sure your travel agent knows the hotels** and other services. Ask about location, room size, beds, and whether it has a pool, room service, or programs for children, if you care about these. Has your agent been there or sent others you can contact?

BUYER, BEWARE

Each year consumers are stranded or lose their money when operators go out of business—even very large ones with excellent reputations. If you can't afford a loss, take the time to **check out the operator**—find out how long the company has been in business, and ask several agents about its reputation. Next, **don't book unless the firm has a consumer-protection program.** Members of the United States Tour Operators Association and the National Tour Association are required to set aside funds exclusively to cover your payments and travel arrangements in case of default. Nonmember operators may instead carry insurance; look for the details in the operator's brochure—and the name of an underwriter with a solid reputation. Note: When it comes to tour operators, **don't trust escrow accounts.** Although there are laws governing those of charter-flight operators, no governmental body prevents tour operators from raiding the till.

Next, **contact your local Better Business Bureau and the attorney general's office** in both your own state and the operator's; have any complaints been filed? Last, **pay with a major credit card.** Then you can cancel payment, provided that you can document your complaint. Always **consider trip-cancellation insurance** (*see* Insurance, *above*).

BIG VS. SMALL➤ An operator that handles several hundred thousand travelers annually can use its purchasing power to give you a good price. Its high volume may also indicate financial stability. But some small companies provide more personalized service; because they tend to specialize, they may also be experts on an area.

USING AN AGENT

Travel agents are an excellent resource. In fact, large operators accept bookings only through travel agents. But it's good to **collect brochures from several agencies,** because some agents' suggestions may be skewed by promotional relationships with tour and package firms that reward them for volume sales. If you have a special interest, **find an agent with expertise in that area;** the American Society of Travel Agents can give you leads in the United States. (Don't rely solely on your agent, though; agents may be unaware of small-niche operators, and some special-interest travel companies only sell direct).

SINGLE TRAVELERS

Prices are usually quoted per person, based on two sharing a room. If traveling solo, you may be required to pay the full double occupancy rate. Some operators eliminate this surcharge if you agree to be matched up with a roommate of the same sex, even if one is not found by departure time.

PACKING FOR THE MARITIME PROVINCES

How you pack will depend on when you go and what you plan to do. Layering is the best defense against Canada's cold winters; a hat, scarf, and gloves are essential. For summer travel, loose-fitting natural-fiber clothes are best; bring a wool sweater and light jacket. If you're planning to spend time in Canada's larger cities, pack both casual clothes for day touring and more formal wear for evenings out. If your visit includes a stay at a large city hotel, bring a bathing suit in any season to take advantage of the indoor pool.

Bring an extra pair of eyeglasses or contact lenses in your carry-on luggage, and if you have a health problem, **pack enough medication** to last the trip or have your doctor write a prescription using the drug's generic name, because brand names vary from country to country (you'll then need a prescription from a local doctor). **Don't put prescription drugs or valuables in luggage to be checked,** for it could go astray. To avoid problems with customs officials, carry medications in original packaging. Also don't forget the addresses of offices that handle refunds of lost traveler's checks.

LUGGAGE

Free airline baggage allowances depend on the airline, the route, and the class of your ticket; ask in advance. In general, on domestic flights and on international flights between the United States and foreign destinations, you are entitled to check two bags—neither exceeding 62 inches, or 158 centimeters (length + width + height), or weighing more than 70 pounds (32 kilograms). A third piece may be brought aboard; its total dimensions are generally limited to less than 45 inches (114 centimeters), so it will fit easily under the seat in front of you or in the overhead compartment. In the United States, the Federal Aviation Administration gives airlines broad latitude to limit carry-on allowances and tailor them to different aircraft and operational conditions. Charges for excess, oversize, or overweight pieces vary.

If you are flying between two foreign destinations, note that baggage allowances may be determined not by piece but by weight—generally 88 pounds (40 kilograms) in first class, 66 pounds (30 kilograms) in business class, and 44 pounds (20 kilograms) in economy. If your flight between two cities abroad *connects* with your transatlantic or transpacific flight, the piece method still applies.

SAFEGUARDING YOUR LUGGAGE➤ Before leaving home, **itemize your bags' contents** and their worth, and label them with your name, address, and phone number. (If you use your home address, cover it so that potential thieves can't see it.)

Inside your bag, **pack a copy of your itinerary.** At check-in, **make sure that your bag is correctly tagged** with the airport's three-letter destination code. If your bags arrive damaged or not at all, file a written report with the airline before leaving the airport.

PASSPORTS
AND VISAS

U.S. CITIZENS

Citizens and legal residents of the United States do not need a passport or a visa to enter Canada, but proof of citizenship (a birth certificate, valid passport, or voter registration card) and proof of identity may be requested. Naturalized U.S. residents should carry their naturalization certificate or "green card." U.S. residents entering Canada from a third country must have a valid passport, naturalization certificate, or "green card."

U.K. CITIZENS

Citizens of the United Kingdom need a valid passport to enter Canada for stays of up to six months. All visitors must also have a return or onward ticket out of Canada. Applications for new and renewal passports are available from main post offices as well as at the passport offices, located in Belfast, Glasgow, Liverpool, London, Newport, and Peterborough. You may apply in person at all passport offices, or by mail to all except the London office. Children

under 16 may travel on an accompanying parent's passport. All passports are valid for 10 years. Allow a month for processing.

While traveling, **keep one photocopy of the data page** separate from your wallet and leave another copy with someone at home. If you lose your passport, promptly call the nearest embassy or consulate, and the local police; having the data page can speed replacement.

R
RAIL TRAVEL

To save money, **look into rail passes** (*see* Important Contacts A to Z, *above*). But be aware that if you don't plan to cover many miles, you may come out ahead by buying individual tickets.

Many travelers assume that rail passes guarantee them seats on the trains they wish to ride. Not so. You need to **book seats ahead even if you are using a rail pass;** seat reservations are required on some European trains, particularly high-speed trains, and are a good idea on trains that may be crowded—particularly in summer on popular routes. You will also need a reservation if you purchase overnight sleeping accommodations.

RENTING A CAR

CUTTING COSTS

To get the best deal, **book through a travel agent and shop around.** When pricing cars, **ask** where the rental lot is located. Some off-airport locations offer lower rates—even though their lots are only minutes away from the terminal via complimentary shuttle. You may also want to **price local car-rental companies,** whose rates may be lower still, although service and maintenance standards may not be up to those of a national firm. Also **ask your travel agent about a company's customer-service record.** How has it responded to late plane arrivals and vehicle mishaps? Are there often lines at the rental counter, and, if - you're traveling during a holiday period, does a confirmed reservation guarantee you a car?

Always **find out what equipment is standard** at your destination before specifying what you want; **do without automatic transmission or air-conditioning** if they're optional.

INSURANCE

When you drive a rented car, you are generally responsible for any damage or personal injury you cause as well as damage to the vehicle. Before you rent, **see what coverage you already have** by means of your personal auto-insurance policy and credit cards. For about $14 a day, rental companies sell insurance, known as a collision damage waiver (CDW), that eliminates your liability for damage to the car; it's always optional and should never be automatically added to your bill.

REQUIREMENTS

Your own driver's license is acceptable. If you have rented in the United States, be sure to keep the rental contract with you to indicate that use in Canada is authorized by the rental agency.

SURCHARGES

Before picking up the car in one city and leaving it in another, **ask about drop-off charges or one-way service fees,** which can be substantial. Note, too, that some rental agencies charge extra if you return the car before the time specified on your contract. To avoid a hefty refueling fee, **fill the tank just before you turn in the car.**

S
SENIOR-CITIZEN DISCOUNTS

VIA Rail Canada (*see* Rail Travel *in* Important Contacts A to Z, *above*) offers those 60 and over a 10% discount on basic transportation for travel any time and with no advance-purchase requirement. This 10% discount can also apply to off-peak reduced fares that have advance-purchase requirements.

To qualify for age-related discounts, **mention your senior-citizen status up front** when booking hotel reservations, not when checking out, and before you're seated in restaurants, not when paying your bill. Note that discounts may be limited to certain menus, days, or hours.

When renting a car, **ask about promotional car-rental discounts**—they can net lower costs than your senior-citizen discount.

STUDENTS ON THE ROAD

Persons under 18 years of age who are not accompanied by their parents should bring a letter from a parent or guardian giving them permission to travel to Canada.

To save money, **look into deals available through student-oriented travel agencies.** To qualify, you'll need to have a bona fide student I.D. card. Members of international student groups also are eligible. *See* Students *in* Important Contacts A to Z, *above*.

T
TELEPHONES

Phones work as they do in the United States. Drop 25¢ in the slot and dial; pay phones accept American coins, unlike U.S. phones, which spit out Canadian money. There are no problems dialing direct to the United States; U.S. telephone credit cards are accepted. For directory assistance, dial 1, the area code, and 555–1212. To place calls outside Canada and the United States, dial "0" and ask for the overseas operator.

LONG-DISTANCE

The long-distance services of AT&T, MCI, and Sprint make calling home relatively convenient and let you avoid hotel surcharges; typically, you dial an 800 number. Before you go, **find out the local access codes** for your destinations.

TIPPING

Tips and service charges are not usually added to a bill in Canada. In general, tip 15% of the total bill. This goes for waiters, waitresses, barbers and hairdressers, taxi drivers, etc. Porters and doormen should get about 50¢–$1 a bag ($1 or more in a luxury hotel). For maid service, $1 a day is sufficient ($2 in luxury hotels).

W
WHEN TO GO

When to go will depend on your itinerary and your interests. In the maritime provinces of Nova Scotia, New Brunswick, and Prince Edward Island, the weather is relatively mild, though snow can remain on the ground well into spring and fog is common year-round. In Newfoundland and Labrador temperatures vary widely; winter days can be about 32°F (0°C) in St. John's—and as low as −50°F (−45°C) in Labrador and on the west coast. The whole of eastern Canada enjoys blooming springs and brilliant autumns.

The following are average daily maximum and minimum temperatures for Halifax, Nova Scotia.

Climate in Canada's Maritime Provinces

HALIFAX

Jan.	33F	1C	May	58F	14C	Sept.	67F	19C
	20	−7		41	5		53	12
Feb.	33F	1C	June	67F	19C	Oct.	58F	14C
	19	−7		50	10		44	7
Mar.	39F	4C	July	73F	23C	Nov.	48F	9C
	26	−3		57	14		36	2
Apr.	48F	9C	Aug.	73F	24C	Dec.	37F	3C
	33	1		58	13		25	4

1 Destination: Canada's Maritime Provinces

SMALL, FRIENDLY, RELAXED

T HAS BEEN ON TRIPS outside the city, to the more far-flung sectors of this most resolutely regional of nations, that I have found Canada at its more extreme, independent, quirky—even romantic, as un-Canadian a word as that is supposed to be. One snow-swept morning in Pouch Cove, a fishing-village-turned-suburb north of St. John's, Newfoundland, I visited William Noseworthy in his white clapboard house high on Noseworthy's Hill. Blue-eyed and ruddy-cheeked, Noseworthy sat in the kitchen by a wood stove, distractedly smoking a cigarette. He was 66 and had just retired the year before after four decades of fishing, but he still stared out the window at the North Atlantic. "There's something that draws you to it," he said in the rich accent of "the Rock."

His son, 31-year-old Barry, sipping a Labatt's beer, recalled that once, when he was 13, his father caught him whistling in a boat. "He was going to throw me overboard," said Barry. "It's just bad luck." William explained: "You don't whistle on the water. You wouldn't dare. You wouldn't launch your boat on Friday either. They're just superstitions, maybe. But several years ago, someone launched a big fishing trawler on a Friday, and she was lost on a Friday, and all the crew members, too." A minute later, William pulled out a shiny red accordion and played a jig, tapping his foot, but his eyes never left the water.

Newfoundland is also a place to sample Canadian regionalism at its most craggy and entrenched. The province's inshore fishermen claim that their very way of life is endangered by declining cod catches, which they blame on offshore trawling, often by foreigners. They blame Ottawa for not looking out for their interests—even 40 years after joining the Confederation, the old refrain still comes quickly to some residents' lips: "A Newfoundlander first, a Canadian second." But in a Pouch Cove twine store, where four diehard fishermen repaired their cod traps while country music drawled from a tape player, Frank Noseworthy, a slim, mustachoied cousin of Barry, said that he rejected the Newfoundlanders first sentiment—and would far rather be Canadian than American. "In the States," he said, "them that's got it, gets more; them that don't, gets less. The Canadian government's more generous toward people that don't have."

In general, Canadians strike me as more outward-looking than Americans. They did not, after all, grow up being told that they already live in the greatest country on earth. "Americans are like TV evangelists," maintained Roger Bill, an Indiana native who is now the Newfoundland-based Atlantic field producer for CBS Radio's *Sunday Morning* show. "They really believe theirs is the best way and everyone else should follow. Canadians aren't nearly so arrogant." They do, however, take a palpable pride in place, with a decided prejudice toward the small, friendly, and relaxed. "I wouldn't live in the States, or in Toronto or Montréal," said Richard Harvey, a high-school principal from Upper Gullies, Newfoundland. "You couldn't pay me enough."

— *Bob Levin*

Originally from Philadelphia, Maclean's *foreign editor Bob Levin moved to Toronto in October 1985. He traveled from coast to coast for this article on an American's impressions of Canada.*

WHAT'S WHERE

Nova Scotia

This little province on the Atlantic coast, compact and distinctive, has a capital city, Halifax, the same size as Christopher Marlowe's London. The days when Nova Scotians were prosperous shipwrights and merchants trading with the world left Victorian mansions in all the salty little ports that dot the coastline and created a uniquely Nova Scotian outlook: worldly, approachable, sturdily independent.

New Brunswick

New Brunswick is where the great Canadian forest, sliced by sweeping river valleys and modern highways, meets the Atlantic. To the north and east, the gentle, warm Gulf Stream washes quiet beaches. Besides the seacoast, there are pure inland streams, pretty towns, and historic cities. The province's dual heritage (35% of its population is Acadian French) provides added spice.

Prince Edward Island

In the Gulf of St. Lawrence north of Nova Scotia and New Brunswick, Prince Edward Island seems too good to be true, with its crisply painted farmhouses, manicured green fields rolling down to sandy beaches, the warmest ocean water north of Florida, lobster boats in trim little harbors, and a vest-pocket capital city, Charlottetown, packed with architectural heritage.

Newfoundland and Labrador

Canada's easternmost province, Newfoundland, was a focus of the world's cod fishing industry for 400 years until the supply ran out in 1992. In summer, Newfoundland's stark cliffs, bogs, and meadows become a riot of wildflowers and greenery, and the sea is dotted with boats and buoys. St. John's, the capital, is a classic harbor city.

PLEASURES & PASTIMES

Biking

Eastern Canada offers some of the best bicycling in the country, from the flats of Prince Edward Island to the varied terrain in New Brunswick and Nova Scotia. Write to the provincial tourist boards for their road maps (which are more detailed than the maps available at gas stations) and information on local cycling associations.

Boating

With the Atlantic coastline, major rivers, and smaller lakes, boating is extremely popular throughout Eastern Canada. Boat rentals are widely available, and provincial tourism departments can provide lists of sources.

Camping

Canada's 2,000-plus campgrounds range from simple roadside turnoffs with sweeping mountain vistas to fully equipped facilities with groomed sites, trailer hookups, recreational facilities, and vacation village atmosphere. Many of the best sites are in Canada's national and provincial parks, with nominal overnight fees. Commercial campgrounds offer more amenities, such as electrical and water hookups, showers, and even game rooms and grocery stores. They cost more and are—some think—antithetical to the point of camping: getting a little closer to nature. Contact tourist offices for listings.

Canoeing and Kayaking

Your degree of expertise and experience will dictate where you canoe. Beginners can try waterways in more settled areas; pros head north to the streams and rivers that flow into the Arctic Ocean. Provincial tourist offices and the federal **Department of Northern Development and Indian Affairs** (Ottawa, Ont. K1A OH4, ☎ 819/997–0002) can be of assistance, especially in locating an outfitter to suit your needs. You can also contact the **Canadian Recreational Canoeing Association** (5–1029 Hyde Park Rd., London, Ont. N0M 1Z0, ☎ 519/473–2109).

Dining

The earliest European settlers of Canada—the British and the French—bequeathed a rather bland diet of meat and potatoes. But though there are few really distinct national dishes here, the strong ethnic presence in Canada makes it difficult not to have a good meal. This is especially true in the larger cities, where Greek, Italian, Chinese, Indian, and other immigrants operate restaurants. In addition, each province is well known for various specialties. **Seafood** usually heads the menu at restaurants in Nova Scotia, New Brunswick, Prince Edward Island, and Newfoundland. In addition, **fiddleheads,** curled young fern fronds picked in the spring, often accompany dishes in these maritime provinces.

Fishing

Anglers can find their catch in virtually any region of the country, though restrictions, seasons, license requirements, and catch limits vary from province to province. In addition, a special fishing permit is required to fish in all national parks; it can be obtained at any national park site, for a nominal fee. **Nova Scotia** has some of the most stringent freshwater restrictions in Canada, but the availability of Atlantic salmon, speckled trout, and striped bass makes the effort worthwhile. Salmon, trout, and black bass are abundant in the waters of **New Brunswick,** and although many salmon pools in the streams and rivers are leased to private freeholders, either individuals or clubs, fly fishing is still readily available for visitors. The waters surrounding **Prince Edward Island** have some of the best deep-sea tuna fishing. **Newfoundland** offers cod, mackerel, salmon, and sea trout in the Atlantic and speckled trout and rainbow trout in its fresh waters.

Hiking

Miles and miles of trails weave through all of Canada's national and provincial parks. Write to the individual provincial tourist offices (*see* Essentials in individual chapters) or the Inquiry Center for the National Parks Department (*see* National Parks, *below*).

National Parks

The country's first national park was established in 1885, and since then the national park system has grown to encompass 34 national parks and 112 national historic sites. Because of Canada's eagerness to preserve its environment, new lands are continually being added to this network. Almost every park offers camping—either primitive camping or campsites with various facilities that can accommodate recreational vehicles. Hiking trails weave their way through each of the parks. One of the most popular preserves is **Fundy National Park** in New Brunswick. Environment Canada (Inquiry Center, Ottawa, Ont. K1A 0H3, ☎ 819/997–2800) publishes *Canada's National Parks* and *Canada's National Historic Sites,* with descriptions and other key information.

Scuba Diving

More than 3,000 shipwrecks lie off the coast of **Nova Scotia,** making it particularly attractive to divers. The provincial Department of Tourism can provide details on the location of wrecks and where to buy or rent equipment.

Shopping

ARTS AND CRAFTS➤ Sweaters, silver objects, pottery, and Acadian crafts can be found in abundance in New Brunswick. For pewter, head for Fredericton. For woven items, visit the village of St. Andrews.

MAPLE SYRUP➤ Eastern Canada is famous for its sugar maples. The trees are tapped in early spring, and the sap is collected in buckets to be boiled down into maple syrup. This natural confection is sold all year. Avoid the tourist shops and department stores; for the best prices and information, stop at farm stands and markets in New Brunswick. A small can of syrup costs about $6 to $9.

Whale-Watching

The Atlantic waters around Newfoundland offer excellent whale-watching, and giant humpback, right whales, finback, and minke whales can be seen in the Bay of Fundy. Boat trips are available from New Brunswick and Nova Scotia.

FODOR'S CHOICE

No two people will agree on what makes a perfect vacation, but it's fun and helpful to know what others think. We hope you'll have a chance to experience some of Fodor's Choices yourself in eastern Canada. For detailed information about each entry, refer to the appropriate chapter.

Historic Sites

★ **Kings Landing Historical Settlement, New Brunswick.** This reconstructed village—more than 60 buildings, including homes, inn, forge, store, church, school, working farms, and sawmill—illustrates life in the central Saint John River valley between 1790 and 1900.

★ **Orwell Corner Historic Village, Prince Edward Island.** A re-created 19th-century rural settlement, this living farm museum employs methods used by Scottish settlers in the 1800s. Here you'll find a beautifully restored 1864 farmhouse, a school, a church, a community hall, and barns.

Parks and Gardens

★ **Cape Breton Highlands National Park, Nova Scotia.** A wilderness of wooded valleys, plateau barrens, and steep cliffs, it stretches across the northern peninsula of Nova Scotia's Cape Breton Island.

★ **Prince Edward Island National Park, Prince Edward Island.** Along the north shore of the island on the Gulf of St. Lawrence, sky and sea meet red sandstone cliffs, rolling dunes, and long stretches of sand.

Views to Remember

★ **Peggy's Cove, Nova Scotia.** At the mouth of a bay facing the open Atlantic, the cove, with its houses huddled around the narrow slit in the boulders, has the only Canadian post office in a lighthouse.

★ **Signal Hill, St. John's, Newfoundland.** Overlooking the snug, punch-bowl harbor of St. John's and the sea, this hilltop was taken and retaken by opposing forces in the 17th century.

Dining

★ **Lobster suppers in New Glasgow, St. Anne's, and North Rustico, Prince Edward Island.** Whether commercial or put on by church or civic groups, these meals feature lobster, rolls, salad, and mountains of sweet, home-baked goodies. $$

★ **Stone House, St. John's, Newfoundland.** You'll feel as though you're dining at a country estate in this restored 19th-century stone cottage. The menu features imported game and provincial specialties such as caribou, rabbit pâté, and broiled salmon with mustard-mint sauce. $$$

Hotels

★ **West Point Lighthouse, West Point, Prince Edward Island.** Still a functioning lighthouse in a provincial park with nature trails, fishing, and biking, this small inn sits next to the beach. $$

★ **Owen House, Campobello Island, New Brunswick.** Built by Admiral Owen (who fancied himself ruler of the island), this 200-year-old house is an artists' haven. Actress Greer Garson stayed here while filming *Sunrise at Campobello*. $$

FESTIVALS AND SEASONAL EVENTS

SPRING
May

NOVA SCOTIA➤ In the Annapolis Valley, the **Apple Blossom Festival** includes dancing, parades, and entertainment.

SUMMER
June

NOVA SCOTIA➤ The **International Blues Festival** draws music lovers to Halifax.

NEW BRUNSWICK➤ **Festival Moncton** highlights internationally acclaimed and regional artists.

PRINCE EDWARD ISLAND➤ **Charlottetown Festival Theatre** offers concerts and musicals (through Sept.).

NEWFOUNDLAND AND LABRADOR➤ The **rainbow trout and salmon fishing** seasons open; **St. John's Day** commemorates the city's birthday and includes a parade, street dance, concerts, and sporting and cultural events.

July

NOVA SCOTIA➤ **Antigonish Highland Games,** staged annually since 1861, has Scottish music, dance, and such ancient sporting events as the caber toss; Halifax hosts both the **Nova Scotia International Tattoo** and the **Atlantic Jazz Festival.**

NEW BRUNSWICK➤ The **Loyalist Festival,** celebrates St. John's founding with parades, dancing, and sidewalk festivities; the **Shediac Lobster Festival** takes place in the town that calls itself the Lobster Capital of the World; there's an **Irish Festival** in Chatham; the **Provincial Fisheries Festival** in Shippagan features The Blessing of the Fishing Vessels.

PRINCE EDWARD ISLAND➤ The **Annual Outdoor Scottish Fiddle and Dance Festival** skirls through Richmond; Rollo Bay hosts a **Fiddle Festival;** Summerside's **Lobster Carnival** is a week-long feast of lobster.

NEWFOUNDLAND AND LABRADOR➤ There's the **Humber Valley Strawberry Jamboree,** the **Hangashore Folk Festival** in Corner Brook, the **Exploits Valley Salmon Festival** in the Grand Falls area, the **Fish, Fun and Folk Festival** in Twillingate, and the **Conception Bay Folk Festival** in Carbonear; **Musicfest** in Stephenville celebrates music from rock and roll to traditional Newfoundland music; **Signal Hill Tattoo** in St. John's (through Aug.) re-enacts the final, 1762 battle of the Seven Years' War between the British and the French; the **Burin Peninsula Festival of Folk Song and Dance** features traditional Newfoundland entertainment.

August

NOVA SCOTIA➤ There's the **Mahone Bay Wooden Boat Festival** and Lunenburg's **Nova Scotia Fisheries Exhibition and Fishermen's Reunion;** the **Nova Scotia Gaelic Mod** in St. Ann's celebrates Scottish culture on the grounds of the only Gaelic college in North America; the **Halifax International Buskerfest** has daily outdoor shows by street performers, a food festival, and stage entertainment.

NEW BRUNSWICK➤ Newcastle's **Miramichi Folk Song Festival** features traditional and contemorary folksongs steeped in Maritime lore. **Foire Brayonne,** in Edmundston, is Canada's largest French festival outside Québec; **Festival by the Sea,** in Saint John, attracts more than 200 entertainers from across Canada and includes cultural and ethnic performances; **Acadian Festival,** at Caraquet, celebrates the region's Acadian heritage with folk singing and indigenous food; the **Chocolate Festival** in St. Stephen includes suppers, displays, and children's events.

PRINCE EDWARD ISLAND➤ Eldon's **Highland Games** gathers Scotsmen; the **Annual Community Harvest Festival** animates Kensington; **Old Home Week** fills Charlottetown with nostalgia.

NEWFOUNDLAND AND LABRADOR➤ Gander's **Festival of Flight** celebrates this town as the aviation "Crossroads of the

World," with dances, parades, and a folk festival; *Une Longue Veillée* folk festival of western Newfoundland's French heritage brings traditional musicians, singers, and dancers to Cape St. George; the **St. John's Regatta** is North America's oldest continuing sporting event; there's also the **Newfoundland and Labrador Folk Festival** in St. John's and the **Labrador Straits Bakeapple Folk Festival** in southern Labrador.

AUTUMN

September

PRINCE EDWARD ISLAND➤ **Festival Acadien de la Region Evangeline** is an agricultural fair with Acadian music, a parade, and lobster suppers, at Wellington Station.

NEWFOUNDLAND AND LABRADOR➤ Deer Lake hosts the **Humber Valley Agricultural Home and Handicraft Exhibition.**

October

NOVA SCOTIA➤ There's the **Shearwater International Air Show.**

WINTER

December

NEWFOUNDLAND AND LABRADOR➤ The nonalcoholic **First Night** New Year's Eve celebration offers dozens of activities and concerts in St. John's.

2 Nova Scotia

This little province on the Atlantic coast, compact and distinctive, has a capital city, Halifax, the same size as Christopher Marlowe's London. The days when Nova Scotians were prosperous shipwrights and merchants trading with the world left Victorian mansions in all the salty little ports that dot the coastline and created a uniquely Nova Scotian outlook: worldly, approachable, sturdily independent.

By Silver
Donald
Cameron

Updated by
Julie V. Watson

I NFINITE RICHES IN A LITTLE ROOM," wrote Elizabethan playwright Christopher Marlowe. Was he referring to Nova Scotia, Canada's second-smallest province, which packs an impossible variety of cultures and landscapes into a mass that's half the size of Ohio?

Nova Scotia's landscapes echo every region of Canada. Mountain clefts in Cape Breton Island could pass for crannies in British Columbia. Stretches of the Tantramar Marshes are as board-flat as the prairies. The glaciated interior, spruce-swathed and peppered with lakes, closely resembles the Canadian Shield in northern Manitoba. The apple blossoms in the Annapolis Valley are as glorious as those in Niagara, and parts of Halifax could masquerade as downtown Toronto. A massive Catholic church in a tiny French village recalls Québec. The warm salt water and long sandy beaches of Prince Edward Island are also found on the mainland side of Northumberland Strait, and the brick-red mudflats of the Bay of Fundy echo their counterparts in New Brunswick. Neil's Harbour looks just like a Newfoundland outport—and sounds like one, too, since many of its people are Newfoundlanders by origin.

As with the land, so with the people. The Micmac Indians have been here for 10,000 years. The French came to the Annapolis Basin in 1605. In the 1750s, cockneys and Irish settled in Halifax and "Foreign Protestants"—chiefly Germans—in Lunenburg. By then Yankees from New England were putting down roots in Liverpool, Cape Sable Island, and the Annapolis Valley. In the 1780s they were joined by thousands of "Loyalists"—many of them black—displaced by the American Revolution. Soon after, the Scots poured into northern Nova Scotia and Cape Breton, evicted from the Highlands by their landlords' preference for sheep. The last wave of immigrants, in the 1890s, became steelworkers and coal miners in Cape Breton. They came from Wales, the West Indies, Poland, Ukraine, and the Middle East. They're all Nova Scotians, and they're all still here, eating their own foods, worshiping in their own churches, speaking in their rich, full-flavored voices.

Infinite riches abound: Gaelic street signs in Pugwash and Mabou, French masses in Cheticamp and Point de l'Eglise, black gospel choirs in Halifax, Micmac handcrafts in Eskasoni, onion-dome churches in Sydney, sauerkraut in Lunenburg, and Yankee Puritanism in Clark's Harbour.

This is a little buried nation, compact and distinctive, with a capital city the same size as Marlowe's London. Before Canada was formed in 1867, Nova Scotians were prosperous shipwrights and merchants, trading with the world. Who created Cunard Lines? A Haligonian, Samuel Cunard. Those spacious days brought democracy to the British colonies, left Victorian mansions in all the salty little ports that dot the coastline, and created a uniquely Nova Scotian outlook: worldly, approachable, sturdily independent.

"Infinite riches in a little room." Kit Marlowe would love it here.

EXPLORING

Tour 1: Halifax and Dartmouth

Numbers in the margin correspond to points of interest on the Nova Scotia and Halifax maps.

❶ Salty and urbane, learned and plain-spoken, **Halifax** is large enough to have the trappings of a capital city, yet small enough to retain the warmth and convenience of a small town.

❷ Begin your walking tour at **Purdy's Wharf**—twin office towers shaped like milk cartons with feet, standing right in the harbor. Much of downtown Halifax is connected by overhead walkways, making it convenient for executives in Purdy's Wharf to get around without venturing outdoors. Take the walkway to the Sheraton, built low to match the historic ironstone buildings next door. If the weather is fine, try the Sheraton's outdoor bar, right on the water, and admire the schooner **Bluenose II** (*see* Guided Tours *in* Nova Scotia Essentials, *below*).

★ ❸ Next door are the warehouses of **Historic Properties,** dating from the early 19th century when trade and war made Halifax prosperous. They were built by such raffish characters as Enos Collins, who did business in the Collins Bank building. A privateer, smuggler, and shipper whose vessels defied Napoléon's blockade to bring American supplies to the Duke of Wellington, Collins was also a prime mover in the Halifax Banking Company, which evolved into the Royal Bank of Canada, the country's largest bank. Look up and to the right: There's the Royal Bank's office tower, three blocks away. When Collins died in 1871, at 99, he was said to be the richest man in Canada. The buildings have been taken over by quality shops and restaurants, boisterous pubs, and chic offices.

❹ Walk along the water behind the modern Law Courts to the **Dartmouth ferry terminal,** jammed with commuters during the rush hour. The terminal is home to the oldest operational salt-water ferry service in North America, which began operation in 1732. Beyond lies the Cable Wharf, so named because it was once home to the ships that laid the undersea telegraph and telephone cables to Europe. There's a fish market here.

❺ Pass the offices of the federal Department of Fisheries (other government offices are in the Central Guaranty Trust tower, across the street) and you'll arrive at the **Maritime Museum of the Atlantic,** housed in a restored chandlery and warehouse. The exhibits include an assortment of small boats once used around the coast, as well as displays describing Nova Scotia's proud heritage of sail—when the province, on its own, was one of the world's foremost shipbuilding and trading nations. There's an exhibit on the Halifax Explosion of 1917. *1675 Lower Water St.,* ☎ *902/424–7490 or 902/424–7491.* ☛ *Admission fee.* ⊙ *June–mid-Oct., Mon. and Wed.–Sat. 9:30–5:30, Tues. 9:30–8, Sun. 1–5:30; mid-Oct.–May, Wed.–Sat. 9:30–5, Tues. 9:30–8, Sun. 1–5.*

The wharves outside the museum are favorite berths for visiting transatlantic yachts and sail-training ships; at any time you may find South American and European square-riggers, classic yachts, and even Viking long ships. The hydrographic steamer *Acadia* is moored here permanently, after a long life of charting the coasts of Labrador and the Arctic.

At the next wharf, in summer, is Canada's naval memorial, HMCS *Sackville,* the sole survivor of a fleet of doughty little corvettes (highly maneuverable warships) that escorted convoys of ships from Halifax to England during World War II. An interpretive center adjacent to the ship explains that the convoys assembled in Bedford Basin, Halifax's vast inner harbor, where the first ships were launched in the early morning and others would follow in a steady stream all day long. The last ones would still be steaming out late at night. *Museum Wharf, Sackville Landing,* ☎ *902/429–5600. Hrs vary so call ahead.*

TIME OUT Between the Maritime Museum and Cornwallis Place (the modern office building just to the south) is an open square and playground at the bottom of Sackville Street. The square is a favorite lunchtime promenade for Halifax office workers, and a setting for concerts associated with the Atlantic Jazz Festival and performances during the Busker Festival. This is a perfect people-watching or picnic spot. Coffee shops and restaurants are within a few blocks, mostly back the way we came.

6 Just south of the square is the **tugboat terminal,** which has become well known to children: Andrew Cochran Associates—a local film company—produces an animated television series called *Theodore Tugboat,* based on the ships' fictional adventures.

7 Leave the tugboats and walk up to Water Street and enter the **Brewery Market,** a sprawling ironstone complex that was once Keith's Brewery (named for Alexander Keith, a 19th-century brewer) but now houses offices, restaurants, and a farmers' market. This area is a favored haunt of knowledgeable Haligonians on Saturday morning.

Take the elevator at the office-end of the complex, and emerge on Hollis Street. Turn left, past several elegant Victorian townhouses—notably Keith Hall (1475 Hollis St.)—once the executive offices of the brewery. Turn right on Bishop Street and walk up to Barrington Street, Halifax's main downtown thoroughfare. Ahead of you is the **Technical University of Nova Scotia,** one of seven Halifax universities; it offers degrees in engineering, architecture, and similar fields.

8 Turn right on Barrington. The stone mansion on your right is **Government House,** the official residence of Nova Scotia's lieutenant-governor, built in 1799 for Sir John Wentworth, the Loyalist governor of New Hampshire, and his racy wife, Fanny. Thomas Raddall's novel *The Governor's Lady* tells their story. Across the street is **The Old Burying Ground,** the city's first cemetery, dating from 1749. One of its residents is General Robert Ross, leader of the attack on Baltimore in 1814 that inspired the anthem "The Star-Spangled Banner." A monument honoring two Halifax heroes of the Crimean War (1853–56) is presently being restored. Maps and information on the stones is available year-round at St. Paul's Church.

Beyond Government House are **St. Matthew's Church** (1859) and **Maritime Centre,** a towering office block above a shopping mall. Turn left on Spring Garden Road and go past the Catholic cathedral church, **St. Mary's Basilica** (1833), with the tallest polished-granite spire in the world.

TIME OUT In the summer, the front lawn of the public library is crowded with people listening to street singers and snacking on french fries bought from **Bud the Spud,** a chip-wagon parked at the curb. Surrounding the lawn are plenty of opportunities for a more substantial take-out lunch.

9 From the library walk west on Spring Garden Road to the South Park Street entrance of the **Halifax Public Gardens,** where the statues of Robbie Burns and Sir Walter Scott face one another from across Spring Garden Road. The gardens were first laid out in 1753, but the present design was created in 1889 by Richard Power, who had been gardener to the Duke of Devonshire. Power's descendants cared for the gardens until the 1960s. Gravel paths wind among ponds, trees, and flower beds, revealing an astonishing variety of plants from all over the world. The centerpiece is a filigreed bandstand erected in 1887 for Queen Victoria's Golden Jubilee.

12

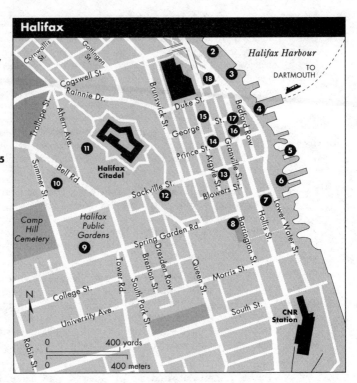

⑩ The **Nova Scotia Museum of Natural History,** located just one block north of the Public Gardens, is a great place for adults and children. One can discover the natural wonders of Nova Scotia by standing next to a real whale skeleton or visiting the life-size models of dinosaurs that once lived nearby. In addition to the natural history collections and displays, the Museum also features an exciting Mi'kmaq and archaeology gallery. Every few months a special exhibit is featured in the changing exhibit hall. The museum is most easily recognized by the huge fiberglass model of the tiny northern spring peeper (a frog) which "clings" to the side of the building May–October, delighting passers-by. *1747 Summer St.,* ☎ *902/424–7353,* FAX *902/424–0560.* ☛ *Admission charged.* ☉ *Mid-May–Oct., Mon., Tues., and Thurs.–Sun. 9:30–5:30, Wed. 9:30–8; Nov.–mid-May, Tues. and Thurs.–Sun. 9:30–5, Wed. 9:30–8.*

★ **⑪** Between the Halifax Commons (a grassy expanse of green space with playing fields and playgrounds) and the compact downtown rises the bulk of **Citadel Hill,** topped by its star-shape fort. The Citadel was the heart of the city's fortifications, and was linked to smaller forts and gun emplacements on the harbor islands and on the bluffs above the harbor entrance. It is now a National Historic Site, with kilted soldiers drilling in front of the **Army Museum,** once the barracks. A cannon is fired every day at noon, and there are audio-visual programs and special events offered several times throughout the year. *Citadel Hill,* ☎ *902/426–5080.* ☛ *Mid-June–Labor Day, $2 adults, $1 children, senior citizens free.* ☉ *July–Labor Day, daily 9–6; Labor Day–mid-June, daily 10–5.*

Most of the city's secondary fortifications have been turned into public parks. **Point Pleasant Park,** a favorite recreation spot, encompasses 186 wooded acres, veined with walking trails and seafront paths. The park was leased from the British Crown by the city for 999 years, at a shilling a year. Its major military installation is a massive round martello tower dating from the late 18th century. Point Pleasant is about 12 blocks down South Park Street from Spring Garden Road.

The handsome four-sided **Town Clock** on Citadel Hill was given to Halifax by Prince Edward, Duke of Kent, military commander from 1794 to 1800. The prince was enamored of round buildings, of which two survive: **St. George's Church,** downtown at Brunswick and Cornwallis streets, and **Julie's Music Room,** on a knoll beside the Bedford Highway. "Julie" was the prince's French mistress, with whom he lived for more than 20 years before being summoned to marry a princess and produce an heir to the British throne. He did his duty, and the result was Queen Victoria.

Pause over the view from the Citadel, and take in the details: the spiky downtown crowded between the hilltop and the harbor; the wooded islands at the harbor's mouth; and the naval dockyard under the Angus L. MacDonald Bridge, the nearer of the two bridges connecting Halifax with its sister city of Dartmouth.

⑫ From the Citadel, walk down Sackville Street toward the harbor. On your right is the **Royal Artillery Park,** with its little-known but excellent military library. The School Board building at Sackville and Brunswick streets is the old Halifax Academy, attended by author Hugh MacLennan.

⑬ Farther down Sackville, where it meets Argyle Street, is the **Neptune Theatre,** Canada's first professional repertory theater, which offers full summer and winter seasons. Argyle Street is the center of the Halifax dining and nightlife scene and a lively place on a Saturday night. A block north of the theater is the **Carleton Hotel,** built of cut stone from the original Fortress of Louisbourg. The hotel, which dates from 1760, was once the home of Richard Bulkeley, one of Halifax's founders, and it later served as a Court of Admiralty.

⑭ Turn left on Barrington Street. A block north is **St. Paul's Church** (1749), Canada's oldest Protestant church, Britain's first overseas cathedral, and the burial site of many colonial notables. Inside, on the north end, a piece of metal is embedded in the wall. It is a fragment of the *Mont Blanc,* one of the two ships whose collision caused the Halifax Explosion of December 6, 1917, the greatest man-made explosion prior to Hiroshima. The blast flattened a square mile of the North End and left 2,000 dead, another 2,000 seriously injured, and 6,000 homeless.

⑮ Leaving St. Paul's, you will find yourself on the **Grand Parade,** facing City Hall. Musicians perform here at noon on fine summer days. From here, look uphill: The tall, stylish brick building is the **World Trade and Convention Centre** and is attached to the 10,000-seat **Halifax Metro Centre**—the site of hockey games, rock concerts, and political conventions. Farther to the right are the office towers above **Scotia Square,** the leading downtown shopping mall.

⑯ Walk downhill a block, and you'll see **Province House,** "a gem of Georgian architecture," according to Charles Dickens. The provincial legislature still meets in this lovely sandstone building, erected in 1819. *Hollis St.,* ☎ *902/424–5982.* ☛ *Free.* ⊙ *Weekdays 9–6, Sat. 9–4.*

⑰ Across Hollis, on Cheapside—a pedestrian-way directly opposite Province House—is the **Art Gallery of Nova Scotia,** which features work by Canadian and international artists. The gallery, housed in a renovated four-story building, displays extensive collections of maritime, Canadian, and folk art, and hosts contemporary traveling exhibitions

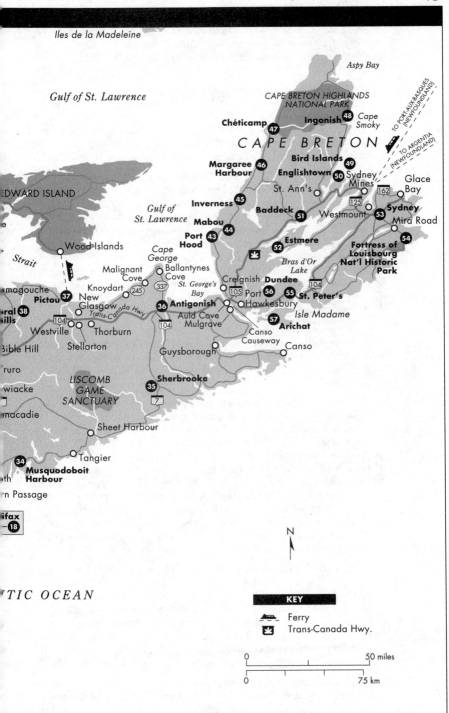

Iles de la Madeleine

Gulf of St. Lawrence

Aspy Bay

CAPE BRETON HIGHLANDS
NATIONAL PARK

Chéticamp 47   Ingonish 48   Cape Smoky

CAPE BRETON

TO PORT AUX BASQUES (NEWFOUNDLAND)
TO ARGENTIA (NEWFOUNDLAND)

Margaree Harbour 46   Bird Islands
Englishtown 49   Sydney Mines 50   Glace Bay
St. Ann's   162
EDWARD ISLAND
Inverness 45   Baddeck 51   Westmount   125   Sydney 53   Mira Road
Gulf of St. Lawrence
Mabou   Estmere 52   Fortress of Louisbourg Nat'l Historic Park 54
Port Hood 43 44
Bras d'Or Lake
Wood Islands
Cape George   Ballantynes Cove
Strait   Malignant Cove 245   337   St. George's Bay   Creignish   Dundee
amagouche   Knoydart   105   Port 56 55 St. Peter's   104
Pictou 37   New Glasgow   Antigonish 36   Hawkesbury
ral 38   Trans-Canada Hwy   Auld Cove   57 Arichat   Isle Madame
ills   104   Mulgrave
Westville   Thorburn   Canso Causeway   Canso
Bible Hill   Stellarton   Guysborough
ruro   Sherbrooke
wiacke   LISCOMB GAME SANCTUARY 35   7
nacadie
Sheet Harbour
34   Tangier
Musquodoboit Harbour
n Passage
ifax 18

TIC OCEAN

N

KEY
Ferry
Trans-Canada Hwy.

0 _____ 50 miles
0 _____ 75 km

from around the world. *1741 Hollis St. at Cheapside,* ☎ *902/424–7542.* ☛ *$2.50 adults, $1.25 students and senior citizens, children under 12 free, $5.50 families.* ☉ *June–Aug., Tues., Wed., and Fri. 10–5, Thurs. 10–9, weekends noon–5; Sept.–May, Tues.–Fri. 10–5, weekends noon–5.*

Return to Province House, turn left, and go one block back to Historic Properties, where this tour began. In addition to owning the warehouses near Purdy's Wharf, Historic Properties also owns the 19th-century buildings between Granville, Duke, and Lower Water streets. The upper floors of most of these buildings are used by the **Nova Scotia College of Art and Design** (NSCAD)—the first degree-granting arts university in Canada and a formidable influence in the world of art.

⑱ Go up the hill a block to Granville Street, past NSCAD's unobtrusive main entrance, and turn right at the Split Crow pub into the one-block **pedestrian mall** with its iron park benches, outdoor cafés, and chic shops. Near the end of the block is the **Anna Leonowens Gallery,** which belongs to NSCAD, and often shows the most challenging exhibits in Halifax. The gallery is named for the college's founder, a remarkable Victorian woman who served the King of Siam as governess and wrote a book about the experience; Rodgers and Hammerstein eventually turned it into the Broadway production of *The King and I,* starring Yul Brynner and Deborah Kerr. *1891 Granville St.,* ☎ *902/422–7381.* ☛ *Free.* ☉ *Tues.–Fri. 11–5, Sat. noon–4.*

Turn right when you leave the gallery. At the end of the block, look toward the harbor: Just across the street are the Sheraton, *Bluenose II,* and Privateer's Warehouse. Welcome back to the beginning of the tour. From here, the tour continues on to two areas: the Northwest Arm and Dartmouth. To continue the tour it will be necessary to travel by car.

"The Arm" is Halifax's recreational secondary harbor, with a popular park, many elegant waterfront homes, and two yacht clubs. From Historic Properties, follow either Duke Street or Cogswell Street (both converge at the Commons) to Quinpool Road, a busy shopping street. Quinpool takes you to a traffic circle called the Armdale Rotary, which heads the Northwest Arm. Take the exit for Purcell's Cove Road (Route 253), which winds along the Arm to the pretty village of **Purcell's Cove,** and passes the Armdale Yacht Club, Flemming Park, the Royal Nova Scotia Yacht Squadron, and the historic cliff-top fortifications of York Redoubt, before ending at the tiny fishing harbor of **Herring Cove.** There is no similar shorefront drive on the Halifax side of the Arm, though several Halifax streets terminate at the Arm's shores.

Dartmouth is Nova Scotia's second city, but it has always been overshadowed by the capital. It was first settled by Quaker whalers from Nantucket, and boasts Canada's largest Coast Guard base and Nova Scotia's most successful industrial park, at Burnside. The 23 lakes within Dartmouth's boundaries provided the Micmacs with a canoe route to the province's interior and to the Bay of Fundy. A 19th-century canal system connected the lakes for a brief time, but today there are only ruins, which have been partially restored as heritage sites.

Halifax-Dartmouth has North America's third-largest concentration of marine scientists, mostly due to the **Bedford Institute of Oceanography,** off Windmill Road just under the A. Murray Mackay Bridge. The institute also has a substantial fleet of specialized ships and submersibles. Visitors can take self-guided walking tours of the facility, or guided tours by reservation; call ahead. *Challenger Dr.,* ☎ *902/426–4093.* ☛ *Free.* ☉ *Weekdays 9–4.*

The **Black Cultural Centre for Nova Scotia,** in Westphal, is located in the heart of the oldest Black community in the area. It is dedicated to the preservation of the history and culture of blacks in Nova Scotia, dating back to the 1600s. *Rte.7 at Cherrybrooke Rd.,* ☎ *902/434–6223.* ☛ *Admission fee.* ☉ *Year-round, weekdays 9–5, Sat. 10–4.*

Tour 2: The South Shore and Annapolis Valley

Mainland Nova Scotia is a long, narrow peninsula; no point in the province is more than 56 kilometers (35 miles) from saltwater. The South Shore is on the Atlantic side, the Annapolis Valley on the Fundy side, and though they are less than an hour apart by car, the two destinations seem like different worlds.

The South Shore is rocky coast, island-dotted bays, fishing villages, and shipyards; the Valley is lumber, farms, vineyards, and orchards. The South Shore is German, French, and Yankee; the Valley is stoutly British. The South Shore is Lutheran, Catholic, and Puritan and boasts a Catholic university; the Valley university is Baptist. The sea is everywhere on the South Shore; in the Valley the sea is blocked from view by a ridge of mountains.

Route 103, Route 3, and various secondary roads form the province's designated Lighthouse Route, which leads from Halifax down the South Shore. It touches the heads of several big bays and small harbors, revealing an ever-changing panorama of shoreline, inlet, and island. Charming little towns are spaced out every 50 kilometers (30 miles) or thereabouts. This tour mostly focuses on the towns along the route, but you should follow the side roads whenever the inclination strikes; the South Shore rewards slow, relaxed exploration.

Leave Halifax on Route 3 or 103—or 333, the scenic road around the shore. **St. Margaret's Bay,** just minutes from Halifax, has always been a favorite summer haunt for Haligonians and is rapidly becoming an outer suburb.

Peggy's Cove, on Route 333, stands at the mouth of the bay facing the open Atlantic. The cove, with its houses huddled around the narrow slit in the boulders, is probably the most photographed village in Canada. It also has the only Canadian post office located in a lighthouse (open April–November). Be careful exploring the bald, rocky shore. Incautious visitors have been swept to their deaths by the towering surf that sometimes breaks here.

Chester, with just over 1,100 people, is the first stop on Lunenburg County's Mahone Bay. The bay has literally hundreds of islands and, according to local claims, there is one for every day of the year. In summer Chester swells with its well-established population of U.S. visitors and Haligonians and with the sailing and yachting community. In mid-August the town celebrates **Chester Race Week,** the largest regatta in Atlantic Canada.

⑲ A passenger-only ferry runs from the dock in Chester to **Big and Little Tancook Islands,** 8 kilometers (5 miles) out in the bay. The boat runs four times daily Monday–Thursday; six times daily Friday; and twice daily on weekend days, and costs $1 for the 45-minute trip. Reflecting its part-German heritage, Big Tancook claims to make the best sauerkraut in Nova Scotia.

Take Route 12 inland for a 20-minute drive from Chester Basin to the **Ross Farm Museum** at New Ross. The restored 19th-century living museum illustrates the evolution of agriculture from 1600 to 1925, and hosts a Heritage Animal Program. Depending on the weather in winter, local farmers sometimes host ice-skating and sleigh-ride events. *Rte. 12, New Ross,* ☎ *902/689–2210.* ☛ *Admission charged.* ☉ *June–mid-Oct., daily 9:30–5:30. Winter programs Jan.–mid-Mar, but phone ahead.*

The town of **Mahone Bay** presents a dramatic face to visitors: Three tall wooden churches—of different denominations—stand side by side, their images reflected in the harbor water. Once a shipbuilding community, Mahone Bay is now a crafts center and also home to the **Wooden Boat Festival,** held during the first week of August, when the works of some of Lunenburg County's top wooden-boat builders are displayed.

★ ⑳ **Lunenburg,** about 9½ kilometers (6 miles) away, is a feast of Victorian-era architecture, wooden boats, steel draggers (a fishing boat that operates a trawl), historic inns, and good restaurants. In the center of town is a national historic district, and the fantastic old school on the hilltop is the region's finest remaining example of Second Empire architecture, an ornate style that began in France.

Lunenburg is also home port to *Bluenose* and *Bluenose II* (*see* Guided Tours *in* Nova Scotia Essentials, *below*), the great racing schooner and its replica. Both were built at the Smith and Rhuland yard here, as was the replica of HMS *Bounty*, used in the film *Mutiny on the Bounty*.

The **Fisheries Museum of the Atlantic,** part of the Nova Scotia Museum, is housed in a renovated fish plant building and adjacent wharf and includes the last of the Grand Bank schooners, the *Theresa E. Connor,* and a steel stern trawler, *Cape Sable.* Also on exhibit is an aquarium, a dory shop, the hall of inshore fisheries, and the *Bluenose* and *August Gale,* among other displays throughout the three floors. There is a gift shop, theater, and restaurant within the museum. *68 Bluenose Dr.,* ☎ *902/634–4794.* ☛ *Admission charged.* ☉ *June–mid-Oct., daily 9:30–5:30; off-season open weekdays by appointment only.*

Before leaving Lunenburg, you may want to visit the **Houston North Gallery,** which represents both trained and self-taught Nova Scotian artists and Inuit (Eskimo) soapstone carvers and printmakers. The gallery, in a large converted house, overlooks the harbor and is near the Fisheries Museum. *110 Montague St.,* ☎ *902/634–8869.* ☉ *Feb.–Dec., Mon.–Sat. 10–6, Sun. 1–6.*

㉑ **Bridgewater,** located at the head of navigation on the La Have River, is the main market town of the South Shore. Another of those towns whose focus was shipping and lumbering, Bridgewater, with its more than 7,000 residents, is now sustained by the large Michelin Tire plant nearby.

The **DesBrisay Museum,** in Bridgewater, explores the nature and people of Lunenburg County. Situated in Bridgewater Woodland Gardens (with a picnic area), DesBrisay presents exhibits on art, nature, science, technology, and history from museums and galleries around the world. It's home to Canada's fifth-oldest historical artifacts collection and presents changing exhibits from the holdings. The gift shop features books by local authors and on topics related to the museum exhibits and art and crafts by local artisans. *130 Jubilee Rd.,* ☎ *902/543–4033.* ☛ *Free.* ☉ *Mid-May–Sept., Mon.–Sat. 9–5, Sun. 1–5; Oct.–mid-May, Tues.–Sun. 1–5, Wed. 1–9.*

Also in Bridgewater, on Route 325, is the **Wile Carding Mill,** which was built in 1860 and retains its original machinery. The mill itself was once powered by an overshot waterwheel. *242 Victoria Rd.,* ☎ *902/543–8233.* ☛ *Free.* ☉ *June–Sept., Mon.–Sat. 9:30–5:30, Sun. 1–5:30.*

Farther down the La Have River, at La Have on Route 331, is **Fort Point Museum,** a former lighthouse-keeper's house that's open daily in the summer.

22 The Lighthouse Route winds on to **Liverpool,** on the estuary of the Mersey River. This community, settled around 1760 by New Englanders, is a fishing and paper-milling town and also serves as a convenient base for visiting the 381-square-kilometer (147-square-mile) **Kejimkujik National Park,** an inland wilderness about 45 minutes away via Route 8. The Mersey is the oldest documented canoe route on the continent; it drains Lake Rossignol, Nova Scotia's largest freshwater lake. The interior of the province here is almost entirely unsettled and is ideally explored by canoe. There is also good trout and salmon fishing. For outfitters, go into the town of Greenfield, on Route 210, off Route 8.

During the American Revolution and the War of 1812, Liverpool was a privateering center; later, it became an important shipping and trading port. In the center of town is the **Simeon Perkins House,** built in 1766, which was the home of a prominent early settler who kept an extensive and revealing diary. The house is now part of the Queens County Museum. *109 Main St.,* ☎ *902/354–4058.* ☞ *Free.* ☉ *June–mid-Oct., Mon.–Sat. 9:30–5:30, Sun. 1–5:30.*

The Perkins diary was used extensively by Thomas Raddall, whose internationally successful novels and stories are sometimes set in and around Liverpool. *His Majesty's Yankees* (1944) is a vivid account of a local family's deeply divided loyalties during the American Revolution, when many Nova Scotians sympathized with the rebels, not the Crown. Raddall still lives in Liverpool.

23 The high noon of **Shelburne** occurred right after the Revolution, when 16,000 Loyalists briefly made it one of the largest communities in North America. Today it is a fishing and shipbuilding town situated on a superb harbor at the mouth of the Roseway River. Many of its homes date back to the Loyalists, including the **Ross-Thomson House** (9 Charlotte La., ☎ 902/875–3141; ☉ June–mid-Oct., daily 9:30–5:30), which is now a provincial museum. Also in Shelburne and worth a visit is the **Dory Shop** (Dock St.; ☉ mid-June–mid-Sept., daily 9:30–5:30), a provincial museum property that was officially opened in 1983 by Prince Charles and Princess Diana. Dories are flat-bottom boats with flaring sides and a sharp bow, well-suited to North Atlantic waters.

South of Shelburne, from Barrington to Digby, is the most prosperous fishing region in the province. With a noticeably milder climate than the rest of Nova Scotia and easy access to the rich fishing grounds of George's Bank, fishermen can work almost year-round to bring in a rich harvest of lobster, scallops, and groundfish.

24 **Barrington** was the home of Captain Benjamin Doane, whose book *Following the Sea* is a fine, lucid account of 19th-century whaling and trading; a more recent native son, Phil Scott, is a nine-time world log-rolling champion. While here, be sure to visit the **Barrington Woolen Mill,** built in 1882 and now a provincial historic site with machinery on display and exhibits that explain how wool is woven into bolts of twills and flannels, blankets, and suitings. Also on the grounds is the Old Meeting House, a national historic site since 1978; the Seal Island Light Museum with its 1906 Fresnel Beacon; and the Western Counties Military Museum. *Rte. 3. Barrington,* ☎ *902/637–2185.* ☞ *Free.* ☉ *Mid-June–Sept., Mon.–Sat. 9:30–5:30, Sun. 1:30–5:30.*

Now turn onto Route 330 for **Cape Sable Island**—a 13 mile loop that includes Nova Scotia's southernmost extremity. Like Barrington, Cape Sable Island is a Yankee community, as common family names attest; everyone seems to be named "Smith" or "Nickerson." Interestingly, there is a bewildering variety of small evangelical churches, which presumably reflects the Puritan enthusiasm for irreconcilable disagreements over fine points of doctrine. The largest community on Cape Sable is **Clark's Harbour** (locally pronounced "Cla'k's Ha'bah," sounding more like a town in Massachusetts), named for Michael Swim, an early settler who could read and write. He was thus described as a clerk or, to the British, a "clark."

The famous Cape Islander fishing boat was developed here. By now you will have seen hundreds of examples of them: Sitting high on the water, with its pilothouse forward and its high, flaring bow and low stern, the Cape Islander is Nova Scotia's standard inshore fishing boat. Boatbuilding (in fiberglass as well as wood) is still carried on along these shores. Successful fishermen buy new boats and sell the older ones, many even turn up as spacious, inexpensive pleasure craft.

Upon reaching **Pubnico** you enter the Acadian milieu; from here to Digby the communities are mostly French-speaking. Favorite local fare includes *fricot,* a stew made mostly of vegetables that sometimes has rabbit meat; and rappie pie, made of meat or poultry with potatoes from which much of the starch has been removed.

You'll no doubt notice that there are no fewer than seven Pubnicos: Lower West Pubnico, Middle West Pubnico, and West Pubnico, all on the west shore of Pubnico Harbour; three East Pubnicos on the eastern shore; and just plain Pubnico, at the top of the harbor. These towns were founded by Phillipe Muis D'Entremont, and they once constituted the only barony in French Acadia. He was a prodigious progenitor: To this day, many of the people in the Pubnicos are D'Entremonts, and most of the rest are D'Eons or Amiraults.

You'll also notice the Acadian flag, tricolored with a gold star representing *stella maris,* the star of the sea. The star guides the Acadians during troubled times, which have been frequent. In 1755, after residing for a century and a half in Nova Scotia, chiefly in the Annapolis Valley, the Acadians were expelled by the British—an event that inspired Longfellow's famous *Evangeline.* Some eluded capture and others slowly crept back, and many settled in New Brunswick and along this shore of Nova Scotia.

㉕ The next stop en route is **Yarmouth,** the largest town (with some 8,500 inhabitants) in southern Nova Scotia, the biggest port west of Halifax, and the point of entry for travelers arriving by ferry from Maine. The ferries are a major reason for Yarmouth's prosperity, as they pull in much revenue by providing quick, inexpensive access for merchants and consumers going to the Boston market for fish, pulpwood, boxes and barrels, knitwear, Irish moss, Christmas trees, and berries.

TIME OUT   Ask locals in Yarmouth where to go for seafood and they'll tell you, "down t' **Harris's Quick 'n' Tasty**" (Rte. 1, Dayton, ☎ 902/742-3467). If you go, you won't be sorry. Specialties include good, old fashioned food such as rappie pie (an Acadian chicken dish) and lobster cooked up more ways than you can imagine.

In the 19th century Yarmouth was an even bigger shipbuilding center than most, and its location put the port on all the early steamship routes. The award-winning **Yarmouth County Museum,** housed in a

Exploring 21

late-19th-century church, does a fine job of unraveling the region's history with its displays of period furniture, costumes, tools, and toys, as well as a significant collection of ship models and paintings. Also in the building is the Research Library and Archives for Yarmouth County, where local history and genealogy are documented. *22 Collins St.,* ☎ *902/742–5539.* ☛ *$2 adults, 50¢ students, 25¢ children under 14, $4 families.* ⊘ *June–mid-Oct., Mon.–Sat. 9–5, Sun. 2–5; mid-Oct.–May, Tues.–Sun. 2–5.*

Yarmouth has another museum that's surprisingly interesting: The **Firefighters Museum of Nova Scotia,** located one block from the waterfront, presents the evolution of fire fighting through its displays of equipment from the leather bucket to the chemical spray. *451 Main St.,* ☎ *902/742–5525.* ☛ *$1 per person, $2 families.* ⊘ *June, Mon.–Sat. 9–5; July and Aug., Mon.–Sat. 9–9, Sun. 10–5; Sept., Mon.–Sat. 9–5; Oct.–May, weekdays 10–noon and 2–4.*

The Lighthouse Route ends here, and the **Evangeline Trail** begins, winding along the shore of St. Mary's Bay, through a succession of Acadian villages collectively known as the French Shore. The villages blend seamlessly into one another for about 32 kilometers (nearly 20 miles), each one, it seems, with its own wharf, fish plant, and enormous Catholic church. Hence, this part of Route 1 is sometimes called "the longest main street in the world."

Along this shore and through Nova Scotia as far east as Truro are nondescript shops called Frenchy's. "Frenchy" refers to Ed Theriault of Meteghan, who hit upon the idea of importing quality used clothing in bulk from Boston and selling it at flat-rate bargain prices. Normally it costs as much to dry-clean the clothes as it does to buy them. Today, even well-heeled Nova Scotians root through the tables at Frenchy's.

㉖ **Point de l'Eglise** (Church Point), past Meteghan River, is the site of **Université Ste-Anne,** the only French-language institution among Nova Scotia's 17 degree-granting colleges and universities. Founded in 1891, this small university is a focus of Acadian studies and culture in the province.

St. Mary's Church (1905) at Point de l'Eglise is the tallest and largest wooden church in North America, at 58 meters (190 feet) long and 56 meters (185 feet) high. The steeple requires 40 tons of rock ballast to keep it steady in the ocean winds. **St. Bernard,** just a few miles farther and marking the end of the French Shore, has an equally impressive granite Gothic church, which seats 1,000 people. Built entirely by local people, beginning in 1910, this monument took 40 years to complete.

The other side of St. Mary's Bay is known as Digby Neck. To explore it, drive on to Digby and follow Route 217. Digby Neck is actually a **㉗** long basalt peninsula extended seaward by two narrow islands, **Long Island** and **Brier Island.** On the far side is the mouth of the Bay of Fundy; ferries going between the islands have to crab sideways against the ferocious Fundy tidal streams that course back and forth through the narrow gaps. The ferries operate hourly, 24 hours a day, and are free to pedestrians ($1 for cars). One of the boats is called *Joshua Slocum* and the other is *Spray;* the former is named for Westport's most famous native, and the latter for the 11-meter (36-foot) oyster sloop that he rebuilt and in which in 1894–96 he became the first man to circumnavigate the world single-handed. At the southern tip of Brier Island is a cairn commemorating the voyage.

An important stop on the "Atlantic Flyway," the islands are an excellent spot for bird-watching; because the surrounding waters are rich in plankton they attract a variety of whales, including fins, humpbacks, minkes, and right whales, as well as harbor porpoises. Whale-watching tours are available through several companies, including **Pirate's Cove Whale Cruises** (Rte. 217, Tiverton, Long Island, ☎ 902/839–2242; $33 adults, $16.50 children 6–14), which operates from June through October.

Digby is the terminus of the ferry service from Saint John, New Brunswick, and an important fishing port with several good restaurants and a major resort, The Pines. The town is located on an otherwise-landlocked Annapolis Basin, into which the Annapolis River flows after its long course through the valley that bears its name. It's particularly famous for its scallops and for smoked herring known as "Digby Chicks." For a real treat go down to the wharf and visit seafood retailers: They'll cook up the delicious scallops and lobster that you buy, fresh from the sea.

Swing inland to **Bear River,** a jewel of a village with a large arts-and-crafts community; or follow the shore of the Basin to the **Upper Clements Park,** a theme park that celebrates Nova Scotia's crafts and heritage and has a variety of rides and attractions, including a water slide, carousel, and roller coaster. *Box 99, Clementsport,* ☎ *902/532–7557 or 800/565–PARK in Atlantic Provinces.* ☛ *Free, but visitors pay for rides.* ⊗ *Mid-May–mid-Oct.*

★ ㉘ Located on the Annapolis River is **Annapolis Royal,** the former capital for both the French and English until 1749. Here you'll find the **Fort Anne National Historic Site,** which was fortified in 1643; the present structures are the remains of the fourth fort erected here and garrisoned by the British, as late as 1854. The officers' quarters are now a museum, with exhibits on the site's history. *On the waterfront (Box 310), Annapolis Royal,* ☎ *902/532–2397 or 902/532–2321.* ☛ *Admission charged.* ⊗ *Mid-May–mid-Oct., daily 9–6; mid-Oct.–mid-May, by appointment.*

Annapolis Royal was Nova Scotia's first capital and first military base. Local businesses (or the tourist information center, located in the Annapolis Royal Tidal Power Building, *see below*) can provide *Footprints with Footnotes,* a self-guided walking tour of the town; guided tours leave from the lighthouse on St. George Street, daily at 10 and 2:30.

Don't miss the **Annapolis Royal Historic Gardens,** 10 acres of magnificent theme gardens connected to a wildlife sanctuary maintained by Ducks Unlimited. *441 St. George St.,* ☎ *902/532–7018.* ☛ *$3.50 adults, $3 students, children under 4 and senior citizens free, $9.75 families.* ⊗ *Mid-May–mid-Oct., daily 8–dusk.*

Located just ¼ mile from Annapolis Royal on the causeway that crosses the Annapolis River to the Granville Ferry is the **Annapolis Royal Tidal Power Project.** Designed to test the feasibility of generating electricity from tidal energy, this pilot project is the only tidal generating station in North America and one of only three operational sites in the world. The interpretive center explains the process with guided tours. ☎ *902/532–5769.* ☛ *Free.* ⊗ *Mid-May–mid-June, daily 9–5:30; mid-June–Aug., daily 9–8; Sept.–mid-Oct., daily 9–5:30.*

Port Royal, established 8 kilometers (5 miles) down the river from Annapolis Royal and on the opposite bank, is one of the oldest European settlements in Canada. It was founded in 1605 by Sieur deMonts, with Samuel de Champlain as his geographer. DeMonts' habitation has been reconstructed and is now the **Port Royal National Historic**

Site, a restored French fur-trading post. Here, amid the hardships of the New World, North America's first social club—the Order of Good Cheer—was founded, and the first theatrical presentation written and produced. ☎ *902/532–2898.* ☛ *Admission charged.* ⊙ *Mid-May–mid-Oct, daily 9–6.*

The **Annapolis Valley** runs northeast like a huge trench, flat on the bottom, sheltered on both sides by the long ridges of the North and South mountains. Occasional roads over the South Mountain lead to the South Shore; short roads over the North Mountain lead to the Fundy shore. The rich soil of the valley bottom supports dairy herds, hay, grain, root vegetables, tobacco, grapes, plums, strawberries, peaches, pears, cherries, and apples, apples, apples. Apple blossom season (late May and early June) or during the fall harvest are the loveliest times to visit.

Like the South Shore, the Valley is punctuated with pleasant small towns, each with a generous supply of extravagant Victorian homes and churches. (Annapolis Royal is especially well supplied with imposing mansions, particularly along the upper end of St. George Street.) For most visitors, the Valley towns go by like charming milestones, among them: Bridgetown, Lawrencetown, Aylesford, Greenwood, Berwick. Each has its distinctions: the Gallery at Saratoga in **Bridgetown** features the paintings of Kenneth Tolmie, whose works reveal Valley scenes and hang in many leading galleries, including the National Gallery of Canada; **Lawrencetown** is the site of the Nova Scotia College of Geographical Sciences, which offers internationally recognized training in cartography, surveying, and various applications of high-technology to geography. Aylesford has a farm zoo; Greenwood is the home of Canada's antisubmarine aircraft squadrons; Berwick is the birthplace (1885) of Alfred Fuller, the original Fuller Brush man. Most of the Valley towns have small museums. But the major impression of the region is one of tranquillity: lush farmland and a settled agricultural society.

Like the South Shore, the Valley is punctuated with pleasant small towns, each with a generous supply of extravagant Victorian homes and churches. (Annapolis Royal is especially well supplied with imposing mansions, particularly along the upper end of St. George Street.) For most visitors, the Valley towns go by like charming milestones, among them: Bridgetown, Lawrencetown, Aylesford, Greenwood, Berwick. Each has its distinctions: the Gallery at Saratoga in **Bridgetown** features the paintings of Kenneth Tolmie, whose works reveal Valley scenes and hang in many leading galleries, including the National Gallery of Canada; **Lawrencetown** is the site of the Nova Scotia College of Geographical Sciences, which offers internationally recognized training in cartography, surveying, and various applications of high-technology to geography. **Aylesford** has a farm zoo; **Greenwood** is the home of Canada's antisubmarine aircraft squadrons; **Berwick** is the birthplace (1885) of Alfred Fuller, the original Fuller Brush man. Most of the Valley towns have small museums. But the major impression of the region is one of tranquillity: lush farmland and a settled agricultural society.

Kentville, New Minas, Greenwich, and Wolfville run into one another almost like the towns of the French Shore; their more than 12,000 residents form the Valley's largest urban cluster. At **Kentville, Agriculture Canada** (☎ 902/678–1093) maintains an important research station on horticulture and poultry; the grounds are beautiful, and free guided tours can be arranged from June through August, weekdays 8–4:30.

㉚ Wolfville, a bucolic college town, is the seat of Acadia University. The school's **Beveridge Art Centre** exhibits contemporary and historic art, including works by Alex Colville, the internationally celebrated realist painter and printmaker who lives here and has served as Acadia's Chancellor. *Acadia University, Highland Ave.,* ☎ *902/542–2201.* ☛ *Free.* ☉ *Sept.–May, Tues.–Fri. 11–5, weekends 1–4; June–Aug., daily noon–5.*

At Greenwich, take Route 358 to Cape Blomidon via Port Williams and Canning for a spectacular view of the Valley and the Bay of Fundy from the **Lookoff.** Cape Blomidon itself rises 231 meters (760 feet) from the Bay. Continue to **Scots Bay,** where rock shelves contain ribbons of amethyst, jasper, and carnelian. A popular hiking trail leads from the end of Route 358 to the dramatic cliffs of Cape Split.

Beyond Wolfville is **Grand Pré,** once a major Acadian site, where a small stone church, at the Grand Pré National Historic Site (☉ Mid-May–mid-Oct., daily 9–6), commemorates Longfellow's hero in *Evangeline,* and houses an exhibit on the 1755 deportation of the Acadians from the Valley.

③ **Windsor,** the last of the Valley towns, was settled in 1703 as an Acadian community, and **Fort Edward** (☎ 902/542–3631; ☉ Mid-June–Labor Day, daily 10–6)—one of the assembly points for the expulsion of the Acadians—still stands as the only remaining colonial blockhouse in Nova Scotia. Flora Macdonald, the Scottish heroine who helped Bonnie Prince Charlie escape to France, spent the winter of 1779 in Windsor while her husband was posted at the fort.

Windsor is also the home of Judge Thomas Chandler Haliburton—lawyer, politician, historian, and humorist. His best-known work, *The Clockmaker,* pillories Nova Scotian follies from the viewpoint of a Yankee clock maker. **Haliburton's Home** (Clifton Ave., ☎ 902/798–2915; ☉ June–Oct. 15, Mon.–Sat. 9:30–5:30, Sun. 1–5:30), set on a manicured 25-acre estate, now belongs to the Nova Scotia Museum.

The tide's average rise and fall at Windsor is over 40 feet, and you can see the tidal bore (the leading edge of the incoming tide) rushing up the Meander River and sometimes reaching a height of 3 feet. The local tourist office (☎ 902/798–2690) can tell you estimated tide times.

Continuing along the Evangeline Trail, Halifax is only about 45 minutes away, but one site 30 miles (18 miles) from Windsor deserves attention: **Uniacke House,** built about 1815 for Richard John Uniacke. During the American Revolution, Uniacke, who was fighting on the rebel side, was captured in Cumberland County, just across the Bay of Fundy. The young Irishman was released through some hazy politics and came to Nova Scotia seeking his fortune. He eventually found it as attorney-general and advocate-general to the Admiralty Court, where his fees in one three-year period during the War of 1812 amounted to the stupendous sum of £50,000. Some of that money went into Uniacke House, a superb example of colonial architecture, situated on spacious grounds near a lake. The house, which is now part of the Nova Scotia Museum, is preserved in its original condition with many authentic furnishings. *758 Windsor Hwy.,* ☎ *902/866–2560.* ☛ *Free.* ☉ *June–Oct. 15, Mon.–Sat., 9:30–5:30, Sun. 1–5:30.*

③ Route 101 cuts across the peninsula through gypsum hills to **Bedford,** at the head of Bedford Basin. Once a tony summer resort, Bedford is now a favored suburb of Halifax. Follow the Bedford Highway to Halifax, noting **Julie's Music Room** (*see* Tour 1, *above*) as you pass through Prince's Lodge. If you take Windsor Street downtown, you will be following the 18th-century route between Windsor and Halifax—a proper conclusion to a memorable tour.

Tour 3: Northern Nova Scotia

This tour takes in parts of three of the official Scenic Trails, including **Marine Drive, The Sunrise Trail,** and **The Glooscap Trail.** Any one leg of the route could be done comfortably as an overnight trip from Halifax; for the whole tour, allow three or four days.

Pick up Route 7 at Dartmouth. The Eastern Shore—the Atlantic coast east of Halifax-Dartmouth—is perhaps the most scenic and unspoiled stretch of coastline in mainland Nova Scotia. Because it is unspoiled, of course, the Eastern Shore's facilities are relatively few and simple. The road winds along a deeply indented, glaciated coastline of rocky waters interspersed with pocket beaches, long narrow fjords, and fishing villages. Take the time to prowl the side roads and discover your own favorite rock pools and islets—there are plenty to find.

③④ **Musquodoboit Harbour,** with about 930 residents, is a substantial village at the mouth of the Musquodoboit River, just east of Dartmouth. The river itself offers good trout and salmon fishing, and the village touches on two slender and lovely harbors. One of the Eastern Shore's best beaches, **Martinique Beach,** is about 12 kilometers (8 miles) south of the village, and other fine beaches are at Clam Bay and Clam Harbour, several kilometers (a few miles) east of Martinique.

The pretty villages slip by: Jeddore, Salmon River, Lake Charlotte. An increasingly important part of their economies is aquaculture: Nearby, in **Ship Harbour,** the provincial Department of Fisheries has developed the **Aquaculture Demonstration Centre** (Rte. 7, ☎ 902/845–2991; ☛ Free; ☉ May–Sept., weekdays 9–3), with a small interpretive center on the hatchery. As you travel a bit farther, take note of the strings of white buoys in Ship Harbour, marking one of North America's largest cultivated mussel farms.

This part of the shore experienced a small gold rush during the first part of this century, complete with a 1936 mine disaster, during which the first live, on-the-spot radio newscasts were made throughout Canada and the world. A small local museum at **Moose River Gold Mines,** about 30 kilometers (19 miles) north of Tangier, commemorates the period. *Rte. 224,* ☎ *902/384–2653.* ☛ *Free.* ☉ *July–Aug. (sometimes extended, depending on weather), Mon.–Sat. 10–6, Sun. 1–6.*

TIME OUT Don't fail to stop in Tangier for some delicious smoked salmon, eel, or mackerel from **Willy Krauch's Danish Smokehouse** (Rte. 7, ☎ 902/772–2188). It's open year-round, weekdays 8–6 and weekends 10–5.

Sheet Harbour is the major service center for the Eastern Shore, with a bank, hospital, accommodations, and campgrounds. Like Musquodoboit, this town straddles two harbors, one of which ships pulpwood to Europe.

The road winds on through a string of uniquely named villages: Necum Teuch, Ecum Secum, Marie Joseph, Spanish Ship Bay. The latter was named for a ghostly galleon, which is said to enter the harbor in flames every seven years. Just beyond, at Liscomb Mills, is Liscomb Lodge, a full-service resort with a very respectable restaurant.

★ ③⑤ The next major center is **Sherbrooke,** which has fewer than 400 residents, but is the Shore's leading tourist center. The St. Mary's River, which flows through the hamlet, is one of Nova Scotia's best salmon rivers, and much of the village itself has been rebuilt by the Nova Scotia Museum to its late 19th-century character, with a blacksmith shop, water-powered sawmill, horse-drawn wagons, tearooms, and stores. Twenty-five buildings have been restored on their original sites for the living history village. ☎ *902/522–2400.* ☛ *Admission charged.* ☺ *June–mid- Oct., daily 9:30–5:30.*

From Sherbrooke you'll have to decide in which direction you wish to go. Marine Drive continues down the shore through wild, harsh, lovely country rarely visited by tourists. To see Nova Scotia unbuttoned, as it were, follow the Drive down to **Canso,** and pick up the Trans-Canada Highway via Guysborough. You will find few tourist attractions, although Canso itself has a stirring history and a National Historic Site; in this part of the province you'll come closer to traditional Nova Scotian ways of life than you will anywhere else.

The alternative is to stay on Route 7, which turns inland up the St. Mary's River through spruce woods and rolling farmland to Antigonish, an hour's drive away. The drive takes you from the Atlantic to the Northumberland Strait, part of the Gulf of St. Lawrence: from cold water and rocky shores to warm water and broad sandy beaches. If water sports are your thing, this is your shore: there are miles of wonderful beaches all along Northumberland Strait.

36 **Antigonish** is the home of **St. Francis Xavier University,** a center for Gaelic studies and for the co-operative movement. Its Coady International Institute offers training to co-op and credit-union workers from foreign countries. It's also a cathedral town with a population of about 5,200.

Follow Route 337, the Sunrise Trail, for a glorious drive along St. George's Bay with its many good swimming beaches, before the road abruptly climbs 1,000 feet up and over to **Cape George.**

TIME OUT   There's a little take-out shop on the wharf at **Ballantyne's Cove,** a tiny artificial harbor near the tip of Cape George, that is said to have the best fish-and-chips in Nova Scotia. Grab an order and enjoy the views.

After following the Cape, high above the sea, the road runs along Northumberland Strait through lonely farmlands and tiny villages, such as Arisaig and Lismore. If, after hearing those names, you have any doubt about the Scottish origin of the people, they will be laid to rest by a stone cairn in Lismore that commemorates Bonnie Prince Charlie's Highland rebels, slaughtered by the English at Culloden in 1746.

Much of the rest of the road runs inland, but the turnoff to Merigomish leads into a maze of inlets, beaches, and islands that are well worth exploring. Either way you go, you'll eventually emerge at Route 104, the Trans-Canada. Turn right 1½ kilometers (1 mile) later, and follow the shore road to **Melmerby Beach**—a favorite local spot—and continue on to New Glasgow by a circuitous shoreside road. Alternatively, stay on the Trans-Canada to reach New Glasgow, a few kilometers (2 miles) away.

New Glasgow is one of five industrial towns on the three rivers that flow into Pictou Harbour. Combined, the five towns have a population of nearly 30,000, making this one of the largest urban centers in the province. New Glasgow is a steel-fabricating and manufacturing center, **Trenton** manufactures railway cars, and **Westville** and **Stellarton** are coal-mining towns.

★ ㊲   For the visitor, the most interesting town by far is **Pictou,** somewhat sullied by a paper mill across the harbor, but nevertheless one of the most engaging communities in Nova Scotia. Lining its streets are typically Scottish-style stone cottage homes and public buildings, and there's a good selection of very attractive small hotels and restaurants. Tour the Grohmann factory on Water Street for a glimpse of knife-making, and visit the factory outlet. Using the main highway system, Pictou can be reached in about two hours from Halifax.

In 1773, the *Hector*—the nearest thing to a Canadian *Mayflower*— came to Pictou Harbour, inaugurating the torrent of Scottish immigration that permanently altered the character of the province and the nation. A replica of the *Hector* is under construction at the *Hector Heritage Quay* (☎ 902/485–8028; admission charged).

Under the inspired leadership of such men as the pioneering educator Thomas McCulloch, Pictou quickly became a center of commerce, education, theological disputation, and radical politics. **McCulloch House,** a restored 1806 building with displays of McCulloch's scientific collection and such personal items as furniture, is preserved as part of the Nova Scotia Museum. *Old Haliburton Rd.,* ☎ *902/485–4563.* ☞ *Free.* ⊙ *June–mid-Oct., Mon.–Sat. 9:30–5:30, Sun. 11:30–5:30.*

Leave Pictou on Route 6, the Sunrise Trail. The road runs beside an apparently endless string of beaches, with many summer homes plunked in the adjoining fields. **River John** is a good meal stop, especially during May, June, and July, when the community prepares lobster suppers, or in August, when chicken barbecues are on the menu.

At Brule, take Route 326 for about 4 kilometers (2½ miles) to the **Sutherland Steam Mill** (Denmark, ☎ 902/657–3365; ⊙ June–Oct. 15, Mon.–Sat. 9:30–5:30, Sun. 1–5:30; admission charged), part of the Nova Scotia Museum complex. Inquire about steamup days, when steam engine enthusiasts get together and fire up their engines. From the mill turn right on Route 256 (at the intersection with Route 311) to reach

㊳   the water-powered gristmill at **Balmoral Mills** (1860), the oldest operating mill in Nova Scotia and one of five that once operated on this stream. It is now a museum with milling demonstrations and a picnic park on the grounds. *Rte. 311,* ☎ *902/657–3016.* ☞ *Admission charged.* ⊙ *June–mid-Oct., Mon.–Sat. 9:30–5:30, Sun. 1–5:30. Demonstrations daily 10–noon and 2–4.*

Turn right off of Route 311 to rejoin the Sunrise Trail. **Tatamagouche,** a market center for farmers and fishermen, is beautifully situated on a ridge overlooking a small estuarine harbor. Beyond Tatamagouche, turn right to Malagash to find **Jost Vineyards** (☎ 902/257–2636 or 800/565– 4567 in Atlantic Canada), one of three farm wineries in the province. Jost produces a surprisingly wide range of very acceptable, award-winning wines, including an ice wine that's making a name for the vineyard. Tours run at 3 PM daily, from mid-June through September.

㊴   The road continues through the small community of Wallace, on another small harbor, to **Pugwash.** This was the home of Cleveland industrialist Cyrus Eaton, at whose estate numerous Thinkers' Conferences brought together leading intellectual figures from the West and the Soviet Union during the 1950s and 1960s. Pugwash is still Scottish terrain, as the Gaelic street signs attest. The town is also the home of **Seagull Pewter** (Durham St., ☎ 902/243–2516) a husband-and-wife crafts operation that has grown into a $25 million business of exporting pewter vessels, picture frames, and other artifacts worldwide. The showroom fronts on the main highway.

From Pugwash, a half-hour drive will take you to Amherst, through rolling hills and along the edge of Amherst Marsh, part of the Tantramar Marsh. The Tantramar covers most of the Isthmus of Chignecto, the narrow neck of land that joins Nova Scotia to the rest of North America, and it is said to be the largest marsh in the world. If you have not yet had your fill of sandy beaches, however, an attractive alternative route leads through Northport, Lorneville, and Tidnish Dock.

Amherst stands on one of the glacial ridges that borders the Tantramar Marsh. Like New Glasgow, Truro, Oxford, and several other towns along what is now the Canadian National main line, Amherst was once a thriving manufacturing center for many products, including pianos and furnaces. During World War II, Amherst's aerospace factories (which still survive, but on a much smaller scale) built hundreds of Anson bombers. The town is historically significant for another reason: In 1917, en route from New York to Russia, the Communist leader Leon Trotsky was confined here for a month in a prisoner-of-war camp.

From Amherst, a two-hour drive via Routes 104 and 102 will return you directly to Halifax. However, the Glooscap Trail from Amherst through Parrsboro to Truro is much more interesting and takes only about an hour longer. Relatively few tourists travel the latter route, which provides some of the most striking scenery in Nova Scotia.

If you opt for the Glooscap Trail, there are several roads that connect Amherst and Parrsboro. Route 2 leads through the coal-mining town of **Springhill,** the site of the famous mine disaster immortalized in the folk song "The Ballad of Springhill" by Peggy Seeger and Ewen McColl. Today the public is invited to tour a real coal mine while visiting the hometown of singer Anne Murray, whose career is celebrated in the **Anne Murray Centre** (Main St., ☎ 902/597–8614; ☛ $5 adults, $4 senior citizens, $3.50 children 7–14, $2 children 3–6; ☉ May–Oct., daily 9–5). Routes 2 and 302 offer the most direct passage to Parrsboro, running through tall hills and farmland to join Route 2 at Southampton.

An alternative—and better—option is to take the Glooscap Trail, which branches off via Route 242 to **Joggins,** where coal-age fossils are embedded in 150-foot sandstone cliffs. Visit the **Joggins Fossil Centre,** where you can learn about the region's geological and archaeological history. Also, guided tours of the fossil cliffs are available, but departure times depend on the tides. *30 Main St., ☎ 902/251–2727. ☛ Center: $3.50 adults, $3 senior citizens, $2 children 5–18. Tours: $10 adults, $8 senior citizens, $4 children 5–18. ☉ June–Sept., daily 9–6:30.*

From Joggins, the Glooscap Trail runs along the shore of Chignecto Bay through Shulie and Sand River to Apple River. You are now on the Bay of Fundy, the third coastline of this tour, where stupendous volumes of water rushing into a narrow shelving bay create the world's highest tides, which sometimes reach heights of 50 feet. **Advocate Harbour** was named by Champlain for his friend Marc Lescarbot, who was a lawyer, or "avocat." Built on flat shore land with a tall ridge backdrop and a broad harbor before it, Advocate is eerily beautiful. The road continues past the spectacular lighthouse at **Cape d'Or,** a piece of land that juts out and divides the waters of the main Bay of Fundy from the narrow enclosure of the Minas Basin. As the tides change, fierce riptides create spectacular waves. The view from the ridge down to the lighthouse is superb; the view from the lighthouse itself is almost equally magnificent, but the road down is rather primitive and should be attempted only in four-wheel drive vehicles.

Route 209 continues through the 19th-century shipbuilding communities of **Spencer's Island** and **Port Greville.** A cairn at Spencer's Island commemorates the construction of the famous *Mary Celeste,* which was found in 1872 sailing in the mid-Atlantic without a crew; she had been abandoned at sea with the table still set for dinner.

㊷ **Parrsboro,** a center for rock hounds and fossil hunters, is the main town on this shore, and hosts the **Rockhound Roundup,** held every August. Among the exhibits and festivities are geological displays, concerts, and other special events. The **Fundy Geological Museum** (6 Two Island Rd., ☎ 902/254–3814; ☛ $3 adults, $1.50 children 5–16, $8 family) stimulates geologists' interests year-round with exhibits from pre-Jurassic to present. Parrsboro is an appropriate setting for the new museum since it's not far from the Minas Basin area, the site where some of the oldest dinosaur fossils in Canada were found. Two-hundred-million-year-old dinosaur fossils are displayed here, alongside exhibits of amethysts, agates, zeolites, and other mineral, plant, and animal relics that have washed out of nearby cliffs; hunting for them is a favorite pastime of the town's visitors. The museum offers workshops on jewelry-making and walking tours to nearby geological sites, led by the museum curator.

If you still haven't gotten your fill of dinosaurmania, check out the "World's Smallest Dinosaur" footprints, on display at the **Parrsboro Rock and Mineral Shop and Museum** (39 Whitehall Rd., ☎ 902/254–2981), run by Eldon George.

Although fossils have become Parrsboro's claim to fame, this harbor town was also a major shipping and shipbuilding port, and its history is described at the **Ottawa House Museum-by-the-Sea.** Ottawa House, which occupies a striking location overlooking the Bay of Fundy, was the summer home of Sir Charles Tupper, a former premier of Nova Scotia who was briefly prime minister of Canada. *Whitehall Rd.,* ☎ *902/ 254–2376.* ☛ *$1.* ⊙ *July–early Sept., daily 10–8.*

From Parrsboro, Route 2 runs along the shore of the Minas Basin to Truro. Almost 5 kilometers (about 3 miles) from Parrsboro is the 125-foot-high **Hidden Falls** (☎ 902/254–2505; ☛ Free; ⊙ Mid-May–Nov.). The gift shop here is a jumble of antique furniture, books, crockery, and bric-a-brac that warrants a visit.

Among the most beautiful scenic areas along Route 2 is **Five Islands,** which, according to Micmac legend, was created when the god Glooscap threw handfuls of sod at Beaver. A provincial park on the shore of Minas Bay includes a campground, a beach, hiking trails, and some interpretation of the region's unusual geology.

Route 2 rejoins the Trans-Canada (Route 104) at **Glenholme.** From here it is a 75-minute drive to Halifax.

Tour 4: Cape Breton Island

Allow three or four days for this meandering tour that begins by entering the island via the Canso Causeway on Route 104; turn left at the rotary, and take Route 19, the Ceilidh Trail. The road winds along the mountainside, with fine views across St. George's Bay to Cape George. This western shoreline of Cape Breton faces the Gulf of St. Lawrence, and is famous for its sandy beaches and warm saltwater.

If Halifax is the heart of Nova Scotia, Cape Breton is its soul, complete with soul music: flying fiddles, boisterous rock, velvet ballads. Cape Breton musicians—weaned on Scottish jigs and reels—are among Canada's finest, and you can hear them all over the island, all summer long, at dozens of local festivals and concerts (*see* Festivals and Seasonal Events *in* Chapter 1).

㊹ Port Hood, with its fine beaches, is the first stop on this tour. Visit **Port Hood Island,** whose 17 traditional homes are now used primarily as a summer retreat by urban refugees. The island has scenic hills, rock formations on the shore, sandy beaches, and warm waters. It's accessible only by an informal ferry operated by Bertie Smith (☎ 902/787–2515), the island's last year-round resident.

㊽ On the way from Port Hood to **Mabou,** the land lies low until Mabou Harbour, where it rises abruptly to the tall hills of the Mabou Highlands. Mabou itself has been called "the prettiest village in Canada," and it is also perhaps the most Scottish, with its Gaelic signs and a deep tradition of Scottish music and dancing. This is the hometown of national recording and performing artists, such as John Allan Cameron and the Rankin Family; stop at a local gift shop and pick up some tapes to play as you drive down the long fjord of Mabou Harbour to **Mabou Mines.** The mines is a place so hauntingly exquisite that you expect to meet the *sidhe,* the Scottish fairies, capering on the hillsides. Within these hills is some of the finest hiking in the province, and above the land fly bald eagles, plentiful in this region. Inquire locally or at the tourist office on Margaree Forks for information about trails. The Ceilidh Trail winds on through green wooded glens and hidden farms.

㊺ The road continues through **Inverness,** a fishing port and former coal-mining town with many services, and on to **Broad Cove,** the site of one of the most venerable Cape Breton Scottish concerts, held annually in late July. The road forks at **Dunvegan,** the home of Alastair MacLeod, whose powerful short stories pierce deeply into the life of these Scottish communities. Look for his collections *The Lost Salt Gift of Blood* or *As Birds Bring Forth the Sun* for a better understanding of the region.

Take Route 219 at Dunvegan, following the coast through **Chimney Corner** and **Whale Cove.** One of the beaches near Chimney Corner has "sonorous sands": When you step on the sand or drag a foot through
㊻ it, it squeaks and moans. The Ceilidh Trail joins the Cabot Trail at **Margaree Harbour** at the mouth of the Margaree River, a famous salmon-fishing stream and a favorite canoe route. Stop at the schooner *Marion Elizabeth,* now the Schooner Village restaurant and free museum, with many small shops and a good selection of books about Cape Breton. On the grounds is writer Farley Mowat's schooner *Happy Adventure,* featured in his book *The Boat That Wouldn't Float.*

The Margaree River is a cultural dividing line: South of the river the settlements are Scottish, up the river they are largely Irish, and north of the river they are Acadian French. The Cabot Trail crosses the river and runs along the shore through Belle Côte and **Cap Le Moine.** Don't miss Joe Delaney's whimsical scarecrow farm and gift shop at Cap Le Moine (Cabot Trail, ☎ 902/235–2108). Most of the harbors on this bold, straight coast are the estuaries of small rivers, with treacherous sandbars at their mouths. Stop at **Friar's Head** and look over the cliff: The tiny cleft in the rocks below was long used as a fishing harbor.

㊼ Chéticamp, an Acadian community, is the best harbor and the largest settlement on the shore. With its tall silver steeple towering over the village, it stands exposed on a wide lip of flat land below a range of bald green hills, behind which lies the high plateau of the Cape Breton Highlands. Cheticamp is famous for its hooked rugs, available at many local gift shops, and for whale cruises, which depart in June, once daily; July and August, three times daily from the government wharf. **Whale Cruis-**

ers Ltd. (☎ 902/224–3376) is one of the reliable charter companies in the area. Cruises cost $25 for adults, $10 for children 6–12.

★ At the outskirts of Cheticamp begins **Cape Breton Highlands National Park,** a 950-square-kilometer (590 mile) wilderness of wooded valleys, plateau barrens, and steep cliffs that stretches across the northern peninsula of Cape Breton from the Gulf Shore to the Atlantic. The highway through the park is magnificent, as it rises to the tops of the coastal mountains and descends through tight switchbacks to the sea. For wildlife watchers there's much to see, including moose, eagle, deer, bear, fox, and bobcat. *In summer* ☎ *902/285–2535, in winter 902/285–2270.* ☛ *May–Oct.: $6 per party per day, $18 for 4-day pass, $30 for seasonal pass; Nov.–Apr., free (includes use of Cabot Trail lookouts within the park, roadside exhibits, walking trails, and picnic areas); camping fee $13–$19.*

Pleasant Bay is a tiny village in a cleft of the mountains, where the Grande Anse River reaches the sea. A spur road creeps along the cliffs to Red River, beyond which is **Gampo Abbey**—the only Tibetan Buddhist monastery in America—situated on a broad flat bench of land high above the sea. The main road climbs North Mountain, past the trail to **Lone Shieling,** a re-creation of a Scottish crofter's lodging. The hut, about a 20-minute scenic walk from the highway, includes displays about the region's history and flora. Its name is taken from the anonymous "Canadian Boat Song," which expresses yearnings for the emigrants' lost Scottish home:

From the lone sheiling on the misty island
Mountains divide us, and the waste of seas;
But still the blood is strong, the heart is Highland
And we in dreams behold the Hebrides.

The most northerly tip of the island is not part of the National Park; turn off to discover **Bay St. Lawrence** and **Meat Cove,** set in an amphitheater of bare green hills, and looking northward to the killer island of **St. Paul's,** site of more than 60 charted shipwrecks. Whale-watching cruises are available June through August, three times daily, through **Whale Watch Bay St. Lawrence** (☎ 902/383–2981; ☛ $22 adults, $11 children 6–12).

The main road reenters the park near **Cabot's Landing,** the long sandy beach in Aspy Bay where Cape Breton folks believe that John Cabot made his landfall in 1497; this theory, however, is vigorously denied in Newfoundland. Dingwall, in the center of the bay, is an archetypal fishing village; so are White Point, New Haven, and Neil's Harbour.

㊽ **Ingonish,** one of the leading holiday destinations on the island, is actually several villages on two bays, divided by a long narrow peninsula called Middle Head. Each bay has a sandy beach, and Middle Head is home to the provincially owned **Keltic Lodge,** a first-class hotel and resort complex located within the national park. It offers a wide range of activities, among them cross-country skiing, golfing on the world-class Highlands Links, swimming, and hiking. Downhill ski facilities are also nearby. Stop at **Lynn's Craft Shop and Art Gallery** (on Rte., ☎ 902/285–2735), which offers the work of noted local artist Christopher Gorey and others.

The road snakes up Cape Smokey and along the face of the mountains, offering spectacular views from high above the sea. **Wreck Cove** is the headquarters of *Cape Breton's Magazine,* an award-winning oral-history publication whose homespun appearance belies its essential sophistication. Look for it on newsstands throughout the island.

Notice the small islands on the far side of the mouth of St. Ann's Bay:
⑭ These are the **Bird Islands,** breeding grounds for Atlantic puffins, black guillemots, razor-billed auks, and cormorants. Boat tours are available from **Bird Islands Boat Tour** (☎ 902/674–2384) in Big Bras d'Or (landing on the islands is forbidden, however). The road descends at last to the flatlands around the mouth of the bay.

If you'd like to extend your drive, take the short ferry ride (runs 24 hours
⑰ and costs 50¢) to **Englishtown,** home of the celebrated Cape Breton Giant, Angus MacAskill. A museum holds the remains of a 7'9" man. ☎ 902/ 929–2106. ☛ *$1 adults, 50¢ children.* ۞ *May–Oct., daily 9–6.*

This alternative route around the head of the bay brings you to **St. Ann's,** home of North America's only **Gaelic College** (☎ 902/295–3441), with the Great Hall of the Clans and a Scottish gift shop. The college offers courses in Gaelic language and literature, Scottish music, and dancing, weaving, and other Scottish arts. In the first week of August Gaelic College hosts the **Gaelic Mod,** a week-long festival of games, theater, and music.

㊶ Turn right on Route 105 for **Baddeck,** the most highly developed tourist center in Cape Breton, with more than 1,000 motel beds, a golf course, many fine gift shops, and numerous restaurants. Baddeck is the main town on the **Bras d'Or Lakes,** a vast, warm, almost-landlocked inlet of the sea, which occupies the entire center of Cape Breton. The coastline of the Lakes is more than 967 kilometers (600 miles) long, and people sail yachts from all over the world to cruise their serene, unspoiled coves and islands. Bald eagles have become so plentiful around the lake that they are now exported to the United States to restock natural habitats. Four of the largest communities along the shore are Micmac Indian reserves.

Baddeck's attractions include the **Centre Bras d'Or Festival of the Arts,** which offers live music and drama every evening during the summer, and the annual regatta of the Bras d'Or Yacht Club, held in the first week of August. Sailing tours and charters are available locally, as are bus tours along the Cabot Trail. A free ferry (passengers only) shuttles between the government wharf and the sandy beach, by the lighthouse at Kidston Island.

The **Alexander Graham Bell National Historic Site** is the most comprehensive collection of Bell's artifacts, mementos, and photographs in the world. Three exhibit halls tell the story of Bell's incredible life and work, including the invention of the telephone. The site is a tribute to the genius and compassion of the great inventor who spent his summers here and is buried on the mountain top above his mansion (which is still owned by his family). People of all ages will find a visit here an entertaining and educational experience; inquire about special summer programs. Picnic facilities are available on these beautiful grounds. *Chebucto St.,* ☎ *902/295–2069, T.D.D. 902/295–1512.* ☛ *Admission charged.* ۞ *July–Aug., daily 9–8, Sept., 9–6, Oct.–June (with reduced services), daily 9–5.*

Continue along the lake shore on Trans-Canada 105 to Exit 6 which leads to **Little Narrows,** then take the ferry (runs 24 hours and costs
㊼ 25¢) to the Washabuck Peninsula. Take Route 223 to **Estmere** and **Iona,** site of the **Nova Scotia Highland Village,** set high on a mountainside, with a spectacular view of Bras d'Or Lake and the narrow Barra Strait.

The village's 10 historic buildings were assembled from all over Cape Breton to depict Highland Scots' way of life from their origins in the Hebrides to the present day. Among the participants at this living-history museum are a smith in the blacksmith shop and a clerk in the store. *Rte. 233,* ☎ *902/725–2272.* ✒ *$4 adults, $3.50 senior citizens, $1 children 5–18, $8 families.* ☉ *Mid-June–mid-Sept., Mon.–Sat. 9–5, Sun. 11–6; mid-Sept.–mid-June (at reception only, no living history), weekdays 9–5.*

The newly constructed Barra Strait Bridge joins Iona to Grand Narrows. A few kilometers (about 2 miles) from the bridge, bear right toward East Bay. (If you miss this turn, don't worry; you'll have just as scenic a drive along St. Andrews Channel.) The East Bay route runs through the Micmac village of **Eskasoni,** the largest native community in the province. This is one of the friendliest villages, with a fascinating cultural heritage: Find an excuse to stop and talk, perhaps at a gift shop or a general store.

❸ Farther on, East Bay becomes a prosperous outer suburb of **Sydney,** the heart of Nova Scotia's second-largest urban cluster. "Industrial Cape Breton" encompasses villages, unorganized districts, and half-a-dozen towns—most of which sprang up around the coal mines, which fed the steel plant at Sydney. These are warmhearted, interesting communities with a diverse ethnic population, including Ukrainians, Welsh, Poles, Lebanese, West Indians, Italians; most residents descended from the miners and steelworkers who arrived a century ago when the area was booming. Sydney is also the only significantly industrialized district in Atlantic Canada, and it has suffered serious environmental damage.

Industrial Cape Breton has the island's only real airport, its only university, and a lively entertainment scene that specializes in Cape Breton music. The **University College of Cape Breton** (1250 Grand Lake Rd., ☎ 902/539–5300) offers many facilities for the public, such as the Boardmore Playhouse, the island's only public art gallery, the Cape Breton Archives, and the Beaton Institute of Cape Breton Studies. A $15 million expansion will include a Cultural Heritage Centre.

Sydney is also a popular departure point: Fast ferries leave from North Sydney for Newfoundland, and scheduled air service to Newfoundland and the French islands of St. Pierre and Miquelon departs from Sydney Airport.

★ ❺ Situated about 30 minutes from Sydney, on Route 22, is **Fortress of Louisbourg National Historic Park,** the most remarkable site in Cape Breton. Louisbourg tends to be chilly, so pack a warm sweater or windbreaker. After the French were forced out of mainland Nova Scotia in 1713, they established their headquarters here, in a walled and fortified town on a low point of land at the mouth of Louisbourg Harbour.

The fortress was twice captured, once by New Englanders and once by the British; after the second siege, in 1758, it was razed to the ground. Its capture essentially ended the French Empire in America. During the past 30 years, a quarter of the original town has been rebuilt on its foundation, just as it was in 1744, before the first siege. Costumed actors re-create the lives and activities of the original inhabitants; you can watch a military drill, see nails and lace being made, and eat food prepared from 18th-century recipes in the town's two inns. Plan on spending at least half a day. Tours available. ☎ *902/733–2280.* ✒ *$7.50 adults, $6 senior citizens, $4.25 children 5–16.* ☉ *June and Sept., daily 9:30–5; July and Aug., daily 9–6.*

While in Louisbourg, consider stopping at the railway museum at the **Sydney and Louisburg Historical Society,** or the **Atlantic Statiquarium,** a marine museum devoted largely to underwater treasure. *Railway Museum: 7336 Main St.,* ☎ *902/733–2720.* ☞ *Free.* ☉ *June–Sept., weekdays 9–5; July and Aug., daily 9–7. Statiquarium: 7523 Main St.,* ☎ *902/733–2721.* ☞ *$2.50 adults, $1 children 5–16, $5 families.* ☉ *June–Sept., daily 10–8.*

To return, you must retrace your tracks, via Route 22, Route 125, and Route 4 to East Bay; continue down the east side of the Bras d'Or Lakes.

TIME OUT   On your return route, about 40 kilometers (25 miles) west of Sydney, you'll come to **Big Pond** (Rte. 4, no ☎), home of singer/songwriter Rita MacNeil, who operates a tearoom in a tranquil setting with seating indoors and out. Stop in for Rita's special blend of tea and home-baked goodies such as oatcakes. A display room contains Rita's awards and memorabilia. A gift shop stocks tapes, CD's, customized merchandise, and local crafts.

Route 4 continues along the lake, sometimes close to the shore and sometimes high in the hills. The Chapel Island Reserve is the site of a major Micmac spiritual and cultural celebration, which draws 5,000 visitors every year during the last weekend in July. The event combines native and Roman Catholic ceremonies, and non-natives are welcome.

⑤⑤ From St. Peter's to Port Hawkesbury the population is largely Acadian French. At **St. Peter's** the Atlantic Ocean is connected with the Bras d'Or Lakes by the century-old St. Peter's Canal, still heavily used by pleasure craft and fishing vessels. The town is a service center for the surrounding region, and offers such amenities as a marina, hotels, restaurants, and a liquor store. From St. Peter's, Route 247 leads through the Acadian villages of Grand Greve and L'Ardoise to a fine beach at Point Michaud.

⑤⑥ The road onward along the Bras d'Or Lakes leads through pretty Acadian villages along the twisting channel of St. Peter's Inlet, with many coves and islands, and then along the main body of the lake to **Dundee,** a large resort with a spectacular hilltop golf course overlooking the island-studded waters of West Bay. The alternative route, equally engaging, leads along the Atlantic coast, through coves and islands past River Tillard and River Bourgeois to Louisdale.

Turn off on Route 320 for Isle Madame, a 27-square-kilometer (17-square-mile) island named for Madame de Maintenon, second wife of Louis XIV. Route 320 leads through the villages of Poulamon and D'Escousse, and overlooks the protected waterway of Lennox Passage, with its spangle of islands. Route 206 meanders through the low hills to a maze of land and water at West Arichat. Together, the two routes encircle the island, meeting at Arichat, the principal town of **Isle Madame.**

⑤⑦ **Arichat** was once the seat of the local Catholic diocese; **Notre Dame de l'Assumption church,** built in 1837, still retains the grandeur of its former cathedral status. The bishop's palace, the only one in Cape Breton, is now a law office. The two cannons overlooking the harbor were installed after the town was sacked by John Paul Jones, founder of the U.S. Navy, during the American Revolution. The town was an important shipbuilding and trading center during the 19th century, and some fine old houses from that period still remain, along with the 18th-century **LeNoir Forge** (☎ 902/226–9364; ☉ May–Sept., weekdays 9–5, Sat. 10–3).

A dead-end road leads to the Acadian villages of Petit de Grat, Sampson's Cove, and **Little Anse;** with its rocky red bluffs, cobble shores, tiny harbor, and brightly painted houses, the latter is particularly attractive to artists and photographers.

From Louisdale, Route 104 passes through the woods and crosses the Inhabitants River to **Port Hawkesbury,** a new industrial center around the deep-water port created when, in 1955, the Canso Causeway blocked the once-fierce currents from the Gulf of St. Lawrence. Port Hawkesbury has a paper mill, an electrical generating station, a gypsum wallboard plant, and an oil trans-shipment depot. It also has all the usual services, including a number of motels.

Eight kilometers (5 miles) farther on is **Port Hastings,** at the Cape Breton end of the Canso Causeway. Crossing the Causeway, Halifax is a three-hour drive away.

SHOPPING

Although the government is reviewing its policy on sales tax refunds, at present you may claim a refund of Nova Scotia's 11% sales tax (nonrefundable on accommodations, meals, and alcohol) paid on goods you transport home. Refund claims must be filed within 90 days of leaving Nova Scotia and must be in excess of $15. (Refunds of the national Goods and Services Tax must be applied for separately; *see* Money and Expenses *in* the Gold Guide's Smart Travel Tips.) For refund forms and information, contact the **Provincial Tax Commission** (Tax Refund Unit, Box 755, Halifax, Nova Scotia B3J 2V4, ☎ 902/424–5946 or 1/424–6708 in Nova Scotia).

Halifax

The Spring Garden Road area has two stylish shopping malls, with shops selling everything from designer clothing to fresh pasta. **Jennifers of Nova Scotia** (5635 Spring Garden Rd., ☎ 902/425–3119) sells locally made jewelry, pottery, wool sweaters, and soaps. You can also find fine crafts in Historic Properties and the Barrington Inn complex, near the waterfront, at such shops as **Pewter House** (1875 Granville St., ☎ 902/423–8843) and the **Stornoway** (1873 Granville St., ☎ 902/422–9507). The **Plaid Place** (1903 Barrington Pl., ☎ 902/429–6872) has a dazzling array of tartans and Highland accessories. The **Wool Sweater Outlet** (1870 Hollis St., ☎ 902/422–9209) offers wool and cotton sweaters at good prices.

Elsewhere in Nova Scotia

SHOPPING MALLS

Shopping malls in Nova Scotia are similar to those in other parts of Canada or in the United States. Two of the largest malls are the **Mic Mac Mall** in Dartmouth, off the A. Murray Mackay Bridge; and the **Halifax Shopping Centre** on Mumford Road. On Route 4 in Sydney you'll find the **Mayflower Mall** on the way to Glace Bay.

SPECIALTY SHOPS

Antiques, gifts, and crafts are especially popular in Cape Breton, but shops selling these items appear in numbers throughout the province. You'll find everything from blacksmithing in East Dover and silversmithing in Waverley to leaded glass ornaments in Purcells Cove, hooked rugs in Cheticamp, woolens in Yarmouth, wooden toys in Middletown, pewter in Wolfville, pottery in Arichat, and apple dolls in Halifax. A good shoppers' guide is the *Buyers Guide to Art and Crafts in*

Nova Scotia, from the Department of Tourism and Culture (*see* Important Addresses and Numbers *in* Nova Scotia Essentials, *below*).

SPORTS AND THE OUTDOORS

The Department of Tourism and Culture (*see* Important Addresses and Numbers *in* Nova Scotia Essentials, *below*) publishes *The Nova Scotia Travel Guide,* which has an Outdoors chapter with information on aviation, diving, kayaking, river rafting, rock-hounding, windsurfing, skiing, and many other sports.

Biking

Bicycle Tours in Nova Scotia (C$5.00) is published by **Bicycle Nova Scotia** (5516 Spring Garden Rd., Box 3010, Halifax B3J 3G6, ☎ 902/425–5450). **Backroads** (1516 5th St., Suite Q333, Berkeley, CA 94710, ☎ 510/527–1555 or 800/245–3874) offers five- and six-day bike trips on the Evangeline Trail.

Bird-Watching

Nova Scotia is located on the "Atlantic Flyway" and is an important staging point for migrating species. An excellent, beautifully illustrated book, *Birds of Nova Scotia,* by Robie Tufts, is a must on every ornithologist's reading list. One of the highest concentrations of bald eagles in North America—about 250 nesting pairs—is located in Cape Breton, along the Bras d'Or Lake region or in Cape Breton Highlands National Park. July and August are the best eagle-watching times. MacNabs Island, in Halifax harbor, has a large osprey population. The Bird Islands, off the coast of Cape Breton, are home to a variety of sea birds, including the rare Atlantic puffin.

Canoeing

Nova Scotia is seamed with small rivers and lakes, by which the Micmac Indians roamed both Cape Breton and the peninsula. Especially good canoe routes are within Kejimkujik National Park (*see* National Parks, *below*). The publication *Canoe Routes of Nova Scotia* and a variety of route maps are available from the Nova Scotia Government Bookstore (Box 637, 1700 Granville St., Halifax B3J 2T3, ☎ 902/424–7580). Information is also available from Canoe NS (Box 3010S, Halifax B3J 3G6, ☎ 902/425–5450, ext. 316; FAX 902/425–5606).

Fishing

Nova Scotia has more than 9,000 lakes and 100 brooks; practically all lakes and streams are open to anglers. The catch includes Atlantic salmon (June–September), brook and sea trout, bass, rainbow trout, and shad. You can get a nonresident fishing license from any Department of Natural Resources office in the province and at most sporting-goods stores.

Golf

Nova Scotia and Cape Breton have 38 golf courses, as well as driving ranges and miniature golf courses. The 9-hole course at Parrsboro and the 18-hole links at Dundee offer spectacular views of the Minas Basin and Bras d'Or Lake, respectively. One of Canada's finest courses is at the Pines Resort Hotel, in Digby (*see* Lodging, *below*), offering 18 challenging holes amid a pine forest.

Hiking

The province has a wide variety of trails along the rugged coastline and inland through forest glades, which enable you to experience otherwise inaccessible scenery, wildlife, and vegetation. *Hiking Trails of*

Nova Scotia ($12.95) is available through **Gooselane Editions** (469 King St., Fredericton, New Brunswick, E3R 1E5, ☎ 506/450–4251).

Windsurfing

Wind and water conditions are often excellent for windsurfing, the fastest-growing aquatic summer sport in Nova Scotia. Lessons and equipment rentals are available from retail outlets throughout the province.

Beaches

The province is one big seashore. The warmest beaches are found on the Northumberland Strait shore and include Heather Beach, Caribou, and Melmerby, all in provincial parks. The west coast of Cape Breton and the Bras d'Or Lakes also offer fine beaches and warm saltwater.

National Parks

Nova Scotia has two national parks: **Cape Breton Highlands National Park** (*see* Tour 4, *above*), through which the Cabot Trail runs; and **Kejimkujik National Park** (*see* Tour 2, *above*), in the interior of the western part of the province. Essentially a wilderness area with many lakes, Kejimkujik offers well-marked canoe routes into the interior, with primitive campsites. Nature trails are marked for hikers, boat rentals are available, and there's freshwater swimming. One precaution: Check for ticks after hiking in the deep woods. Kejimkujik also operates the Seaside Adjunct near Port Joli on the Atlantic shore that protects one of the last undeveloped tracts of coastline on the Eastern Seaboard. There are two mile-long beaches, both reached by hiking trails (no visitor services; day use only). *To Kejimkujik: Take Rte. 8 from Liverpool or Annapolis Royal, Box 36, Maitland Bridge, B0T 1N0, ☎ 902/682–2772.* ☞ *Park fee: $4 per vehicle per day, $9 for 4-day pass, $25 for annual pass. Camping fee: $8.50–$13 per day.*

DINING AND LODGING

Dining

Many of Halifax's restaurants are set in refurbished historic homes or other restored quarters. The menus almost always center on seafood, including Malpeque oysters, Fundy lobster, and Digby scallops.

Along the main highways, your best bet for a meal will be at truck stops, particularly the **Irving Big Stops.** Expect nothing fancy, just generous helpings of plain, solid food at reasonable prices.

What to Wear

Unless otherwise noted, dress at restaurants throughout Nova Scotia is casual; only at expensive properties is a jacket required.

CATEGORY	COST*
$$$$	over $50
$$$	$35–$50
$$	$15–$35
$	under $15

per person, excluding drinks, service, 7% GST, and 11% sales tax on meals costing more than $3.

Lodging

Nova Scotia has a superb computerized system called **Check In** (☎ 800/565–0000; in Halifax-Dartmouth, 902/425–5781; in the continental

U.S., 800/341–6096; in Maine, 800/492–0643), which provides information and makes reservations with more than 700 hotels, motels, inns, campgrounds, and car-rental agencies. Check In also represents most properties in Prince Edward Island and some in New Brunswick.

Several hotel and motel chains operate in Nova Scotia. **Best Western** (☎ 800/528–1234) and **Wandlyn Inn** (in eastern Canada, ☎ 800/561–0000; in the U.S., 800/561–0006) are mid-range chains, quite suitable for families. **Comfort Inn** (☎ 800/668–4200) is a chain of budget hotels with clean and pleasant rooms, but no eating facilities.

In addition to the reliable chains, Halifax-Dartmouth has a number of excellent hotels; reservations are necessary year-round, and can be made by calling Check In (*see above*). Expect to pay considerably more in the capital district than elsewhere. Those on a budget might try a hostel, country inn, or bed-and-breakfast.

CATEGORY	COST*
$$$$	over $80
$$$	$65–$80
$$	$45–$65
$	under $45

All prices are for a standard double room, excluding 10% service charge.

Halifax-Dartmouth

Dining

$$$ MacAskill's Restaurant. Experience a continuing tradition of Nova Scotian hospitality in this romantic dining room overlooking beautiful Halifax Harbor. Award-winning chefs will delight you with a unique selection of seafood dishes prepared using only the finest, freshest fish available. Specialties include pepper steak, flambéed table-side. ✕ *88 Alderney Dr., Dartmouth Ferry Terminal Bldg.,* ☎ *902/466–3100. AE, DC, MC, V.*

$$–$$$ Birmingham Bar & Grill. This perennial Halifax favorite offers a unique and varied menu focusing on current trends, accompanied by an extensive wine and beverage list. Open-air dining in the summer and live jazz music enhance the setting at this fun, friendly place. ✕ *5657 Spring Garden Rd. (upper level, Park Lane),* ☎ *902/420–9622. Reservations advised. AE, MC, V.*

$$–$$$ Ryan Duffy's. Steaks are the specialty at this spot, in the Spring Garden Place, where you can select your own cut by the ounce; other options include an array of seafood and lamb. Upstairs, corner window seats allow you to watch the world walk by from inside this brass and wood-paneled dining room. The green-and-burgundy color scheme adds to Ryan Duffy's old-time atmosphere. ✕ *5640 Spring Garden Rd.,* ☎ *902/421–1116. Reservations advised for dining room. AE, MC, V.*

$$–$$$ Salty's on the Waterfront. This restaurant gets the prize for the best
★ location in the city: It overlooks Privateer's Wharf and the entire harbor. Request a table with a window view, and save room for their famous dessert, called "Cadix" (chocolate moussse over praline crust). The **Salty Dog Bar** on the ground level is less expensive, and serves lunches outside on the wharf in summer. ✕ *1869 Upper Water St.,* ☎ *902/432–6818. Reservations advised. AE, DC, MC, V.*

$$ Da Maurizio. This popular northern Italian restaurant is located in the Brewery Center. Chef-owner Maurizio serves homemade pastas with olive oil, ravioli stuffed with duck or rabbit, grilled fish and meats, and the only risotto in town. The brewery has enormously high ceilings—

15 and 20 feet—and stone-and-brick walls adorned with paintings and masks of a Venetian carnival theme. Fresh flowers are placed at linen-draped tables set with gleaming silver. There's a wide wine selection by the bottle and by the glass, and food is served in the wine bar, too. ✕ *1496 Lower Water St., ☎ 902/423–0859. Reservations advised. AE, MC, V. Closed Sun. No lunch Sat.*

$$ **Old Man Morias.** Authentic Greek specialties at this turn-of-the-cen-
★ tury Halifax town house include lamb on a spit and moussaka. Greek music, tapestries, and archways set the mood for a traditionally Greek evening, and full-flavored dishes enrich the spirit; sample the fried squid and fried cheese appetizers. ✕ *1150 Barrington St., ☎ 902/422–7960. Reservations advised. AE, DC, MC, V. Closed Sun. No lunch.*

$–$$ **Privateer's Warehouse.** History surrounds you in this 200-year-old build-ing, where three restaurants share the early 18th-century stone walls and hewn beams, serving food in descending order of elegance. **The Upper Deck Waterfront Fishery & Grill** (☎ 902/422–1289), where you can experience a nautical setting with great views of the harbor, special-izes in Nova Scotian regional cuisine such as oysters, fresh Atlantic salmon, and lobster straight from their holding tank. The **Middle Deck Pasta Works & Beverage Co.** (☎ 902/426–1500) has a bistro-style, relaxed atmosphere. The varied menu features innovative pastas, spe-cialty drinks, and traditional cuisine; a children's menu is also avail-able. The **Lower Deck Good Time Pub** (☎ 902/426–1501) is a boisterous bar with long trestle tables, a patio, beer mugs for thumping, and lots of hand-holding and singing of traditional Maritime, Irish, and Scot-tish songs; fish and chips and other pub food is served. ✕ *Historic Prop-erties, Lower Water St. AE, DC, MC, V.*

$ **A.K.'s Food & Beverage Emporium.** When you're hungry for the good old days, relax amidst mementos of Bogie and Bacall, Chaplin and Churchill, and dig into a hearty meal. From innovative salads to meaty sandwiches to full dinners, there is something for everyone, along with a selection of imported beers. ✕ *Brewery Market, 1496 Lower Water St., Halifax, ☎ 902/492–2441. AE, DC, MC, V. Closed Sun.*

$ **Satisfaction Feast.** This small, vegetarian restaurant and bakery is in-formal, friendly, and usually packed at lunchtime. The food is simple and wholesome; try the fresh whole-wheat bread and one of the daily curries. Smoking is not permitted. ✕ *1581 Grafton St., ☎ 902/422–3540. MC, V.*

Lodging

$$$$ **Cambridge Suites.** "A suite for the price of a room" is this hotel's motto . . . and a good one it is. Choose among three suite sizes; all have sitting room and kitchenette. What makes this lodging even more de-sirable is its convenient location near the Citadel and the Spring Gar-den Road shopping district, and it's only a short walk from downtown. Complimentary Continental breakfast is served. ☎ *1583 Brunswick St., B3J 3P5, ☎ 902/420–0555 or 800/565–1263 in Canada, FAX 902/420–9379. 200 mini-suites and 1-bedrooms. Pool, hot tub, sauna, ex-ercise room. AE, D, MC, V.*

$$$$ **Chateau Halifax.** This first-class Canadian Pacific hotel offers spacious, attractive rooms in a perfect location, near Scotia Square and Historic Properties. There's a good dining room and an upbeat bar with live entertainment. ☎ *1990 Barrington St., B3J 1P2, ☎ 902/425–6700 or 800/441–1414. 279 rooms, 21 suites. Restaurant, coffee shop, bar, in-door pool, hot tub, sauna, exercise equipment. AE, DC, MC, V.*

$$$$ **Citadel Inn Halifax.** Situated at the base of Citadel Hill, this business-oriented hotel is still within walking distance of the action. Rooms with a harbor view are recommended, though they will cost more than those without. Free parking is an asset in car-clogged Halifax. Continental breakfast is included in the room rate. ☎ *1960 Brunswick St., B3J 2G7,* ☎ *902/422–1391. 261 rooms, 6 suites. Restaurant, indoor pool, hot tub, sauna, exercise room. AE, DC, MC, V.*

$$$$ **Halliburton House Inn.** Halifax's only four-star registered heritage property, this hotel is an elegant renovation of three 19th-century town houses. Twenty-seven comfortable rooms are furnished with period antiques, lending a homey ambience to the inn. All have private baths. Several suites have working fireplaces. Continental breakfast is included in the room rate. ☎ *5184 Morris St., B3H 1B3,* ☎ *902/420–0658,* FAX *902/423–2324. 24 rooms, 3 suites. Dining room, library. AE, DC, MC, V.*

$$$$ **Holiday Inn Halifax Centre.** This first-class property overlooking Halifax Commons is 1 kilometer (½ mile) from Scotia Square and the harbor. The property's new renovations include appointments in the guest rooms and an elegant lobby. ☎ *1980 Robie St., B3H 3G5,* ☎ *902/423–1161,* FAX *902/423–9069. 232 rooms, 4 suites. Restaurant, bar, indoor pool, hot tub, sauna, exercise room, 7 meeting rooms, parking. AE, DC, MC, V.*

$$$$ **Prince George Hotel.** The Prince George is a luxurious and understated business-oriented hotel. The contemporary mahogany furnishings include a writing desk. The building is conveniently connected by underground tunnel to the World Trade and Convention Center. ☎ *1725 Market St., B3J 3N9,* ☎ *902/425–1986 or 800/565–1567 in Canada. 208 rooms, 3 suites. Restaurant, 2 bars, café, pub, pool, hot tub, exercise room, concierge. AE, DC, MC, V.*

$$$$ **Ramada Renaissance.** Located in Dartmouth's Burnside Industrial Park, this luxury hotel is aimed at the business traveler as well as families. There is an 108-foot indoor water slide. ☎ *240 Brownlow Ave., Dartmouth, B3B 1X6,* ☎ *902/468–8888 or 800/561–3733 in Canada,* FAX *902/468–8765. 178 rooms, 30 suites. Restaurant, bar, room service, pool, hot tub, sauna, exercise room, meeting rooms. AE, DC, MC, V.*

$$$$ **Sheraton Halifax.** The convenient location, in Historic Properties, contributes to the elegance of this waterfront hotel. Other assets include the hotel's indoor pool with a summer sun deck and spa facilities. There's also docking space for yachts. In summer you can sit on an outdoor terrace at the **Grand Banker** restaurant and eat lobster while you watch the ships go by. ☎ *1919 Upper Water St., B3J 3J5,* ☎ *902/421–1700 or 800/325–3535. 333 rooms, 20 suites. 2 restaurants, bar, deli, room service, dock, concierge, meeting rooms. AE, DC, MC, V.*

$$ **Waken'n Eggs B&B.** Situated across the Common from the Citadel is this Victorian, originally built as two homes, but now a single house. The comfortable, eclectic furnishings include antiques and folk art, and the helpful service makes this a hospitable B&B. ☎ *2114 Windsor St., B3K 5B4,* ☎ *902/422–4737. 3 rooms, 1 with private bath. No credit cards.*

Mainland Nova Scotia

Annapolis Royal

LODGING

$$ **Auberge Wandlyn Royal Anne Motel.** This modern, no-frills motel offers clean rooms at reasonable rates. Enjoy the pleasant, quiet, country setting by taking a walk on the motel's 20 acres of land. ☎ *Rte. 1 (Box 628), B0S 1A0,* ☎ *902/532–2323,* FAX *902/532–7277. 30 rooms. Hot tub, sauna, meeting rooms. AE, DC, MC, V.*

$ **Moorings Bed & Breakfast.** This tall, beautiful home overlooking Annapolis Basin, built in 1881 by sea captain Joseph Hall and the former home of author H. R. Percy, comes complete with fireplace, tin ceilings, antiques, and contemporary art. ⊡ *Box 118, Granville Ferry B0S 1K0,* ☎ *902/532–2146. 3 rooms, 2 with half-bath, 2 with shared full bath. Nov.–May, by reservation only. V.*

Antigonish
DINING
$$ Lobster Treat Restaurant. Once a two-room schoolhouse, this property has since been converted into a cozily decorated brick, pine, and stained-glass restaurant. Located on the Trans-Canada Highway, it's convenient for travelers following the Sunrise Trail. The varied menu features fresh seafood and vegetables year-round, as well as bread and pies baked on the premises. Because of a relaxed atmosphere and a varied menu, including a separate list for children, families enjoy coming here. ✗ *241 Post Rd.,* ☎ *902/863–5465,* ℻ *902/863–2944. Reservations advised in summer. AE, DC, MC, V. Closed Nov.–mid-Apr.*

Bedford
DINING
$$ Pictures Restaurant. A fun place to eat with the family, this spot is also popular for business lunches. The restaurant takes its name from the collection of vintage photographs of Bedford that adorn the walls. Pasta plays a big part in the picture, and there's a special children's menu. ✗ *1516 Bedford Hwy.,* ☎ *902/835–8082. AE, DC, MC, V.*

Chester
DINING
$ The Galley. Decked out in nautical bric-a-brac and providing a spectacular view of the ocean, this restaurant offers a pleasant, relaxed atmosphere. The menu features seafood chowder, live lobster from their in-house pound, and homemade desserts. ✗ *Rte. 3, on the Marina (take exit 8 off 103),* ☎ *902/275–4700. Reservations advised. AE, MC, V. Closed mid-Dec.–mid-Mar.*

Digby
DINING AND LODGING
$$$$ The Pines Resort Hotel. Complete with fireplaces, sitting rooms, a bistro, dining room, and a view of Annapolis Basin, this elegant property offers myriad amenities. Seafood with a French touch is served daily in the restaurant, and the lounge is perfect for quiet relaxation. ⊡ *Box 70, Shore Rd., B0V 1A0,* ☎ *902/245–2511 or 800/667–4637,* ℻ *902/ 245-6133. 83 rooms in main lodge, 61 in cottages. Restaurant, bar, pool, sauna, 18-hole golf course, 2 tennis courts. AE, DC, MC, V. Closed mid-Oct.–May.*

Lorneville
DINING AND LODGING
$$$ Amherst Shore Country Inn. This seaside country inn with a beautiful ★ view of Northumberland Straight has comfortable rooms, suites and seaside cottages fronting 600 feet of private beach. Incredibly well-prepared four-course dinners are served at one daily seating (7:30 PM, by reservation only). ⊡ *32 km (20 mi) from Amherst on Rte. 366, R.R. 2, Amherst, B4H 3X9,* ☎ *902/661–4800. 5 rooms, suites, cottages. Restaurant. AE, DC, MC, V. Closed late Oct.–Apr.*

Lunenburg
LODGING
$$-$$$ Bluenose Lodge. This 130-year-old mansion has nine large bedrooms and offers a full complimentary breakfast featuring such treats as freshly baked muffins, stewed rhubarb, and quiche. The bedrooms and

sitting areas are furnished with distinctive antiques. Solomon Gundy's, an award-winning seafood restaurant, is on the premises. ⊠ *Box 399, 10 Falkland St., B0J 2C0,* ☎ *902/634–8851 or 800/565–8851. 9 rooms. AE, D, MC, V.*

$$–$$$ **Boscawen Inn.** Antiques and fireplaces decorate this elegant mansion built in 1888, located in the center of this National Heritage Town. The inn has views of the town's harbor. Afternoon tea is served in the drawing rooms or on the balcony. McLachlan House, an annex, has four harbor-view suites which opened in 1994. ⊠ *150 Cumberland St., Box 1343, B0J 2C0,* ☎ *902/634–3325. 17 rooms. AE, MC, V. Closed Jan.–Easter.*

Masstown
LODGING

$$–$$$ **Shady Maple B&B.** Here's a unique property: a working dairy farm where you can breakfast on fresh eggs and the farm's own maple syrup, jams, and jellies. Enjoy the smoke-free rooms and sun-dried bed linen, and take a dip in the pool. One of the three rooms is a deluxe suite with a waterbed. ⊠ *R.R. 1, B0M 1G0,* ☎ *902/662–3565. 3 rooms. Pool. MC, V.*

Musquodoboit Harbour
LODGING

$$–$$$ **Salmon River House.** About 35 minutes east of Dartmouth, where Route 7 crosses the Salmon River, is this unpretentious white-frame inn, situated on 30 acres and providing glorious views. The home has a licensed dining room, sun room, wheelchair-accessible guest room, and one room with a waterbed and whirlpool bath. ⊠ *R.R. 2, head of Jeddore, B0J 1P0,* ☎ *902/889–3353 or 800/565–3353,* 𝔽𝔸𝕏 *902/889–3653. 6 rooms with bath or shower. Dining room, boating, fishing. MC, V.*

Pictou
DINING AND LODGING

$$–$$$ **Braeside Inn.** Built in 1938, this inn, situated on a 5-acre hillside site in the center of historic Pictou, has been totally refurbished and now offers well-appointed accommodations and fine food. Beaches are nearby. The dining room specializes in fresh seafood dishes. ⊠ *126 Front St., Box 1810, B0K 1H0,* ☎ *902/485–5046,* 𝔽𝔸𝕏 *902/485–1701. 20 rooms with bath. 2 dining rooms, pool, meeting room. AE, MC, V.*

LODGING

$$ **Walker Inn.** A hospitable and energetic Swiss couple run this downtown inn in their brick Georgian-style town house, built in 1865. Every room is different, the dining room is fully licensed, and there's a new library-conference room. A Continental breakfast buffet is included in the room rate. ⊠ *34 Coleraine St., Box 629, B0K 1H0,* ☎ *902/485–1433. 10 no-smoking rooms with bath. Restaurant, meeting room. AE, MC, V.*

Wolfville
DINING AND LODGING

$$$ **Blomidon Inn.** This 19th-century sea captain's mansion, located in the beautiful Annapolis Valley, was restored in 1981. Guestrooms are uniquely furnished, most with four-poster beds. Relax over lunch or dinner in one of the dining rooms or on the terrace, enjoying the fresh fare from the valley and sea. Lobster bisque, and salmon and scallop Florentine are among the menu favorites. Afternoon tea is served daily, and there's a weekend brunch (reservations advised). ⊠ *127 Main St., Box 839, B0P 1X0,* ☎ *902/542–2291,* 𝔽𝔸𝕏 *902/542–7461. 26 rooms. 2 dining rooms, tennis court, horseshoes, shuffleboard, meeting room. MC, V. Closed Dec. 25.*

Yarmouth
DINING AND LODGING

$$ Manor Inn. With superior rooms and good food in pleasant surroundings, this colonial mansion beside Doctors Lake on Route 1 is a nice find. There are four settings and price ranges to choose from: coachhouse units, lakeside or rose-garden motels, or the main estate. Steak and lobster are the specialties in the dining room; reservations are required. ☎ *Box 56, Hebron, B0W 1X0,* ☎ *902/742–2487,* FAX *902/742–8094. 53 rooms. 2 dining rooms, 2 bars, outdoor café, pool, hot tub, tennis court. AE, DC, MC, V.*

Cape Breton Island

Baddeck
LODGING

$$$$ Inverary Inn Resort. Located on the shores of the magnificent Bras d'Or Lakes, this resort offers stunning views and a lot of activities for the money. Choose from cozy pine-paneled cottages, modern hotel units, or the elegant 100-year-old main lodge. The property offers boating and swimming and close proximity to the village, but the resort remains tranquil. Families will appreciate the on-site children's playground and the choice of dining in the Lakeside Cafe or the elegant main dining room. The main lodge with its paneled walls, stone fireplace, and polished horse brasses, has a strong Scottish flavor. ☎ *Box 190, B0E 1B0,* ☎ *902/295–2674,* FAX *902/295–5660. 137 rooms. Restaurant, indoor pool, sauna, 3 tennis courts, chapel. AE, D, MC, V.*

Iona
DINING AND LODGING

$$ Highland Heights Inn. The rural surroundings, the Scottish home-style cooking served near the dining room's huge stone fireplace, and the unspoiled view of the lake substitute nicely for the Scottish Highlands. The inn is located on a hillside beside the Nova Scotia Highland Village, overlooking the village of Iona, where some residents still speak the Gaelic language of their ancestors. Enjoy the salmon (or any fish in season), fresh-baked oat cakes, and homemade desserts. ☎ *Box 19, Iona,* ☎ *902/725–2360,* FAX *902/725–2800. 26 rooms. Dining room. D, MC, V. Closed mid-Oct.–mid-May.*

Margaree Valley
LODGING

$$ Normaway Inn. This secluded 1920s inn, nestled on 250 acres in the hills of the valley at the beginning of the Cabot Trail, offers distinctive rooms and cabins, most with woodstoves and screened porches; some have hot tubs. Take advantage of the traditional entertainment or films featured nightly, and the weekly square dances in the "Barn." The inn is known for its gourmet country cuisine, all of which is prepared on the premises. The owners will organize whale watches, boat tours, horseback riding, and salmon- and trout-fishing trips for interested guests. ☎ *Box 326, B0E 2C0,* ☎ *902/248–2987 or 800/565–9463,* FAX *902/248–2600. 9 rooms, 19 cabins. Restaurant, tennis court, hiking, bicycles. MC, V. Closed mid-Oct.–mid-June.*

Northeast Margaree
LODGING

$–$$ Heart of Hart's Tourist Farm. This 100-year-old rural farmhouse on the Cabot Trail is within walking distance of the village. The theme is "very country," with woodstove, antiques, colonial colored glass, and an array of flowers in the gardens. Hot homemade oatmeal, Red River cereal (oatmeal), and garden-fresh rhubarb juice are among the specialties served with the full breakfast that's included in the room rate. Salmon- and trout-fishing trips can be arranged upon request. ☏ *Cabot Trail B0E 2H0,* ☎ *902/248–2765. 5 rooms. MC, V. Closed Nov.–Apr.*

Sydney

DINING

$$ Joe's Warehouse. For excellent food in the heart of town, stop here, where the specialties include local seafood and prime rib. The porridge rolls and homemade scones also win rave reviews. In summer, when the patio is open, the restaurant seats 200 people. Dress is casual and the atmosphere fun. After dinner head downstairs for live music and dancing at Smooth Herman's. ✗ *424 Charlotte St.,* ☎ *902/539–6686. AE, DC, MC, V.*

LODGING

$$$ Delta Sydney. This hotel is located on the harbor, beside the yacht club and close to the center of town. The attractively decorated guest rooms each have a view of the harbor. The intimate dining room specializes in seafood and Continental cuisine. ☏ *300 Esplanade, B1P 6J4,* ☎ *in Canada, 902/562–7500 or 800/268–1133; 800/887–1133 in the U.S; FAX 902/562–3023. 152 rooms. Restaurant, lounge, indoor pool, sauna, exercise room. AE, DC, MC, V.*

THE ARTS AND NIGHTLIFE

The Arts

Film

Halifax has a dynamic and growing film industry, which presents current work during the **Atlantic Film Festival,** held in Halifax the third week in September. The festival also showcases feature films, TV movies, and documentaries made elsewhere in the Atlantic Provinces. **Wormwood's Dog and Monkey Cinema** (2015 Gottingen St., ☎ 902/422–3700) shows Canadian, foreign-language, and experimental films.

Music

Live concerts and musical presentations are held in Halifax at the **Metro Centre** (Brunswick and Duke Sts., ☎ 902/451–1202) and the **Rebecca Cohn Auditorium** (6101 University Ave., ☎ 902/494–2646). **Symphony Nova Scotia** normally appears at "the Cohn."

Scotia Festival of Music (☎ 902/429–9469) presents internationally recognized classical musicians in concerts and master classes each May and June at various locations in Halifax. **Musique Royale** hosts an August series of superb Renaissance and baroque concerts in historic buildings around the province. The **Atlantic Jazz Festival** takes place in Halifax in mid-July.

Talented musicians abound in Nova Scotia, ranging from traditional fiddlers to folk singers and rock bands. They appear in clubs, concerts, dances, and a constant stream of open-air festivals. Names to watch for include The Rankin Family, The Barra MacNeills, the Minglewood Band, Sam Moon, Rita MacNeil, David MacIsaac, Scott Macmillan, and such traditional fiddlers as Buddy MacMaster, Ashley MacIsaac, Sandy MacIntyre, Lee Cremo, Jerry Holland, and Natalie MacMaster. An annual **Nova Scotia Bluegrass and Oldtime Music Festival** is held in Ardoise the last weekend in July; the **Lunenburg Folk Harbour Festival,** devoted to acoustic instruments and authentic folk music, takes place in early August; many leading fiddlers appear at Cape Breton's **Big Cove Concert** in mid-July.

Theater

Canada's oldest professional repertory theater, the **Neptune Theatre** (5216 Sackville St., Halifax, ☎ 902/429–7300), presents a full season each summer and winter of performances from classics to contemporary Canadian drama. The **Mulgrave Road Co-Op Theatre** (☎ 902/533–2092) is a small but active professional company performing all over the Maritime Provinces, producing original plays based on local history. **Mermaid Theatre** (☎ 902/798–5841), based in Windsor, travels the world with original children's plays that make extensive use of masks and puppets.

The **Cape Breton Summertime Revue,** based in Sydney, performs an annual original revue of music and comedy that tours Nova Scotia during June and August.

The **Atlantic Fringe Festival** presents 40 shows in eight venues during the first week of September. Dinner theaters in Halifax include the **Historic Feast Company** (☎ 902/420–1840), which presents shows set in the 19th century at Historic Properties Thursday, Friday, and Saturday evenings; and the **Grafton Street Dinner Theatre** (1741 Grafton St., ☎ 902/425–1961), where shows run Wednesday through Saturday.

Parrsboro's professional **Ship's Company Theatre** (☎ 902/254–2003) offers a summer season of plays based on historical events of the region, performed aboard the MV *Kipawo,* a former Minas Basin ferry. The **Chester Summer Theatre** (☎ 902/275–2933) operates throughout the summer. Among the best of Nova Scotia's thriving amateur companies are the **Kipawo Show Boat Company** (☎ 902/542–3500), which performs in Wolfville on summer weekends, and **Theatre Antigonish** (☎ 902/867–3954), which performs at St. Francis Xavier University in Antigonish.

Many other towns have theaters that present touring shows and occasional local productions, notably Chester, Liverpool, Yarmouth, Annapolis Royal, Middle Musquodoboit, Pictou, and Sydney. Glace Bay's opulent old opera house, the **Savoy Theatre,** is the home of the summer-long Festival on the Bay.

Nightlife

The multilevel entertainment center in Historic Properties, **Privateer's Warehouse** (☎ 902/422–1289), is a popular night-time hangout. At the ground-level Lower Deck tavern you can quaff a beer to Celtic music.

Other popular Halifax night spots include **Cheers** (1743 Grafton St., ☎ 902/421–1655), with bands and entertainment nightly, and **O'Carroll's** (1860 Upper Water St., ☎ 902/423–4405), a restaurant, oyster bar, and lounge where you can hear live Irish music nightly.

NOVA SCOTIA ESSENTIALS

Arriving and Departing

By Bus

Greyhound Lines (800/231–2222) from New York, and **Voyageur Inc.** (☎ 613/238–5900) from Montréal, connect with **Scotia Motor Tours** or **SMT** (☎ 506/458–6000) through New Brunswick, which links (rather inconveniently) with **Acadian Lines Limited** (☎ 902/454–8279), which provides inter-urban services within Nova Scotia.

By Car
The Trans-Canada Highway reaches Nova Scotia through New Brunswick. Entering the province at Amherst, it becomes Route 104. To reach Halifax, pick up Route 102 at Truro. To reach Cape Breton, continue on Route 104.

Throughout Nova Scotia, the highways numbered from 100 to 199 are all-weather, limited-access roads, with 100-kilometer-per-hour (62-mile-per-hour) speed limits. The last two digits usually match the number of an older trunk highway along the same route, numbered from 1 to 99. Thus, Route 102, between Halifax and Truro, matches the older Route 2, between the same towns. Roads numbered from 200 to 399 are secondary roads that usually link villages. Unless otherwise posted, the speed limit on these and any roads other than the 100-series highways is 80 kilometers per hour (50 miles per hour).

Most highways in the province lead to Halifax and Dartmouth. Routes 3/103, 7, 2/102, and 1/101 terminate in the twin cities.

CAR RENTAL
Halifax is the most convenient place from which to begin your driving tour of the province. The following list details city and airport venues of rental-car agencies: **Avis** (5600 Sackville St., ☏ 902/423–6303; airport, ☏ 902/873–3523); **Budget** (1558 Hollis St., ☏ 902/421–1242; airport, ☏ 902/873–3509); **Hertz** (Halifax Sheraton, ☏ 902/421–1763; airport, ☏ 902/873–3700); **Thrifty** (6930 Lady Hammond, ☏ 902/422–4455; airport, ☏ 902/873–3527); **Tilden** (1130 Hollis St., ☏ 902/422–4433; airport, ☏ 902/873–3505).

For information about motor-home rentals call the **Nova Scotia Reservation System** (☏ 800/565–0000 in Canada or 800/341–6096 in the U.S.).

By Ferry
Three car ferries connect Nova Scotia with Maine and New Brunswick. **Marine Atlantic** (☏ 800/341–7981 in the U.S., 902/794–5700 in Canada) sails from Bar Harbor, Maine; and **Prince of Fundy Cruises** (☏ 800/341–7540) from Portland; both arrive in Yarmouth. From Saint John, New Brunswick, to Digby, Nova Scotia, ferry service is provided by **Marine Atlantic** (☏ 800/565–9470 in Canada or 800/341–7981 in the U.S.).

Marine Atlantic also operates ferries between New Brunswick and Prince Edward Island, and between Cape Breton and Newfoundland. In Nova Scotia, call 902/794–5700; in Newfoundland, 709/772–7701, in the U.S. call 800/341–7981. Between May and December, **Northumberland Ferries** (☏ 902/566–3838; or 800/565–0201 in Nova Scotia and Prince Edward Island) operate between Caribou, Nova Scotia, and Wood Islands, Prince Edward Island.

By Plane
The **Halifax International Airport** is 40 kilometers (25 miles) northeast of downtown Halifax. **Sydney Airport** is 13 kilometers (8 miles) east of Sydney.

Air Canada (☏ 902/429–7111 or 800/776–3000) provides regular, daily service to Halifax and Sydney, Nova Scotia, from New York, Boston, Toronto, Montréal, and St. John's, Newfoundland. **Canadian Airlines International** (☏ 800/527–8499) has service to Halifax via Toronto and Montréal. **Air Nova** (☏ 902/429–7111 or 800/776–3000) and **Air Atlantic** (☏ 800/426–7000 or 800/665–1177 in Canada) provide regional service to both airports with flights to Toronto, Montréal, and

Boston. **KLM** (☎ 902/455–8282) provides three weekly flights between Halifax and Amsterdam, with connections to the United Kingdom and continental Europe.

Limousine and taxi service, as well as car rentals, are available at Halifax, Sydney, and Yarmouth airports. Airport bus service to most Halifax and Dartmouth hotels costs $20 round-trip, $12 one-way. Regular taxi fare is $35 each way, but if you book in advance with **Aero Cab** (☎ 902/445–3393) the fare is $26 if you pay cash, slightly more with a credit card (MC, V). The trip takes 30–40 minutes.

By Train

VIA Rail (☎ 800/561–3949) provides service from Montréal to Halifax via Moncton, in New Brunswick, and Amherst and Truro, in Nova Scotia.

Amtrak (☎ 800/USA–RAIL) from New York City makes connections in Montréal.

Getting Around

Halifax

Walking and biking are excellent ways to get around and see the city, especially on weekdays when parking in the downtown area can be a problem. A pleasant alternative, however, is to take one of the rickshaws, available downtown during summer.

BY BUS

Metro Transit (☎ 902/421–6600) provides bus service throughout the cities of Halifax and Dartmouth, the town of Bedford, and (to a limited extent) the county of Halifax. The base fare is $1.25 adults, 75¢ children 5–15; exact change only.

BY FERRY

Metro Transit (☎ 902/421–6600) also runs three passenger ferries from the Halifax Ferry Terminal on the hour and half-hour from 6:30 AM to 11:57 PM. During the weekday commuter rush, ferries cross continuously to the Woodside Terminal from 6:52 AM to 10:04 AM and 3:37 PM to 6:19 PM only. Ferries also operate on Sundays during the summer (June–September). Free transfers are available from the ferry to the bus system (and vice-versa). The fare for a single crossing is $1, and is well worth it considering you get an up-close view of both waterfronts.

BY TAXI

Rates begin at about $2.50 and increase based on mileage and time. A crosstown trip should cost $5–$6, depending on traffic. Hailing a taxi can be difficult, but there are taxi stands at major hotels and shopping malls. Most Haligonians simply phone for a taxi service. Call **Aero Cab** (☎ 902/445–3393).

Elsewhere in Nova Scotia

You will need a car to explore the province beyond Halifax. For rental car information, *see* Car Rental *in* Arriving and Departing by Car, *above*.

As you explore Nova Scotia, be on the lookout for the 10 designated "Scenic Travelways" that appear throughout the province and are easily identified by roadside signs with icons that correspond with trail names. These routes, as well as tourist literature (maps and the provincial *Travel Guide*) published in accordance with this scheme, have been developed by the Nova Scotia Department of Tourism and Culture.

Guided Tours

Boat Tours

Murphy's on the Water (☎ 902/420–1015) sails various vessels: *Harbour Queen I*, a paddle wheeler; *Haligonian III*, an enclosed motor launch; *Stormy Weather I*, a 40-foot Cape Islander (fishing boat); and *Mar II*, a 75-foot sailing ketch. All operate from mid-May to late October, from berths at 1751 Lower Water Street on Cable Wharf, next to the Historic Properties in Halifax. Costs vary, but a basic tour of the harbor ranges from $10 to $15 adults, discount for children and senior citizens, children under 5 free, $30 families. Available for private parties.

Bluenose II (☎ 902/422–2678 or 902/424–5000) is an exact replica of Nova Scotia's 143-foot fishing schooner *Bluenose,* the ship that was the undefeated champion in international schooner racing for nearly 20 years and is featured on the Canadian dime. *Bluenose II* undertakes private sailings and charters in Halifax Harbour during the summer and participates in festivals throughout Nova Scotia. When available for public sailings, the schooner departs from Privateer's Wharf three times daily on a two-hour harbor sail. Fares are charged, and are approximately $15 for adults, $8 for senior citizens and children, but are subject to change. Reservations are required.

Bus Tours

Both **Gray Line Sightseeing** (☎ 902/454–8279) and **Cabana Tours** (☎ 902/423–6066) run coach tours through Halifax-Dartmouth and Peggy's Cove. **Halifax Double Decker Tours** (☎ 902/420–1155) offers two-hour tours on double-decker buses that leave daily from Historic Properties. You can also charter a bus from **Metro Transit** (☎ 902/421–6600) for a narrated tour.

Important Addresses and Numbers

Emergencies

Dial **"0"** for operator in emergencies; check the front of the local phone book for specific medical services.

Visitor Information

The **Nova Scotia Department of Tourism and Culture** (Box 130, Halifax, Nova Scotia B3J 2M7, ☎ 902/424–5000, 800/565–0000 in Canada or 800/341–6096 in the U.S.; FAX 902/420–1286) publishes a range of literature, including an exhaustive annual travel guide to sights, accommodations, and transportation.

The **Nova Scotia Tourism Information Centre** (Old Red Store at Historic Properties, Halifax, ☎ 902/424–4247), and **Tourism Halifax** (City Hall, Duke and Barrington Sts., ☎ 902/421–8736 or 902/421–2842) are open mid-June–Labor Day, daily 9–6; Labor Day–mid-June, weekdays 9–4:30.

3 Excursions from Nova Scotia to Coastal Maine

Purists hold that the Maine coast begins at Penobscot Bay. Here you'll find the rugged, "downeast" experience: classic townscapes, rocky shorelines, sandy beaches, and quaint downtown districts. Maine's principal tourist attraction, Acadia National Park, has 34,000 acres to explore. Others go to explore Freeport, north of Portland, where a bewildering assortment of outlets has sprung up around the famous outfitter L.L. Bean.

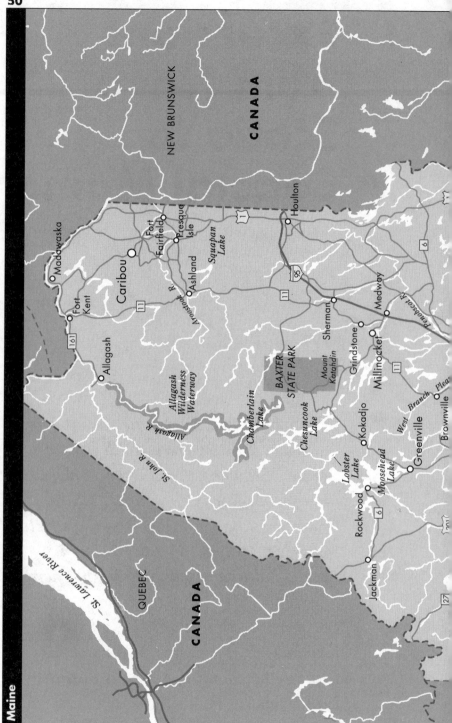

Maine

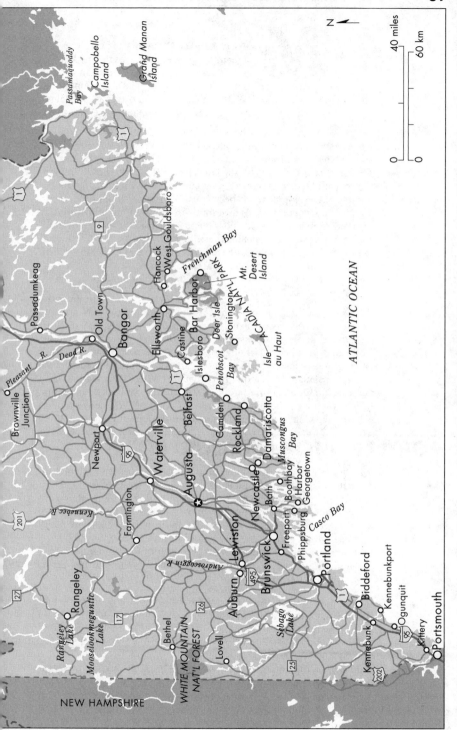

ATLANTIC OCEAN

NEW HAMPSHIRE

MAINE IS A LIKELY EXCURSION from Nova Scotia thanks to two ferry systems that make commuting easy. Boats depart from Yarmouth, Nova Scotia, and arrive in either Portland or Bar Harbor, Maine. Consider taking your car across, though, so you can travel up the Maine coast, taking in history, seafood, and fine shopping in the many outlet shops.

The coast is several places in one. South of the rapidly gentrifying city of Portland, such resort towns as Ogunquit, Kennebunkport, and Old Orchard Beach (sometimes called the Québec Riviera because of its popularity with French Canadians) predominate along a reasonably smooth shoreline. Development has been considerable; north of Portland and Casco Bay, secondary roads turn south off Route 1 onto so many oddly chiseled peninsulas that it's possible to drive for days without retracing your route and to conclude that motels, discount outlets, and fried-clam stands are taking over the domain of presidents and lobstermen. Freeport is an entity unto itself, a place where a bewildering assortment of off-price, name-brand outlets has sprung up around the famous outfitter L. L. Bean.

The visitor seeking an untouched fishing village with locals gathered around a pot-bellied stove in the general store may be sadly disappointed; that innocent age has passed in all but the most remote of villages. Tourism has supplanted fishing, logging, and potato farming as Maine's number one industry, and most areas are well equipped to receive the annual onslaught of visitors. But whether you are stepping outside a motel room for an evening walk or watching a boat rock at its anchor, you can sense the infinity of the natural world. Wilderness is always nearby, growing to the edges of the most urbanized spots.

PORTLAND TO PEMAQUID POINT

Maine's largest city, small enough to be seen in a day or two, Portland is undergoing a cultural and economic renaissance. New hotels and a bright new performing arts center have joined the neighborhoods of historic homes; the Old Port Exchange, perhaps the finest urban renovation project on the East Coast, balances modern commercial enterprise with a salty waterfront character in an area bustling with restaurants, shops, and galleries. The piers of Commercial Street abound with opportunities for water tours of the harbor and excursions to the Calendar Islands.

Freeport, north of Portland, is a town made famous by the L. L. Bean store, whose success led to the opening of scores of other clothing stores and outlets. Brunswick is best known for Bowdoin College. Bath has been a shipbuilding center since 1607, and the Maine Maritime Museum preserves its history.

The Boothbays—the coastal areas of Boothbay Harbor, East Boothbay, Linekin Neck, Southport Island, and the inland town of Boothbay—attract hordes of vacationing families and flotillas of pleasure craft. The Pemaquid peninsula juts into the Atlantic south of Damariscotta and just east of the Boothbays, and near Pemaquid Beach one can view the objects unearthed at the Colonial Pemaquid Restoration.

Southern Maine Coast

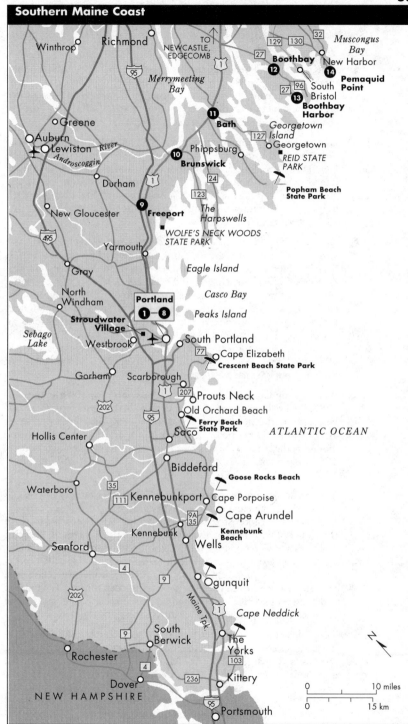

Winthrop
Richmond
TO
NEWCASTLE,
EDGECOMB
1
Merrymeeting
Bay
95
Muscongus
Bay
129 130 32
27 **Boothbay** New Harbor
12 **14** **Pemaquid
Point**
27 96 South
Bristol
13 **Boothbay
Harbor**
11 **Bath**
Georgetown
Island
127
Georgetown
**REID STATE
PARK**
Greene
Auburn
Lewiston River
Androscoggin
Phippsburg
10
Brunswick
Popham Beach
State Park
24
Durham
1
123
New Gloucester
9 **Freeport**
The
Harpswells
495
Yarmouth
WOLFE'S NECK WOODS
STATE PARK
Eagle Island
Gray
Casco Bay
North
Windham
Portland
1 — **8**
Peaks Island
**Stroudwater
Village**
Sebago
Lake
Westbrook
South Portland
77 Cape Elizabeth
Crescent Beach State Park
Gorham
Scarborough
1
207 Prouts Neck
Old Orchard Beach
95
Ferry Beach
State Park
Saco
ATLANTIC OCEAN
Hollis Center
Biddeford
Goose Rocks Beach
Waterboro
35
111 Kennebunkport Cape Porpoise
9A
35 Cape Arundel
Kennebunk Beach
Kennebunk
Sanford Wells
4
9
Ogunquit
202
Maine Tpk.
1 Cape Neddick
South
Berwick
The
Yorks
9
103
Rochester
4
236 Kittery
Dover
NEW HAMPSHIRE
0   10 miles
0   15 km
95
Portsmouth

202

Exploring

Numbers in the margin correspond to points of interest on the Southern Maine Coast and Portland maps.

❶ Congress Street, **Portland**'s main street, runs the length of the peninsular city from the Western Promenade in the southwest to the Eastern Promenade in the northeast, passing through the small downtown area. A few blocks southeast of downtown, the bustling Old Port Exchange sprawls along the waterfront.

❷ One of the notable homes on Congress Street is the **Neal Dow Memorial,** a brick mansion built in 1829 in the late Federal style by General Neal Dow, a zealous abolitionist and prohibitionist. The library has fine ornamental ironwork, and the furnishings include the family china, silver, and portraits. Don't miss the grandfather clocks and the original deed granted by James II. *714 Congress St., ☎ 207/773–7773.* ☛ *Free.* ⊙ *Tours weekdays 11–4.*

❸ On Congress Square, the distinguished **Portland Museum of Art** has a strong collection of seascapes and landscapes by such masters as Winslow Homer, John Marin, Andrew Wyeth, and Marsden Hartley. Homer's *Pulling the Dory* and *Weatherbeaten,* two quintessential Maine coast images, are here. The Joan Whitney Payson Collection includes works by Monet, Picasso, and Renoir. The strikingly modern Charles Shipman Payson building was designed by Harry N. Cobb, an associate of I. M. Pei, in 1983. *7 Congress Sq., ☎ 207/775–6148 or 207/773–2787.* ☛ *$6 adults, $5 senior citizens and students, $1 children 6–12, free Thurs. evenings 5–9.* ⊙ *Tues.–Sat. 10–5 (Thurs. until 9), Sun. noon–5. Call for winter hrs.*

❹ Walk east on Congress Street to the **Wadsworth Longfellow House** of 1785, the boyhood home of the poet and the first brick house in Portland. The late-Colonial-style structure sits well back from the street and has a small portico over its entrance and four chimneys surmounting the hip roof. Most of the furnishings are original to the house. *485 Congress St., ☎ 207/879–0427.* ☛ *$4 adults, $1 children under 12.* ⊙ *June–Oct., Tues.–Sun. 10–4.*

❺ You can walk from downtown to the **Old Port Exchange,** or you can drive and park your car either at the city garage on Fore Street (between Exchange and Union streets) or opposite the U.S. Customs House at the corner of Fore and Pearl streets. Like the Customs House, the brick buildings and warehouses of the Old Port Exchange were built following the Great Fire of 1866 and were intended to last for ages. When the city's economy slumped in the middle of the present century, however, the Old Port declined and seemed slated for demolition. Then artists and craftspeople began opening shops here in the late 1960s, and in time restaurants, chic boutiques, bookstores, and gift shops followed.

The Old Port is best explored on foot. Allow a couple of hours to wander at leisure on Market, Exchange, Middle, and Fore streets. The
❻ Mariner's Church (376 Fore St.) has a fine facade of granite columns, and the Elias Thomas Block on Commercial Street demonstrates the graceful use of bricks in commercial architecture. Inevitably the salty smell of the sea will draw you to one of the wharves off Commercial Street; Custom House Wharf retains some of the older, rougher waterfront atmosphere.

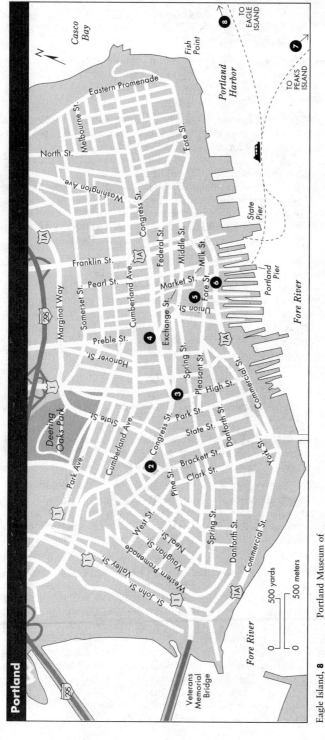

Portland

Eagle Island, **8**
Mariner s Church, **6**
Neal Dow
Memorial, **2**
Old Port
Exchange, **5**
Peaks Island, **7**

Portland Museum of
Art, **3**
Wadsworth
Longfellow
House, **4**

0   500 yards
0   500 meters

The brightly painted ferries of **Casco Bay Lines** (☎ 207/774–7871) are the lifeline to the Calendar Islands of Casco Bay, which number about 136, depending on the tides and how one defines an island.

❼ **Peaks Island,** nearest Portland, is the most developed, and some residents commute to work in Portland. Yet you can still commune with the wind and the sea on Peaks, explore an old fort, and ramble along the alternately rocky and sandy shore.

❽ The 17-acre **Eagle Island,** owned by the State of Maine and open to the public for day trips in summer, was the home of Admiral Robert E. Peary, the American explorer of the North Pole. Peary built a stone-and-wood house on the island as a summer retreat in 1904, then made it his permanent residence. The house remains as it was when Peary was here with his stuffed Arctic birds and the quartz he brought home and set into the fieldstone fireplace. The *Kristy K.,* departing from Long Wharf, makes a four-hour narrated tour. *Long Wharf,* ☎ *207/774– 6498.* ☛ *Excursion tour: $15 adults, $12 senior citizens, $9 children 5–12.* ☉ *Departures mid-June–Labor Day, daily 10 AM.*

❾ **Freeport,** on Route 1, 15 miles northeast of Portland, has charming back streets lined with old clapboard houses and even a small harbor on the Harraseeket River, but the overwhelming majority of visitors come to shop, and L. L. Bean is the store that put Freeport on the map. Founded in 1912 as a small mail-order merchandiser of products for hunters, guides, and fisherfolk, L. L. Bean now attracts some 3.5 million shoppers a year to its giant store in the heart of Freeport's shopping district on Route 1. Here you can still find the original hunting boots, along with cotton, wool, and silk sweaters; camping and ski equipment; comforters; and hundreds of other items for the home, car, boat, or campsite. Across the street from the main store, a Bean factory outlet has seconds and discontinued merchandise at discount prices. *Rte. 1, Freeport,* ☎ *800/341–4341.* ☉ *24 hrs.*

All around L. L. Bean, like seedlings under a mighty spruce, some 70 outlets have sprouted, offering designer clothes, shoes, housewares, and toys at discount prices (*see* Shopping, *below*).

❿ It's 9 miles northeast on Route 1 from Freeport to **Brunswick.** Follow the signs to the Brunswick business district, Pleasant Street, and—at the end of Pleasant Street—Maine Street, which claims to be the widest (198 feet across) in the state. Friday from May through October sees a fine farmer's market on the town mall, between Maine Street and Park Row.

Maine Street takes you to the 110-acre campus of **Bowdoin College,** an enclave of distinguished architecture, gardens, and grassy quadrangles in the middle of town. Campus tours (☎ 207/725–3000) depart every day but Sunday from Chamberlain Hall, the admissions office. Among the historic buildings are Massachusetts Hall, a stout, sober, hip-roofed brick structure that dates from 1802 and that once housed the entire college. Hubbard Hall, an imposing 1902 neo-Gothic building is home to Maine's only gargoyle. In addition, it houses the **Peary-MacMillan Arctic Museum.** The museum contains photographs, navigational instruments, and artifacts from the first successful expedition to the North Pole, in 1909, by two of Bowdoin's most famous alumni, Admiral Robert E. Peary and Donald B. MacMillan. ☎ *207/725–3416.* ☛ *Free.* ☉ *Tues.–Sat. 10–5, Sun. 2–5.*

Don't miss the **Bowdoin College Museum of Art,** a splendid limestone, brick, and granite structure in a Renaissance Revival style, with three galleries upstairs, and four more downstairs, radiating from a rotunda. Designed in 1894 by Charles F. McKim, the building stands on a rise, its facade adorned with classical statues and the entrance set off by a triumphal arch. The collections encompass Assyrian and Classical art and that of the Dutch, Italian, French, and Flemish old masters; a superb gathering of Colonial and Federal paintings, notably the Gilbert Stuart portraits of Madison and Jefferson; and a Winslow Homer Gallery of engravings, etchings, and memorabilia (open summer only). The museum's collection also includes 19th- and 20th-century American painting and sculpture, with works by Mary Cassatt, Andrew Wyeth, John Sloan, Rockwell Kent, Jim Dine, and Robert Rauschenberg. *Walker Art Bldg.,* ☎ *207/725–3275.* ☛ *Free.* ☉ *Tues.–Sat. 10–5, Sun. 2–5.*

Before going on to Bath, drive down Route 123 or Route 24 to the peninsulas and islands known collectively as the **Harpswells.** The numerous small coves along Harpswell Neck shelter the boats of local lobstermen, and summer cottages are tucked away amid the birch and spruce trees.

⓫ **Bath,** 7 miles east of Brunswick on Route 1, has been a shipbuilding center since 1607. Today the Bath Iron Works turns out guided-missile frigates for the U.S. Navy and merchant container ships.

The **Maine Maritime Museum and Shipyard** in Bath (take the Bath Business District exit from Route 1, turn right on Washington Street, and follow the signs) has ship models, journals, photographs, and other artifacts to stir the nautical dreams of old salts and young. The 142-foot Grand Banks fishing schooner *Sherman Zwicker,* one of the last of its kind, is on display when in port. You can watch apprentice boatbuilders wield their tools on classic Maine boats at the restored Percy & Small Shipyard and Apprentice Shop. The outdoor shipyard is open May–November; during these months visitors may take scenic tours of the Kennebec River on the *Summertime.* During off-season, the Maritime History Building has indoor exhibits, videos, and activities. *243 Washington St.,* ☎ *207/443–1316.* ☛ *$6.50 adults, $5.85 senior citizens, $4 children 6–17.* ☉ *Daily 9:30–5.*

From Bath it's 10 miles northeast on Route 1 to Wiscasset, where the huge rotting hulls of the schooners *Hester* and *Luther Little* rest, testaments to the town's once-busy harbor. Those who appreciate both music and antiques will enjoy a visit to the **Musical Wonder House** to see and hear the vast collection of antique music boxes from around the world. *18 High St.,* ☎ *207/882–7163.* ☛ *1-hr presentation on main floor: $10 adults, $7.50 children under 12 and senior citizens; 3-hr tour of entire house: $30 or $50 for 2 people.* ☉ *May 15–Oct. 15, daily 10–6. Last tour usually 4 PM; call ahead for 3-hr tours.*

TIME OUT **Treats** (Main St., ☎ 207/882-6192) is a good spot to pick up a gourmet snack, a cappuccino or espresso, or picnic fixings. Take your treat down to the waterfront park or across the street to the Hidden Garden, a small park made in an old foundation.

Across the river, drive south on Route 27 to reach the **Boothbay Railway Village,** about a mile north of **Boothbay,** where you can ride 1½ ⓬ miles on a narrow-gauge steam train through a re-creation of a turn-of-the-century New England village. Among the 24 village buildings is a museum with more than 50 antique automobiles and trucks. *Rte. 27, Boothbay,* ☎ *207/633–4727.* ☛ *$6 adults, $3 children 2–12.* ☉ *Weekends Memorial Day–mid-Oct., 9:30–5; 9:30–5 daily June 10–*

Columbus Day; special Halloween schedule; closed Columbus Day–Memorial Day.

⑬ Continue south on Route 27 into Boothbay Harbor, bear right on Oak Street, and follow it to the waterfront parking lots. **Boothbay Harbor** is a town to wander through: Commercial Street, Wharf Street, the By-Way, and Townsend Avenue are lined with shops, galleries, and ice-cream parlors. Excursion boats (*see* Sports and the Outdoors, *below*) leave from the piers off Commercial Street.

Having explored Boothbay Harbor, return to Route 27 and head north again to Route 1. Proceed north to Business Route 1, and follow it through Damariscotta, an appealing shipbuilding town on the Damariscotta River. Bear right on the Bristol Road (Rte. 129/130), and when the highway splits, stay on Route 130, which leads to Bristol and
⑭ terminates at **Pemaquid Point.**

About 5 miles south of Bristol you'll come to New Harbor, where a right turn will take you to Pemaquid Beach and the **Colonial Pemaquid Restoration.** Here, on a small peninsula jutting into the Pemaquid River, English mariners established a fishing and trading settlement in the early 17th century. The excavations at **Ft. William Henry,** begun in the mid-1960s, have turned up thousands of artifacts from the Colonial settlement, including the remains of an old customs house, tavern, jail, forge, and homes, and from even earlier Native American settlements. The State of Maine operates a museum displaying many of the artifacts. *Rte. 130, Pemaquid Point,* ☎ *207/677–2423.* ☛ *$1.50 adults, 50¢ children 6–12.* ☉ *Memorial Day–Labor Day, daily 9:30–5.*

Route 130 terminates at the **Pemaquid Point Light,** which looks as though it sprouted from the ragged, tilted chunk of granite that it commands. The former lighthouse-keeper's cottage is now the **Fishermen's Museum,** with photographs, models, and artifacts that explore commercial fishing in Maine. Here, too, is the Pemaquid Art Gallery, which mounts changing exhibitions from July 1 through Labor Day. *Rte. 130,* ☎ *207/677–2494.* ☛ *Donation requested.* ☉ *Memorial Day–Columbus Day, Mon.–Sat. 10–5, Sun. 11–5.*

What to See and Do with Children

Boothbay Railway Village, Boothbay
Children's Museum of Maine. Touching is okay at this museum where little ones can pretend they are lobstermen, shopkeepers, or computer experts. Camera Obscura, a new permanent exhibit on the third floor, charges a separate admission fee ($2). *142 Free St., Portland,* ☎ *207/ 828–1234.* ☛ *$4 adults and children over 1.* ☉ *Mon., Wed., Thurs. 10–5, Fri. 10–8, Tues. and Sun. noon–5.*
Maine Coast Railroad. Travel from Wiscasset to Newcastle in restored 1930s coaches. *Rte. 1, Wiscasset,* ☎ *207/882–8000.* ☛ *$10 adults, $5 children ages 5–12, under 5 free when not occupying a separate seat, $25 family (2 adults, 4 children).*

Off the Beaten Path

Stroudwater Village, 3 miles west of Portland, was spared the devastation of the fire of 1866 and thus contains some of the best examples of 18th- and early 19th-century architecture in the region. Here are the remains of mills, canals, and historic homes, including the Tate House, built in 1755 with paneling from England. It overlooks the old mast yard where George Tate, Mast Agent to the King, prepared tall pines for the ships of the Royal Navy. The furnishings date to the late 18th century. *Tate House, 1270 Westbrook St.,* ☎ *207/774–9781.* ☛ *$3 adults, $1 children.* ⊙ *July–Sept. 15, Tues.–Sat. 10–4, Sun. 1–4.*

Shopping

The best shopping in Portland is at the Old Port Exchange, where many shops are concentrated along Fore and Exchange streets. Freeport's name is almost synonymous with shopping: **L. L. Bean** and the 70 factory outlets that opened during the 1980s are here. Outlet stores are in the Fashion Outlet Mall (2 Depot St.) and the Freeport Crossing (200 Lower Main St.), and many others crowd Main Street and Bow Street. The *Freeport Visitors Guide* (Freeport Merchants Association, Box 452, Freeport 04032, ☎ 207/865–1212) has a complete listing. Boothbay Harbor, and Commercial Street in particular, is chockablock with gift shops, T-shirt shops, and other seasonal emporia catering to visitors.

Antiques
F. O. Bailey Antiquarians (141 Middle St., Portland, ☎ 207/774–1479), Portland's largest retail showroom, features antique and reproduction furniture and jewelry, paintings, rugs, and china. **Harrington House Museum Store** (45 Main St., Freeport, ☎ 207/865–0477) is a restored 19th-century merchant's home owned by the Freeport Historical Society; all the period reproductions that furnish the rooms are for sale. In addition, you can buy books, rugs, jewelry, crafts, Shaker items, toys, and kitchen utensils. **Maine Trading Post** (80 Commercial St., Boothbay Harbor, ☎ 207/633–2760) sells antiques and fine reproductions that include rolltop desks able to accommodate personal computers, as well as gifts and decorative accessories.

Books and Maps
Carlson and Turner (241 Congress St., Portland, ☎ 207/773–4200) is an antiquarian book dealer with an estimated 75,000 titles. **DeLorme's Map Store** (Rte. 1, Freeport, ☎ 207/865–4171) carries an exceptional selection of maps and atlases of Maine, New England, and the rest of the world; nautical charts; and travel books. **Maine Coast Book Shop** (Main St., Damariscotta, ☎ 207/563–3207) carries a good selection of books and magazines and often hosts author signings. **Raffles Cafe Bookstore** (555 Congress St., Portland, ☎ 207/761–3930) presents an impressive selection of fiction and nonfiction, plus the best selection of periodicals north of Boston. Coffee and a light lunch are served, and there are frequent readings and literary gatherings.

Clothing
House of Logan (Townsend Ave., Boothbay Harbor, ☎ 207/633–2293) has specialty clothing for men and women, plus children's clothes next door at the Village Store. **Joseph's** (410 Fore St., ☎ 207/773–1274) has elegant tailored designer clothing for men and women.

Crafts
Edgecomb Potters (Rte. 27, Edgecomb, ☎ 207/882–6802) sells glazed porcelain pottery and other crafts. **Sheepscot River Pottery** (Rte. 1, Edgecomb, ☎ 207/882–9410) has original hand-painted pottery as well as a large collection of American-made crafts including jewelry, kitchenware, furniture, and home accessories.

Galleries
Abacus (44 Exchange St., Portland, ☎ 207/772–4880) has unusual gift items in glass, wood, and textiles, plus fine modern jewelry. **Franciska Needham Gallery,** (Water St., Damariscotta ☎ 207/563–1227) has contemporary paintings and sculpture by Maine and New York artists.

The **Gil Whitman Gallery** (Rte. 1, N. Edgecomb, ☎ 207/882–7705) exhibits the work of bronze sculptor Gil Whitman in a barn gallery and an outdoor sculpture garden, where giant metal flowers bloom amidst the real thing. The studio and workshop areas also are open to visitors. The **Pine Tree Shop & Bayview Gallery** (75 Market St., Portland, ☎ 207/773–3007 or 800/244–3007) has original art and prints by prominent Maine painters. **Stein Glass Gallery** (20 Milk St., Portland, ☎ 207/772–9072) specializes in contemporary glass, both decorative and utilitarian. The **Wiscasset Bay Gallery** (Water St., Wiscasset, ☎ 207/882–7682) emphasizes 19th- and 20th-century American and European artists.

Sports and the Outdoors

Boat Trips

BOOTHBAY HARBOR

Appledore (☎ 207/633–6598), a 66-foot windjammer, departs from Pier 6 at 9:30, noon, 3, and 6 for voyages to the outer islands. **Argo Cruises** (☎ 207/633–2500) runs the *Islander* for morning cruises, Bath Hellgate cruises, whale watching, and the popular Cabbage Island Clambake; the *Islander II* for 1½-hour trips to Seal Rocks; the *Miss Boothbay*, a licensed lobster boat, for lobster-trap hauling trips. Biweekly evening cruises feature R&B or reggae. Departures are from Pier 6. **Balmy Day Cruises** (☎ 207/633–2284 or 800/298–2284) has day trips to Monhegan Island and tours of the harbor and nearby lighthouses. *Bay Lady* (☎ 207/633–6990), a 31-foot Friendship sloop, offers sailing trips of under 2 hours from Pier 8. **Cap'n Fish's Boat Trips** (☎ 207/633–3244) offers sightseeing cruises throughout the region, including puffin cruises, lobster-hauling and whale-watching rides, trips to Damariscove Harbor, Pemaquid Point, and up the Kennebec River to Bath, departing from Pier 1. *Eastward* (☎ 207/633–4780) is a Friendship sloop with six-passenger capacity that departs from Ocean Point Road in East Boothbay for full- or half-day sailing trips. Itineraries vary with passengers' desires and the weather.

FREEPORT

Atlantic Seal Cruises (S. Freeport, ☎ 207/865–6112) has daily trips to Eagle Island, where you can tour Admiral Peary's museum home, and evening seal and osprey watches on the *Atlantic Seal.*

PORTLAND

For tours of the harbor, Casco Bay, and the nearby islands, try **Bay View Cruises** (Fisherman's Wharf, ☎ 207/761–0496), **The Buccaneer** (Long Wharf, ☎ 207/799–8188), **Casco Bay Lines** (Maine State Pier, ☎ 207/774–7871), **Eagle Tours** (Long Wharf, ☎ 207/774–6498), or **Old Port Mariner Fleet** (Long Wharf, ☎ 207/775–0727).

Deep-Sea Fishing

Half- and full-day fishing charter boats are operated out of Portland by *Devils Den* (DeMillo's Marina, ☎ 207/761–4466). Operating out of Boothbay Harbor, **Cap'n Fish's Deep Sea Fishing** (☎ 207/633–3244) schedules full- and half-day trips, departing from Pier 1, and **Lucky Star Charters** (☎ 207/633–4624) runs full- and half-day private charters for up to six people, with departures from Pier 8.

Nature Walks

Wolfe's Neck Woods State Park has self-guided trails along Casco Bay, the Harraseeket River, and a fringe salt marsh, as well as walks led by naturalists. Picnic tables and grills are available, but there's no camping. Follow Bow Street opposite L. L. Bean off Route 1. *Wolfe's Neck*

Rd., ☎ 207/865–4465. ☛ Memorial Day–Labor Day: $2 adults ($1 off-season), 50¢ children 5–11.

Sea Kayaking

H2Outfitters (Orr's Island, ☎ 207/833–5257) offers instruction, rentals, and half-day through multi-day trips. **Maine Island Kayak Co.** (70 Luther St., Peak's Island, ☎ 800/796–2373) provides instruction, expeditions, and tours all along the Maine coast.

Beaches

Crescent Beach State Park (Rte. 77, Cape Elizabeth, ☎ 207/767–3625; ☛ Late Apr.–mid-Oct.: $2.50 adults [$1 off-season], 50¢ children 5–11), about 8 miles from Portland, has a sand beach, picnic tables, seasonal snack bar, and bathhouse. **Ferry Beach State Park** (follow signs off Rte. 9 in Saco, ☎ 207/283–0067; ☛ Late Apr.–mid-Oct.: $2 adults, 50¢ children 5–11), near Old Orchard Beach, has picnic facilities with grills and extensive nature trails. **Popham Beach State Park** (Phippsburg, ☎ 207/389–1335; ☛ $2 adults [$1 Nov.–Apr.], 50¢ children 5–11), at the end of Route 209, south of Bath, has a good sand beach, a marsh area, and picnic tables. **Reid State Park** (☎ 207/371–2303; ☛ Late Apr.–mid-Oct.: , $2.50 adults, 50¢ children 5–11), on Georgetown Island, off Route 127, has 1½ miles of sand on three beaches. Facilities include bathhouses, picnic tables, fireplaces, and snack bar. Parking lots fill by 11 AM on summer Sundays and holidays.

Dining and Lodging

Many of Portland's best restaurants are in the Old Port Exchange district.

Bath

DINING

$$ **Kristina's Restaurant & Bakery.** This frame house-turned-restaurant, with a front deck built around a huge maple tree, turns out some of the finest pies, pastries, and cakes on the coast. A satisfying dinner menu features new American cuisine, including fresh seafood and grilled meats. All meals can be packed to go. ✕ *160 Centre St., ☎ 207/442–8577. D, MC, V. No dinner Sun. Call ahead in winter.*

LODGING

$$$ **Fairhaven Inn.** This cedar-shingle house built in 1790 is set on 27 acres of pine woods and meadows sloping down to the Kennebec River. Guest rooms are furnished with handmade quilts and mahogany pineapple four-poster beds. The home-cooked breakfast offers such treats as peach soup, blintzes, and apple upside-down French toast. ▨ *R.R. 2, Box 85, N. Bath, 04530, ☎ 207/443–4391. 7 rooms, 5 with bath. Hiking, cross-country skiing. Full breakfast included. AE, MC, V.*

Boothbay

LODGING

$$–$$$ **Kenniston Hill Inn.** The oldest inn in Boothbay (circa 1786), this classic center-chimney colonial with its white clapboards and columned porch offers comfortably old-fashioned accommodations on 4 acres of land only minutes from Boothbay Harbor. Four guest rooms have fireplaces, some have four-poster beds, rocking chairs, and gilt mirrors. ▨ *Rte. 27, Box 125, 04537, ☎ 207/633–2159. 10 rooms with bath. Full breakfast included. MC, V.*

Boothbay Harbor

DINING

$$–$$$ **Black Orchid.** The classic Italian fare includes fettuccine Alfredo with fresh lobster and mushrooms, and *petit filet à la diabolo* (fillets of Angus steak with marsala sauce). The upstairs and downstairs dining rooms sport a Roman-trattoria ambience, with frilly leaves and fruit hanging from the rafters and little else in the way of decor. In the summer there is a raw bar outdoors. ✗ *5 By-Way,* ☎ *207/633–6659. AE, MC, V. No lunch. Closed Nov.–Apr.*

$$ **Andrew's Harborside.** The seafood menu is typical of the area—lobster, fried clams and oysters, haddock with seafood stuffing—but the harbor view makes it memorable. Lunch features lobster and crab rolls; children's and seniors' menus are available. You can dine outdoors on a harborside screened porch during the summer. ✗ *8 Bridge St.,* ☎ *207/ 633–4074. Dinner reservations accepted for 5 or more. MC, V. Closed mid-Oct.–mid-May.*

LODGING

$$$–$$$$ **Fisherman's Wharf Inn.** All rooms overlook the water at this Colonial-style motel built 200 feet out over the harbor. The large dining room has floor-to-ceiling windows, and several day-trip cruises leave from this location. ☎ *42 Commercial St., 04538,* ☎ *and* FAX *207/633–5090 ext. 602 or 800/628–6872. 54 rooms with bath. Restaurant. AE, D, DC, MC, V. Closed late Oct.–mid-May.*

$$$ **Anchor Watch.** This country Colonial on the water overlooks the outer harbor and lies within easy walking distance of town. Guest rooms are decorated with quilts and stenciling and are named for the Monhegan ferries that ran in the 1920s. Breakfast includes apple puff pancake, muffins, fruit, omelets, blueberry blintzes, and more. ☎ *3 Eames Rd., 04538,* ☎ *207/633–7565. 4 rooms with bath. Pier. Full breakfast included. MC, V. Closed Jan.*

$$ **The Pines.** Families seeking a secluded setting with lots of room for little ones to run will be interested in this motel on a hillside a mile from town. Rooms have sliding glass doors opening onto private decks, two double beds, and small refrigerators. ☎ *Sunset Rd., Box 693, 04538,* ☎ *207/633–4555. 29 rooms with bath. Pool, tennis, playground. D, MC, V. Closed mid-Oct.–early May.*

Brunswick

DINING

$–$$ **The Great Impasta.** This small, storefront restaurant is a great spot for lunch, tea, or dinner. Try the seafood lasagna, or match your favorite pasta and sauce to create your own dish. ✗ *42 Maine St.,* ☎ *207/729– 5858. No reservations. AE, D, DC, MC, V.*

DINING AND LODGING

$$$–$$$$ **Captain Daniel Stone Inn.** This Federal inn overlooks the Androscoggin River. While no two rooms are furnished identically, all offer executive-style comforts and many have whirlpool baths and pullout sofas in addition to queen-size beds. A guest parlor, 24-hour breakfast room, and excellent service in the Narcissa Stone Restaurant make this an upscale escape from college-town funk. ☎ *10 Water St., 04011,* ☎ *and* FAX *207/725–9898. 32 rooms with bath. CP. Restaurant (no lunch Sat.). AE, DC, MC, V.*

Freeport

DINING

$–$$ **Freeport Cafe.** This small restaurant south of Freeport's shopping district serves creative homemade food, including soups, salads, sandwiches, and dinner entrées. Breakfast is available all day. ✕ *Rte. 1, ☎ 207/865–3106. MC, V.*

$ **Harraseeket Lunch & Lobster Co.** This no-frills, bare-bones, genuine lobster pound and fried-seafood place is located beside the town landing in South Freeport. Seafood baskets and lobster dinners are what it's all about; there are picnic tables outside and a dining room inside. ✕ *Main St., S. Freeport, ☎ 207/865–4888. No reservations. No credit cards. ⊙ May 1–Oct. 15.*

DINING AND LODGING

$$$$ **Harraseeket Inn.** This gracious Greek Revival home of 1850, just two blocks from the biggest retailing explosion ever to hit Maine, includes a three-story addition that looks like an old New England inn—white clapboard with green shutters—but is in fact a steel and concrete structure with elevators, whirlpools, and modern fireplaces. Despite these modern appointments, the Harraseeket gives its visitors a country-inn experience, with afternoon tea served in the mahogany drawing room. Guest rooms (vintage 1989) have reproductions of Federal canopy beds and bright, coordinated fabrics. The formal, no-smoking dining room upstairs, serving New England–influenced Continental cuisine, is a simply decorated, light and airy space with picture windows facing the inn's garden courtyard. The Broad Arrow Tavern downstairs appears to have been furnished by L. L. Bean, with fly rods, snowshoes, moose heads, and other hunting-lodge trappings; the hearty fare includes ribs, burgers, and charbroiled skewered shrimp and scallops. ☎ *162 Main St., 04032, ☎ 207/865–9377 or 800/342–6423, FAX 207/865–1684. 48 rooms, 6 suites. Restaurant (reservations advised; collar shirt at dinner), bar, croquet. AE, D, DC, MC, V.*

Georgetown

DINING

$$$–$$$$ **The Osprey.** Located in a marina on the way to Reid State Park, this gourmet restaurant may be reached both by land and sea. The appetizers alone are worth the stop: homemade garlic and Sicilian sausages; artichoke strudel with three cheeses; and warm braised duck salad with Oriental vegetables in rice paper. Entrées might include such classics as saltimbocca or such originals as salmon en papillote with julienne leeks, carrots, and fresh herbs. The wine list is excellent. The glassed-in porch offers water views and breezes. ✕ *6 mi down Rte. 127, turn left at restaurant sign on Robinhood Rd., ☎ 207/371–2530. Reservations advised. MC, V. Call ahead for off-season hrs.*

Newcastle

LODGING

$$$$ **Newcastle Inn.** The white-clapboard house, vintage mid-19th century,
★ has a romantic living room with a fireplace, loveseat, plenty of books, and river views. It also has a sun porch with white wicker furniture and ice-cream parlor chairs. The "Stencil Room," a favorite common room, has a hand-decorated hardwood floor. Guest rooms have been carefully appointed with unique beds—an old spool bed, wrought-iron beds, a brass-pewter bed, a sleigh bed, and several canopy beds—and rabbits are everywhere: stuffed, wooden, ceramic. Breakfast is a gourmet affair that might include scrambled eggs with caviar in puff pastry, ricotta cheese pie, or frittata. The five-course dinner served nightly brings people back again and again. ☎ *River Rd., 04553, ☎ 207/563–5685 or 800/832–8669. 15 rooms with bath. 2 dining rooms, pub. Full breakfast included; MAP available. MC, V.*

Peaks Island

LODGING

$$ Keller's B&B. This turn-of-the-century home provides rustic accommodations with deck views of Casco Bay and the Portland skyline. The beach is only steps away from your room. Guests select breakfast from a menu. ⌨ *20 Island Ave.,* ☎ *207/766–2441. 4 rooms with bath. Full breakfast included. No credit cards.*

Pemaquid Point

DINING AND LODGING

$$$–$$$$ Bradley Inn. Within walking distance of the Pemaquid Point lighthouse, beach, and fort, the 1900 Bradley Inn began as a rooming house for summer rusticators and alternated between abandonment and operation as a B&B until its complete renovation in the early 1990s. Rooms are comfortable and uncluttered; ask for one of the cathedral-ceiling, waterside rooms on the third floor, which deliver breathtaking views of the sun setting over the water. The Ship's Restaurant has a frequently rotating menu, including a variety of fresh seafood dishes; there's light entertainment in the pub on weekends. ⌨ *Rte. 130, HC 61, Box 361, New Harbor 04554,* ☎ *207/677–2105,* ℻ *207/677–3367. 12 rooms with bath, 1 cottage, 1 carriage house. Restaurant, pub, croquet, bicycles. CP. AE, D, MC, V. Closed Jan.–Mar.*

Portland

DINING

$$$–$$$$ Back Bay Grill. Mellow jazz, a 28-foot mural, an impressive wine list,
★ and good food make this simple, elegant restaurant a popular spot. Appetizers such as black-pepper raviolis of red swiss chard, pancetta, and Fontina cheese in chicken broth are followed by grilled chicken, halibut, oysters, salmon, trout, veal chops, or steak. Don't miss the desserts—the crème brûlée is legendary. ✗ *65 Portland St.,* ☎ *207/772– 8833. Reservations advised. AE, D, DC, MC, V. Closed Sun.*

$$–$$$ Cafe Always. White linen tablecloths, candles, and Victorian-style mu-
★ rals by local artists set the mood for innovative cuisine. Begin with Pemaquid Point oysters seasoned with pink peppercorns and champagne, or grilled duck, before choosing from vegetarian dishes, pasta, or more substantial entrées, such as grilled tuna with a fiery Japanese sauce or leg of lamb with goat cheese and sweet peppers. ✗ *7 Middle St.,* ☎ *207/774–9399. Reservations advised. MC, V. Closed Sun., Mon.*

$$–$$$ Seamen's Club. Built just after Portland's Great Fire of 1866, and an actual sailors' club in the 1940s, this restaurant has become an Old Port Exchange landmark, with its Gothic windows and carved medallions. Seafood is an understandable favorite—moist, blackened tuna, salmon, and swordfish prepared differently each day and lobster fettuccine are among the highlights. ✗ *375 Fore St.,* ☎ *207/772–7311. Reservations advised. AE, DC, MC, V.*

$$–$$$ Street and Co. You enter through the kitchen, with all its wonderful aro-
★ mas, and dine amid dried herbs and shelves of staples on one of a dozen copper-topped tables (so your waiter can place a skillet of steaming seafood directly in front of you). A second dining room for walk-ins was added in 1994. Begin with lobster bisque or grilled eggplant—vegetarian dishes are the only alternatives to fish. Choose from an array of superb entrées, ranging from calamari, clams, or shrimp served over linguine, to blackened, broiled, pan-seared, or grilled seafood. The desserts are top-notch. ✗ *33 Wharf St.,* ☎ *207/775–0887. Reservations advised. AE, MC, V. No lunch.*

$$ Katahdin. Somehow, the painted tables, flea-market decor, mismatched dinnerware, and log pile bar work together here. The cuisine, large portions of home-cooked New England fare, is equally unpretentious and fun: Try the chicken potpie, fried trout, crab cakes, or the nightly Blue Plate special—and save room for the fruit cobbler. ✕ *106 High St., ☎ 207/774–1740. No reservations. MC, V.*

LODGING

$$$$ Pomegranate Inn. Clever touches such as faux marbling on the moldings and mustard-colored rag-rolling in the hallways give this bed-and-breakfast a bright, postmodern air. Most guest rooms are spacious and bright, accented with original paintings on floral and tropical motifs; the location on a quiet street in the city's Victorian Western Promenade district ensures serenity. Telephones and televisions make this a good choice for businesspeople. ☷ *49 Neal St., 04102, ☎ 207/772–1006 or 800/356–0408. 7 rooms with bath, 1 suite. Full breakfast included. AE, D, MC, V.*

$$$–$$$$ Portland Regency Hotel. The only major hotel in the center of the Old
★ Port Exchange, the Regency building was Portland's armory in the late 19th century and is now the city's most luxurious, most distinctive hotel. The bright, plush, airy rooms have four-poster beds, tall standing mirrors, floral curtains, and loveseats. The health club, the best in the city, offers massage and has an aerobics studio, free weights, Nautilus equipment, a large whirlpool, sauna, and steam room. ☷ *20 Milk St., 04101, ☎ 207/774–4200 or 800/727–3436, FAX 207/775–2150. 95 rooms with bath, 8 suites. Restaurant, health club, nightclub, banquet and convention rooms. AE, D, DC, MC, V.*

$$–$$$ Eastland Plaza. Although it's a bit dowdy, this 1927 hotel has a prime location in Portland's up-and-coming arts district. Rooms in the tower section (added in 1961) have floor-to-ceiling windows; higher floors have harbor views. The small health room offers Universal gym equipment, rowing machines, stationary bikes, and a sauna. ☷ *157 High St., 04101, ☎ 207/775–5411 or 800/777–6246, FAX 207/775–2872. 204 rooms with bath. 2 restaurants, 2 bars, exercise room with sauna, banquet and convention rooms. AE, D, DC, MC, V.*

The Arts

Chocolate Church Arts Center (804 Washington St., ☎ 207/442–8455) offers changing exhibits by Maine artists in a variety of mediums, including textiles, photography, painting, and sculpture. The center also hosts folk, jazz, and classical concerts; theater productions; and performances for children, including puppet shows and Portland Symphony Orchestra Kinderkonzerts. Sign up for classes and workshops in visual and performing arts. **Portland Performing Arts Center** (25A Forest Ave., Portland, ☎ 207/774–0465) hosts music, dance, and theater performances. **Round Top Center for the Arts** (Business Rte. 1, Damariscotta, ☎ 207/563–1507) has exhibits, concerts, shows, and classes. The **State Theatre** (609 Congress St., ☎ 207/879–1112) has come along way from its days as Portland's porn-film house—it's now one of the star attractions in Portland's up-and-coming arts district. Among the numerous events hosted here are film premieres and concerts by nationally known artists.

Music

Bowdoin Summer Music Festival (Bowdoin College, Brunswick, ☎ 207/725–3322 for information or ☎ 207/725–3895 for tickets) is a six-week concert series featuring performances by students, faculty, and prestigious guest artists. **Carousel Music Theater** ("The Meadows," Boothbay Harbor, ☎ 207/633–5297) mounts musical revues from Memorial Day to Columbus Day. **Cumberland County Civic Center** (1 Civic

Center Sq., Portland, ☎ 207/775–3458) hosts concerts, sporting events, and family shows in a 9,000-seat auditorium. **Portland Symphony Orchestra** (30 Myrtle St., Portland, ☎ 207/773–8191) gives concerts October through August.

Theater
Mad Horse Theatre Company (955 Forest Ave., Portland, ☎ 207/797–3338) performs contemporary and original works. **Maine State Music Theater** (Pickard Theater, Bowdoin College, Brunswick, ☎ 207/725–8769) stages musicals from mid-June through August. **Portland Stage Company** (25A Forest Ave., Portland, ☎ 207/774–0465), a producer of national reputation, mounts six productions, from October through May, at the Portland Performing Arts Center. **Theater Project of Brunswick** (14 School St., Brunswick, ☎ 207/729–8584) performs from late June through August.

Nightlife

Portland's hot nightspot, **Brian Boru** (57 Center St., Portland, ☎ 207/780–1506) is a traditional Irish pub serving up hearty fare and entertainment. For dancing, head to **Granny Killam's** (55 Market St., Portland, ☎ 207/761–2787). **Gritty McDuff's—Portland's Original Brew Pub** (396 Fore St., Portland, ☎ 207/772–2739) serves fine ales, brewed on the premises, along with British pub fare and local seafood dishes. **Khalidi's Creative Seafoods** (36 Market St., Portland, ☎ 207/871–1881) has a good selection of Maine microbrewery beers on draft. **Three Dollar Dewey's** (446 Fore St., Portland, ☎ 207/772–3310), long a popular night spot, is an English-style ale house. **Top of the East** (Sonesta Hotel, 157 High St., Portland, ☎ 207/775–5411) has a view of the city and live entertainment—jazz, piano, and comedy. **McSeagull's Gulf Dock** (Boothbay Harbor, ☎ 207/633–4041) draws young singles with live music and a loud bar scene.

Portland to Pemaquid Point Essentials

Getting Around
BY BUS
Greater Portland's **Metro** (☎ 207/774–0351) runs seven bus routes in Portland, South Portland, and Westbrook. The fare is $1 for adults, 50¢ for senior citizens, people with disabilities, and children (under 5 free); exact change ($1 bills accepted) is required. Buses run from 5:30 AM to 11:45 PM.

BY CAR
The Congress Street exit from I–295 takes you into the heart of Portland. Numerous city parking lots have hourly rates of 50¢ to 85¢; the Gateway Garage on High Street, off Congress, is a convenient place to leave your car while exploring downtown. North of Portland, I–95 takes you to Exit 20 and Route 1, Freeport's Main Street, which continues on to Brunswick and Bath. East of Wiscasset you can take Route 27 south to the Boothbays, where Route 96 is a good choice for further exploration.

Important Addresses and Numbers
EMERGENCIES
Maine Medical Center (22 Bramhall St., Portland, ☎ 207/871–0111). **Mid Coast Hospital** (1356 Washington St., Bath, ☎ 207/443–5524; 58 Baribeau Dr., Brunswick, ☎ 207/729–0181). **St. Andrews Hospital** (3 St. Andrews Ln., Boothbay Harbor, ☎ 207/633–2121).

VISITOR INFORMATION
Off-season, most information offices are open weekdays 9–5; the hours below are for summer only.

Boothbay Harbor Region Chamber of Commerce (Box 356, Boothbay Harbor, ☎ 207/633–2353; ☉ Weekdays 9–5, Sat. 11–4, Sun. noon–4). **Chamber of Commerce of the Bath Brunswick Region** (45 Front St., Bath, ☎ 207/443–9751, and 59 Pleasant St., Brunswick, ☎ 207/725–8797; ☉ Weekdays 8:30–5). **Convention and Visitors Bureau of Greater Portland** (305 Commercial St., ☎ 207/772–5800; ☉ Weekdays 8–6 and weekends 10–6 from June 1 to Columbus Day; weekdays 8–5 and weekends 10–3 from Columbus Day to June 1). **Freeport Merchants Association** (Box 452, Freeport, ☎ 207/865–1212; ☉ Weekdays 9–5). **Greater Portland Chamber of Commerce** (145 Middle St., Portland, ☎ 207/772–2811; ☉ Weekdays 8–5). **Maine Publicity Bureau, the Maine Information Center** (Rte. 1 [Exit 17 off I-95], Yarmouth, ☎ 207/846–0833).

PENOBSCOT BAY

Purists hold that the Maine coast begins at Penobscot Bay, where the vistas over the water are wider and bluer, the shore a jumble of broken granite boulders, cobblestones, and gravel punctuated by small sand beaches, and the water numbingly cold. Port Clyde in the southwest and Stonington in the southeast are the outer limits of Maine's largest bay, 35 miles apart across the bay waters but separated by a drive of almost 100 miles on scenic but slow two-lane highways.

Rockland, the largest town on the bay, is Maine's major lobster distribution center and the port of departure for several bay islands. The Camden Hills, looming green over Camden's fashionable waterfront, turn bluer and fainter as one moves on to Castine, the elegant small town across the bay. In between Camden and Castine is the Mayberryesque town of Belfast and the flea-market mecca of Searsport. Because both communities are less glitzy than other bay towns, they offer value dining and lodging. Deer Isle is connected to the mainland by a slender, high-arching bridge, but Isle au Haut, accessible from Deer Isle's fishing town of Stonington, can be reached by passenger ferry only: More than half of this steep, wooded island is wilderness, the most remote section of Acadia National Park.

Exploring

Numbers in the margin correspond to points of interest on the Penobscot Bay map.

From Pemaquid Point at the western extremity of Muscongus Bay to Port Clyde at its eastern extent, it's less than 15 miles across the water, but it's 50 miles for the motorist, who must return north to Route 1 to reach the far shore.

Travelers on Route 1 can make an easy detour south through Tenants Harbor and Port Clyde before reaching Rockland. Turn onto Route 131S at Thomaston, 5 miles west of Rockland, and follow the winding road past waterside fields, spruce woods, ramshackle barns, and
❶ trim houses. **Tenants Harbor,** 7 miles from Thomaston, is a quintessential Maine fishing town, its harbor dominated by lobster boats, its shores rocky and slippery, its center a scattering of clapboard houses, a church, a general store. The fictional Dunnet Landing of Sarah Orne Jewett's classic book, *The Country of the Pointed Firs,* is based on this region.

Route 131 ends at Port Clyde, a fishing village that is the point of departure for the *Laura B.* (☎ 207/372–8848 for schedules), the mailboat that serves Monhegan Island. Tiny, remote **Monhegan Island,** with its high cliffs, fronting the open sea was known to Basque, Portuguese, and Breton fishermen well before Columbus "discovered" America. About a century ago Monhegan was discovered again by some of America's finest painters, including Rockwell Kent, Robert Henri, and Edward Hopper, who sailed out to paint the savage cliffs, the meadows, the wild ocean views, and the shacks of fisherfolk. Tourists followed, and today Monhegan is overrun with visitors in summer.

❸ Returning north to Route 1, you have less than 5 miles to go to **Rockland** on Penobscot Bay. This large fishing port is the commercial hub of the coast, with working boats moored alongside a growing flotilla of cruise schooners. Although Rockland retains its working-class flavor, the recent expansion of the Farnsworth Museum, combined with new boutiques, restaurants, and bed-and-breakfasts is making Rockland a good stop for coastal travelers. This also is the point of departure for popular day trips to Vinal Haven, North Haven, and Matinicus islands.

The outer harbor is bisected by a nearly mile-long granite breakwater, which begins on Samoset Road and ends with a lighthouse that was built in 1888. Next to the breakwater, on the Rockland–Rockport town line, is the **Samoset Resort** (Warrenton St., Rockport, ☎ 207/594–2511 or, outside ME, 800/341–1650), a sprawling oceanside resort providing an 18-hole golf course, indoor and outdoor swimming pools, tennis, racquetball, restaurant, and fitness center.

In downtown Rockland is the **William A. Farnsworth Library and Art Museum.** Here are oil and watercolor landscapes of the coastal areas you have just seen, among them N. C. Wyeth's *Eight Bells* and Andrew Wyeth's *Her Room.* Jamie Wyeth is also represented in the collections, as are Winslow Homer, Rockwell Kent, and the sculptor Louise Nevelson. Next door, and part of the museum's holdings, is the Farnsworth Homestead, a handsome Greek Revival dwelling furnished in the Victorian style. Also operated by the museum is the **Olson House** in Cushing, approximately 14 miles away, which was made famous by Andrew Wyeth's painting, *Christina's World. 352 Main St.,* ☎ *207/596–6457.* ☛ *Museum and homestead: $5 adults, $2 senior citizens, $1 children 8–18. Olson House: $3 adults, $1 children 8–18.* ☯ *Mon.–Sat. 10–5, Sun. 1–5. Museum closed Mon. Oct.–May. Olson House open Wed.–Sun. 11–4. Closed Oct.–May.*

❹ From Rockland it's 8 miles north on Route 1 to **Camden,** "Where the mountains meet the sea"—an apt description, as you will discover when you step out of your car and look up from the harbor. Camden is famous not only for geography but for the nation's largest fleet of windjammers—relics and replicas from the age of sail. At just about any hour during the warmer months you're likely to see at least one windjammer tied up in the harbor, and windjammer cruises are a superb way to explore the ports and islands of Penobscot Bay.

TIME OUT   **Ayer's Fish Market** (43 Main St.) has the best fish chowder in town; take a cup to the pleasant park at the head of the harbor when you're ready for a break from the shops on Bay View and Main streets.

The entrance to the 5,500-acre **Camden Hills State Park** (☎ 207/236–3109) is 2 miles north of Camden on Route 1. If you're accustomed to the Rockies or the Alps, you may not be impressed with heights of not much more than 1,000 feet, yet the Camden Hills are landmarks

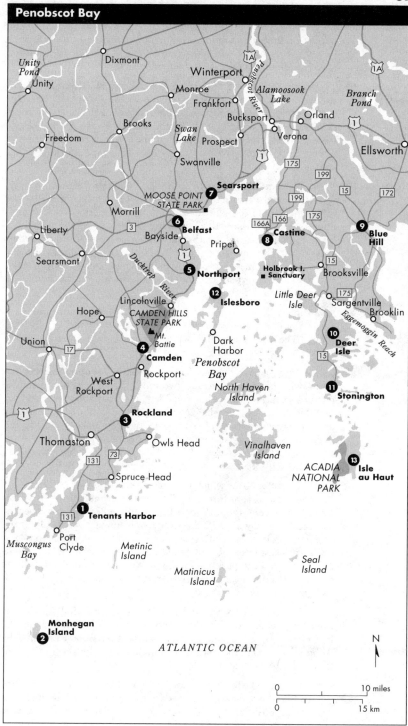

Penobscot Bay

Unity Pond
Unity
Dixmont
Monroe
Frankfort
Winterport
Penobscot River
Alamoosook Lake
Branch Pond
1A
Brooks
Bucksport
Orland
1
Verona
Ellsworth
Swan Lake
Prospect
Freedom
1
Swanville
7 Searsport
175
199
MOOSE POINT STATE PARK
199
15
172
Morrill
6 Belfast
166A 166
175
9 Blue Hill
Liberty
Bayside
Pripet
8 Castine
3
1
Searsmont
5 Northport
Holbrook I. Sanctuary
15
Brooksville
Ducktrap River
12 Islesboro
Little Deer Isle
175
Sargentville
Brooklin
Lincolnville
CAMDEN HILLS STATE PARK
Hope
Dark Harbor
Eggemoggin Reach
10 Deer Isle
Union
17
Mt. Battie
4 Camden
Penobscot Bay
15
Rockport
North Haven Island
West Rockport
11 Stonington
1
3 Rockland
Thomaston
Owls Head
Vinalhaven Island
ACADIA NATIONAL PARK
13 Isle au Haut
131 73
Spruce Head
131 **1** Tenants Harbor
Port Clyde
Muscongus Bay
Metinic Island
Seal Island
Matinicus Island
Monhegan Island
2
ATLANTIC OCEAN
N

0 — 10 miles
0 — 15 km

for miles along the low, rolling reaches of the Maine coast. The park contains 20 miles of trails, including the easy Nature Trail up Mount Battie. The 112-site camping area, open mid-May through mid-October, has flush toilets and hot showers. ☛ *Trails and auto road up Mount Battie: $2 adults, 50¢ children 5–11.*

⑤ The lovely community of Bayside, a section of **Northport** that is off Route 1 on the way to Belfast, is dotted with 150-year-old Queen Anne cottages that have freshly painted porches and exquisite architectural details. Some of these homes line the main one-car thoroughfare of George Street; others are clustered on bluffs with water views around town greens complete with flagpoles and swings; yet others are on the shore.

⑥ Back on Route 1, the next town north is **Belfast,** which has a lively waterfront and a charming Main Street. Architectural buffs will want to do the 1-mile self-guided walking tour of period sea captain's homes, reminders of the town's heyday in the 1800s: Belfast was once home to more sea captains than any other port in the world. Belfast also offers trains rides along the water and through fall foliage; a bay excursion on a former Mississippi riverboat; sailing; and kayaking. Belfast also has an active artistic community, and is included in the book, *The 100 Best Small Art Towns in America.*

⑦ Seven miles north on Route 1, **Searsport**—Maine's second-largest deepwater port (after Portland)—claims to be the antiques capital of Maine. The town's stretch of Route 1 hosts a seasonal weekend flea market in addition to its antiques shops.

Searsport preserves a rich nautical history at the **Penobscot Marine Museum,** where eight historic and two modern buildings document the region's seafaring way of life. Included are display photos of 284 sea captains, artifacts of the whaling industry (lots of scrimshaw), hundreds of paintings and models of famous ships, navigational instruments, and treasures collected by seafarers. *Church St.,* ☎ *207/548–2529.* ☛ *$5 adults, $3.50 senior citizens, $1.50 children 7–15.* ۞ *June–mid-Oct., Mon.–Sat. 10–5, Sun. noon–5.*

⑧ Historic **Castine,** over which the French, the British, the Dutch, and the Americans fought from the 17th century to the War of 1812, has two museums and the ruins of a British fort, but the finest aspect of Castine is the town itself: the lively, welcoming town landing, the serene Federal and Greek Revival houses, and the town common. Castine invites strolling, and you would do well to start at the town landing, where you can park your car, and walk up Main Street past the two inns and on toward the white Trinitarian Federated Church with its tapering spire.

Turn right on Court Street and walk to the town common, which is ringed by a collection of white-clapboard buildings that includes the Ives House (once the summer home of the poet Robert Lowell), the Abbott School, and the Unitarian Church, capped by a whimsical belfry that suggests a gazebo.

⑨ From Castine, take Route 166 north to Route 199 and follow the signs to **Blue Hill.** Castine may have the edge over Blue Hill in charm, for its Main Street is not a major thoroughfare and it claims a more dramatic perch over its harbor, yet Blue Hill is certainly appealing and boasts a better selection of shops and galleries. Blue Hill is renowned for its pottery, and two good shops are right in town.

The scenic Route 15 south from Blue Hill passes through Brooksville and on to the graceful suspension bridge that crosses Eggemoggin
❿ Reach to **Deer Isle.** The turnout and picnic area at Caterpillar Hill, 1 mile south of the junction of routes 15 and 175, commands a fabulous view of Penobscot Bay, the hundreds of dark green islands, and the Camden Hills across the bay, which from this perspective look like a range of mountains dwarfed and faded by an immense distance—yet they are less than 25 miles away.

Route 15 continues the length of Deer Isle—a sparsely settled landscape of thick woods opening to tidal coves, shingled houses with lobster traps stacked in the yards, and dirt roads that lead to summer cottages—to
⓫ **Stonington,** an emphatically ungentrified community that tolerates summer visitors but makes no effort to cater to them. Main Street has gift shops and galleries, but this is a working port town, and the principal activity is at the waterfront, where fishing boats arrive with the day's catch. The high, sloped island that rises beyond the archipelago of Merchants Row is Isle au Haut (accessible by mailboat from Stonington), which contains sections of Acadia National Park.

Island Excursions

⓬ **Islesboro,** reached by car-and-passenger ferry (Maine State Ferry Service, ☎ 207/734–6935 or 800/491–4883) from Lincolnville Beach, on Route 1 north of Camden, has been a retreat of wealthy, very private families for more than a century. The long, narrow, mostly wooded island has no real town to speak of; there are scatterings of mansions as well as humbler homes at Dark Harbor (where celebrity couples Kirstie Alley and Parker Stevenson and John Travolta and Kelly Preston live) and at Pripet near the north end. Since the amenities on Islesboro are quite spread out, you don't want to come on foot. If you plan to spend the night here, you should make a reservation well in advance (*see* Islesboro *in* Dining and Lodging, *below*).

TIME OUT   **Dark Harbor Shop** (Main Rd., ☎ 207/734–8878; ⊙ Memorial Day–Labor Day) on Islesboro is an old-fashioned ice cream parlor where tourists, locals, and summer folk gather for sandwiches, newspapers, gossip, and gifts.

⓭ **Isle au Haut** thrusts its steeply ridged back out of the sea 7 miles south of Stonington. Accessible only by passenger mailboat (☎ 207/367–5193), the island is worth visiting for the ferry ride alone, a half-hour cruise amid the tiny, pink-shore islands of Merchants Row, where you may see terns, guillemots, and harbor seals. More than half the island is part of Acadia National Park; 17½ miles of trails extend through quiet spruce and birch woods, along cobble beaches and seaside cliffs, and over the spine of the central mountain ridge. From late June to mid-September, the mailboat docks at Duck Harbor within the park. The small campground here, with five Adirondack-type lean-tos (⊙ Mid-May–mid-Oct.), fills up quickly; reservations are essential, and they can be made only after April 1 by writing to Acadia National Park (Box 177, Bar Harbor 04609).

What to See and Do with Children

Belfast & Moosehead Lake Railroad, one of the oldest railroads in the country, has two narrated scenic rail trips in Waldo County. A diesel train leaves from Belfast's waterfront and runs along an inland river. The other railhead is in Unity, 35 miles inland, where a steam locomotive passes over Unity Pond and alongside working farmlands and small villages. A staged train robbery is fun for children, as is the pre-ride demonstration of turning the engine around at Unity station. Both locations have dining facilities and offer seating in first-class, coach, or open-air cars, which are the most fun in good weather. There are special fall foliage tours that are longer than the usual 1½ hour excursions, and there's a discount if you ride both the railroad and Belfast's river-boat, **Voyager.** *One Depot Square, Unity ME. 04988,* ☎ *207/948–5500 or 800/392–5500.* ☛ *$14 adults, $7 children 3–16.* ☺ *May–Oct. Call for schedule information and directions.*

Owls Head Transportation Museum, 2 miles south of Rockland on Route 73, displays antique aircraft, cars, and engines and stages weekend air shows. *Rte. 73, Owls Head,* ☎ *207/594–4418.* ☛ *$6 adults, $3 children 6–12, $12 family (2 adults and all children under 18).* ☺ *May–Oct., daily 10–5; Nov.–Apr., weekdays 10–4, weekends 10–3.*

Off the Beaten Path

Haystack Mountain School of Crafts, on Deer Isle, attracts internationally renowned glassblowers, potters, sculptors, jewelers, blacksmiths, print-makers, and weavers to its summer institute. You can attend evening lectures or visit the studios of artisans at work (by appointment only). *South of Deer Isle Village on Rte. 15, turn left at Gulf gas station and follow signs for 6 mi,* ☎ *207/348–2306.* ☛ *Free.* ☺ *June–Sept.*

Shopping

The most promising shopping areas are Main and Bay View streets in Camden, Main Street in Blue Hill, and Main Street in Stonington. Antiques shops are clustered in Searsport and scattered around the outskirts of villages, in farmhouses and barns; yard sales abound in summertime.

Antiques

Old Cove Antiques (Rte. 15, Sargentville, ☎ 207/359–2031) has folk art, quilts, hooked rugs, and folk carvings. **Old Deer Isle Parish House Antiques** (Rte. 15, Deer Isle Village, ☎ 207/348–9964) is a place for poking around in the jumbles of old kitchenware, glassware, books, and linen. Billing itself the antiques capital of Maine, Searsport hosts a massive weekend **flea market** on Route 1 during the summer months. Indoor shops, most of them in old houses and barns, are also on Route 1, in Lincolnville Beach as well as in Searsport. Shops are open daily during the summer months, by chance or by appointment from mid-October through the end of May.

Art Galleries

Blue Heron Gallery & Studio (Church St., Deer Isle Village, ☎ 207/348–6051) features the work of the Haystack Mountain School of Crafts faculty. **Deer Isle Artists Association** (Rte. 15, Deer Isle Village, no ☎) has group exhibits of prints, drawings, and sculpture from mid-June through Labor Day. **J. S. Ames Fine Art** (68 Main St., Belfast, ☎ 207/338–1558) carries contemporary art in all media. **Leighton Gallery** (Parker Point Rd., Blue Hill, ☎ 207/374–5001) shows oil paintings, lithographs, watercolors, and other contemporary art in the gallery, and sculpture in its garden. **Maine's Massachusetts House Galleries** (Rte. 1, Lincolnville, ☎ 207/789–5705) offers a broad selection of regional art, including bronzes, carvings, sculptures, and landscapes and seascapes in pencil, oil, and watercolor. The **Pine Tree Shop & Bayview Gallery** (33 Bay View St., Camden, ☎ 207/236–4534) specializes in original art, prints, and posters—almost all with Maine themes.

Books

The **Owl and Turtle Bookshop** (8 Bay View St., Camden, ☎ 207/236–4769) sells a thoughtfully chosen selection of books, CDs, cassettes, and cards, including Maine-published works. The two-story shop has special rooms devoted to marine books and children's books. The **Personal Bookstore** (78 Main St, Thomaston, ☎ 207/354–8058 or 800/391–8058) is a booklover's treasure. Maine authors frequently do book-signings; browsers will find some autographed copies on the shelves. **Reading Corner** (408 Main St., Rockland, ☎ 207/596–6651) carries an extensive inventory of cookbooks, children's books, Maine titles, best-sellers, and one of the area's best newspaper and magazine selections.

Crafts and Pottery

Chris Murray Waterfowl Carver (Upper Main St., Castine, ☎ 207/326–9033) sells award-winning wildfowl carvings and offers carving instruction. **Handworks Gallery** (Main St., Blue Hill, ☎ 207/374–5613) carries unusual crafts, jewelry, and clothing. **North Country Textiles** (Main St., Blue Hill, ☎ 207/374–2715) specializes in fine woven shawls, placemats, throws, baby blankets, and pillows in subtle patterns and color schemes. **Rackliffe Pottery** (Rte. 172, Blue Hill, ☎ 207/374–2297) is famous for its vivid blue pottery, including plates, tea and coffee sets, pitchers, casseroles, and canisters. **Rowantrees Pottery** (Union St., Blue Hill, ☎ 207/374–5535) has an extensive selection of styles and patterns in dinnerware, tea sets, vases, and decorative items.

Furniture

The **Windsor Chairmakers** (Rte. 1, Lincolnville, ☎ 207/789–5188 or 800/789–5188) sells custom-made, handcrafted beds, chests, china cabinets, dining tables, highboys—and, of course, chairs.

Gourmet Supplies

The Good Table (72 Main St., Belfast, ☎ 207/338–4880) carries an imaginative array of gifts and gourmet items. **Heather Harland** (37 Bay View St., Camden, ☎ 207/236–9661) is a two-story cornucopia of cookbooks, imported pottery and cookware, designer linens, and unusual condiments. **The Store** (435 Main St., Rockland, ☎ 207/594–9246) features top-of-the-line cookware, table accessories, and an outstanding card selection.

Skiing

Camden Snowbowl

Box 1209, Camden 04843
☎ *207/236–3438*

DOWNHILL

No other ski area can boast a view over island-studded Penobscot Bay like Camden Snowbowl. The Currier & Ives setting includes the 950-foot-vertical mountain adjacent to a small lake that is cleared for ice skating. Also on premises is a 400-foot toboggan run that shoots sledders out onto the lake. There is a small lodge with cafeteria, a ski school, and ski and toboggan rentals. Camden Snowbowl has 11 trails accessed by one double chair and two T-bars. It also has night skiing.

CROSS-COUNTRY

There are 16 kilometers (10 miles) of cross-country skiing trails at the **Camden Hills State Park** SM (☎ 207/236–9849), and 20 kilometers (12½ miles) at the **Tanglewood 4-H Camp** in Lincolnville (☎ 207/789–5868), about 5 miles away.

Other Sports

Boat Trips

Windjammers create a stir whenever they sail into Camden harbor, and a voyage around the bay on one of them, whether for an afternoon or a week, is unforgettable. The season for the excursions is June through September. Excursion boats, too, provide a great opportunity for getting afloat on the waters of Penobscot Bay.

The 150-passenger *Voyageur* (☎ 800/392–5500) leaves Belfast twice daily in season for 1½-hour narrated tours of the bay. Sightings of seals and cormorants are common; dolphins show up more rarely. This former Mississippi riverboat has both open and enclosed decks and food-and-beverage service. Sailing schedules coordinate with that of the Belfast & Moosehead Lake Railroad; a discount applies if you employ both.

CAMDEN
Angelique (Yankee Packet Co., Box 736, ☎ 207/236–8873 or 800/282–9989) makes three- and six-day trips. *Appledore* (0 Lily Pond Dr., ☎ 207/236–8353 or 800/233–7437) has two-hour day sails as well as private charters. *Betselma* (35 Pearl St., ☎ 207/236–4446) offers two two-hour excursions and eight one-hour trips from Camden's Public Landing every day between June and October. No reservations needed. **Maine Windjammer Cruises** (Box 617, ☎ 207/236–2938 or 800/736–7981) has three two-masted schooners making two-, four-, and six-day trips along the coast and to the islands. *Roseway* (Box 696, ☎ 207/236–4449 or 800/255–4449) takes three-, four-, and six-day cruises.

ROCKLAND
North End Shipyard Schooners (Box 482, ☎ 800/648–4544) operates three- and six-day cruises on the schooners *American Eagle, Isaac H. Evans,* and *Heritage.* The **Vessels of Windjammer Wharf** (Box 1050, ☎ 207/236–3520 or 800/999–7352) organizes three- and six-day cruises on the *Pauline,* a 12-passenger motor yacht, and the *Stephen Taber,* a windjammer.

ROCKPORT
Timberwind (Box 247, ☎ 207/236–0801 or 800/759–9250) is a 100-foot windjammer that sails out of Rockport harbor on three- and six-day trips.

STONINGTON
Palmer Day IV (☎ 207/367–2207) departs Stonington Harbor each day at 2 between July 1 and Labor Day for a two-hour excursion. Each Thursday morning, a special four-hour cruise stops at North Haven and Vinalhaven Islands.

Biking

Maine Sport (Rte. 1, Rockport, ☎ 207/236–8797) rents bikes, camping and fishing gear, canoes, kayaks, cross-country skis, ice skates, and skis.

Deep-Sea Fishing

The 42-foot *Henrietta* (☎ 207/594–5411) departs the Rockland Landings Marina (end of Sea St.) at 7:30 daily, returning at 5, from late May through September, weather permitting. Bait and tackle are provided, alcohol is prohibited, reservations are essential.

Flightseeing

Ace Aviation (Belfast Municipal Airport, Belfast, ☎ 207/338–2970) takes up to three people, at approximately $25 per 15 minutes, for panoramic views of the jagged coastline, lighthouses, and islands. Planes are available for charter.

Water Sports

Eggemoggin Reach is a famous cruising ground for yachts, as are the coves and inlets around Deer Isle and the Penobscot Bay waters between Castine and Camden. **Bay Island Yacht Charters** (Box 639, Camden, ☎ 207/236–2776 or 800/421–2492) offers bareboat and charters, daysailer rentals, and sailing lessons. **Belfast Kayak Tours** (RR 1, Box 715, Freedom, ☎ 207/382–6204) guides paddlers of all levels by the hour in sturdy double kayaks. **Chance Along** (140 High St., Belfast, ☎ 207/338–6003 or in Maine 800/286–6696) offers sailing instructions and outings, sailboat rentals and bareboat charters, and boat repairs and storage. **Indian Island Kayak Co.** (16 Mountain St., Camden, ☎ 207/236–4088) gives one- and multi-day kayaking tours. **Maine Sport** (Rte. 1, Rockport, ☎ 207/236–8797), the best sports outfitter north of Freeport, rents sailboards and organizes whitewater-rafting and sea-kayaking expeditions, starting at the store. The **Phoenix Centre** (Rte. 175, Blue Hill Falls, ☎ 207/374–2113) gives sea-kayaking tours of Blue Hill Bay and Eggemoggin Reach.

State Parks

Holbrook Island Sanctuary (on Penobscot Bay in Brooksville, ☎ 207/326–4012) has a gravelly beach with a splendid view; hiking trails through meadow and forest; no camping facilities. **Moose Point State Park** (Rte. 1, between Belfast and Searsport, ☎ 207/548–2882) is ideal for hikes and picnics overlooking Penobscot Bay; no camping facilities.

Dining and Lodging

The Camden-Rockport area has the greatest variety of restaurants, bed-and-breakfasts, and inns in the region.

Belfast

DINING

$–$$ **90 Main.** This family-run restaurant with an outdoor patio in the back is helmed by young chef and owner Sheila Costello. Using Pemaquid oysters, Maine blueberries, organic vegetables grown on a nearby farm, and other fresh, local ingredients, Costello creates flavorful dishes that delight all the senses. Choose from a chalkboard full of specials that always includes a macrobiotic option, or start with the smoked seafood and pâté sampler or the spinach salad topped with sautéed chicken, sweet peppers, hazelnuts and a warmed raspberry vinaigrette. Entreés include ribeye steak and seafood linguine fra diablo. ✕ *90 Main St.,* ☎ *207/338–1106. Reservations accepted for 5 or more. AE, MC, V.*

$ **Weathervane.** Because this small northeastern chain has cut out the middleman—buying directly from fishers and self-distributing their goods—an average meal of very fresh raw, grilled, fried, broiled, or sautéed seafood costs under $10. Shellfish such as littleneck clams and the ubiquitous Maine lobster, tender rings of calamari, and fish from smelt to swordfish are available in combination platters. There are also token non-seafood items like sirloin and chicken tenders. This location has outdoor waterfront seating. ✕ *Main St.,* ☎ *207/338–1774. No reservations. MC, V.*

LODGING

$$ **The Inn on Primrose Hill.** Built in 1812 and once the home of a navy admiral, this 14-room inn near the waterfront is the most elegant in town. The inn's Ionic columns belie its original Federal architecture. The two acres that surround it have formal gardens, a terrace with wrought-iron furniture, and both horseshoes and a boccie court; a porch swing is an agreeable addition. Owners Pat and Linus Heinz have taken great care to keep and restore authentic details like ornate Waterford chandeliers, a mahogany dining set, and black marble fireplace. There are several spacious public rooms including double parlors, a library with a large-screen cable TV, and a sunny conservatory with wicker and plump, upholstered furniture. Guest rooms are large and have partial bay views. ☎ *100 High St., ☎ 207/338–6982. 2 rooms, 1 with private bath, 1 with shared bath. Boccie, horseshoes. Full breakfast included. No credit cards.*

$–$$ **Thomas Pitcher House.** Easygoing hosts Fran and Ron Kresge run a cheerful bed and breakfast that's one block from Belfast's Main Street. Bright common areas include a small library, a formal dining room with Chippendale furnishings, and a parlor with a marble fireplace and Victorian touches. Upstairs, carefully decorated guest rooms have supremely comfortable beds and floral, paisley, and/or striped accents. Ron is a master breakfast chef—beg for his ham and cheese soufflé. ☎ *5 Franklin St., ☎ 207/338–6454. 4 rooms with bath. Full breakfast included. No credit cards. No children under 12.*

Blue Hill

DINING

$$–$$$ **The Firepond.** Reopened in 1994 after a two-year hiatus, the Firepond
★   attracts customers from all over the region. The upstairs dining room has the air of an English country gentleman's library, with built-in bookshelves, antiques, and Oriental carpets; a new street-level dining area increases the seating capacity to 120. The kitchen delivers old favorites like lobster Firepond—with three cheeses, served over pasta—and new veal, pork, and scallop specialties. ✗ *Main St., ☎ 207/374–9970. Reservations advised. AE, MC, V. Closed Jan.–Apr.*

$$ **Jonathan's.** The downstairs room has captain's chairs, linen tablecloths, and local art; in the post-and-beam upstairs, there's wood everywhere, plus candles with hurricane globes and high-back chairs. The menu may include chicken breast in a fennel sauce with peppers, garlic, rosemary, and shallots; shrimp *scorpio* (served on linguine with a touch of ouzo and feta cheese); pan-seared medallions of venison with sweet-potato pancakes; and several fresh-fish entrées. The wine list has 200 selections from French and California vineyards as well as from the Bartlett Maine Estate Winery in Gouldshore. ✗ *Main St., ☎ 207/374–5226. Reservations advised in summer. MC, V.*

LODGING

$$$$ **John Peters Inn.** The John Peters is unsurpassed for the privacy of its
★   location and the good taste in the decor of its guest rooms. The living room has two fireplaces, books and games, a baby grand piano, and Empire furniture. Oriental rugs are everywhere. Huge breakfasts in the light and airy dining rooms include the famous lobster omelet, served complete with lobster-claw shells as decoration. The Surry Room, one of the best rooms, has a king-size bed, a fireplace, curly-maple chest, gilt mirror, and six windows. The large rooms in the carriage house, a stone's throw down the hill from the inn, have dining areas, cherry floors and woodwork, wicker and brass accents, and a modern feel. ☎ *Peters Point, Box 916, 04614, ☎ 207/374–2116. 7 rooms with bath and 1 suite in inn; 6 rooms with bath in carriage house. Pool, pond, boating. Full breakfast included. MC, V. Closed Nov.–Apr.*

Camden

DINING

$$ Waterfront Restaurant. A ringside seat on Camden Harbor can be had here; the best view is from the outdoor deck, open in warm weather. The fare is primarily seafood: boiled lobster, scallops, bouillabaisse, steamed mussels, Cajun barbecued shrimp. Lunchtime highlights include Tex-Mex dishes, lobster and crabmeat salads, and tuna niçoise. ✕ *Bay View St.,* ☎ *207/236–3747. No reservations. AE, MC, V.*

$–$$ Cappy's Chowder House. Lobster traps, a moose head, and a barber-shop pole decorate the bar in this lively but cozy eatery; the Crow's Nest dining room upstairs is quieter and has a harbor view. Simple fare is the rule here: burgers, sandwiches, seafood, and, of course, chowder. A bakery downstairs sells breads, cookies, and filled croissants to go. ✕ *1 Main St.,* ☎ *207/236–2254. No reservations. MC, V.*

DINING AND LODGING

$$$$ Whitehall Inn. Camden's best-known inn, just north of town on Route
★ 1, is an 1843 white-clapboard, wide-porch ship-captain's home with a turn-of-the-century wing. Just off the comfortable main lobby with its faded Oriental rugs, the Millay Room preserves memorabilia of the poet Edna St. Vincent Millay, who grew up in the area. Rooms are sparsely furnished, with dark-wood bedsteads, white bedspreads, and clawfoot bathtubs. Some rooms have ocean views. The dining room, serving traditional and creative American cuisine, is open to the public. Dinner entrées include Eastern salmon in puff pastry, swordfish grilled with roast red pepper sauce, and lamb tenderloin. ☎ *52 High St. (Rte. 1), Box 558, 04843,* ☎ *207/236–3391 or 800/789–6565,* FAX *207/236– 4427. 44 rooms with bath. Restaurant (reservations advised; no lunch), shuffleboard, golf privileges, tennis courts. MAP. AE, MC, V. Closed mid-Oct.–late May.*

LODGING

$$$$ Norumbega. This stone castle, built in 1886 amid Camden's elegant
★ clapboard houses, was obviously the fulfillment of a fantasy. The public rooms have gleaming parquet floors, oak and mahogany paneling, richly carved wood mantels over four fireplaces on the first floor alone, gilt mirrors, and Empire furnishings. At the back of the house, several decks and balconies overlook the garden, the gazebo, and the bay. The view improves as you ascend; the penthouse suite has a small deck, private bar, and a skylight in the bedroom. On arrival, guests are welcomed with complimentary aperitifs. ☎ *61 High St., 04843,* ☎ *207/ 236–4646,* FAX *207/236–0824. 12 rooms with bath. Full breakfast included. AE, MC, V.*

$$$–$$$$ Blackberry Inn. This Victorian painted lady furnishes nine rooms decorated in the minimalist Victorian style and a carriage-house suite, complete with kitchen, which is ideal for traveling families. Also in the carriage house, two renovated garden rooms have fireplaces, whirlpool tubs, and separate entrances. ☎ *82 Elm St., 04843,* ☎ *207/346– 6060,* FAX *207/236–4117. 7 rooms with bath, 2 rooms share shower, 1 suite with kitchen. Full breakfast included. MC, V.*

$$$–$$$$ Windward House. A choice bed-and-breakfast, this Greek Revival house of 1854, at the edge of downtown, has rooms furnished with fishnet lace canopy beds, cherry highboys, curly-maple bedsteads, and clawfoot mahogany dressers. Guests are welcome to use any of three sitting rooms, including the Wicker Room with its glass-top white wicker table where morning coffee is served. Breakfasts may include quiche, apple puff pancakes, peaches-and-cream French toast, or soufflés. A pleasant, private deck in back overlooks extensive English cutting gardens. ☒ *6 High St., 04843,* ☎ *207/236–9656. 7 rooms with bath, 1 suite. Full breakfast included. AE, MC, V.*

Castine

DINING AND LODGING

$$$$ **The Pentagoet.** The rambling, pale-yellow Pentagoet, a block from Castine's waterfront, has been a favorite stopping place for more than a century. The porch wraps around three sides of the inn and has two charming "courting swings." Decor in guest rooms includes hooked rugs, a mix of Victorian antiques, and floral wallpapers. Dinner in the deep-rose-and-cream formal dining room is an elaborate affair; entrées always include lobster creatively prepared, plus two other selections, such as grilled salmon with Dijon sauce, or pork loin braised in apple cider. Complimentary hors d'oeuvres are served evenings in the library-cum-music room, where there is often live chamber music. Inn guests can choose from a hearty breakfast or a lighter breakfast buffet. ☒ *Main St., 04421,* ☎ *207/326–8616 or 800/845–1701. 16 rooms with bath. Restaurant (reservations required; no lunch). MAP. MC, V. Closed Nov.–late May.*

$$–$$$$ **The Castine Inn.** Light, airy rooms, upholstered easy chairs, and fine
★ prints and paintings are typical of the guest-room furnishings here. One room has a pineapple four-poster bed. The third floor has the best views: the harbor over the handsome formal gardens on one side, the village on the other. The dining room, decorated with a wraparound mural of Castine and its harbor, is open to the public for breakfast and dinner; the menu includes traditional New England fare—Maine lobster, crabmeat cakes with mustard sauce, roast leg of lamb, and chicken-and-leek potpie—plus such creative entrées as sweetbreads with hazelnut butter and roast duck with peach chutney. In the snug, English-style pub off the lobby are small tables, a fireplace, and antique spirit jars over the mantel. ☒ *Main St., Box 41, 04421,* ☎ *207/326–4365,* ℻ *207/326–4570. 17 rooms with bath, 3 suites. Restaurant, pub. Full breakfast included. MC, V. Closed Nov.–mid-Apr.*

Deer Isle

DINING AND LODGING

$$$$ **Pilgrim's Inn.** The bright red, four-story, gambrel-roof house dating from
★ about 1793 overlooks a mill pond and harbor in Deer Isle Village. The library has wing chairs and Oriental rugs; a downstairs taproom has a huge brick fireplace, pine furniture, braided rugs, and parson's benches. A generous array of hors d'oeuvres is served in the taproom and common room before dinner each evening. Guest rooms, each with its own character, sport English fabrics and select antiques. The dining room is in the attached barn, an open space both rustic and elegant, with farm implements, French oil lamps, and tiny windows. The five-course, single-entrée menu changes nightly; it might include rack of lamb or fresh local seafood, scallop bisque, asparagus and smoked salmon, and poached pear tart for dessert. ☒ *Rte. 15A, Deer Isle 04627,* ☎ *207/348–6615. 13 rooms, 8 with bath, 1 seaside cottage. Restaurant (reservations required; no lunch), bicycles. Full breakfast included; MAP available. No credit cards. Closed mid-Oct.–mid-May.*

$$–$$$ **Goose Cove Lodge.** The heavily wooded property at the end of a back road has 2,500 feet of ocean frontage, two sandy beaches, a long sandbar that leads to the Barred Island nature preserve, and nature trails. Some cottages and suites are in secluded woodlands, some on the shore, some attached, some with a single large room, others with one or two bedrooms. All but two units have fireplaces. The restaurant's prix-fixe four-course repast (always superb and always including at least one vegetarian entrée) is preceded by complimentary hors d'oeuvres. Friday nights, there's a lobster feast on the inn's private beach. ☒ *Box 40, Sunset 04683,* ☎ *207/348–2508,* ℻ *207/348–2624. 11 cottages, 10 suites. Restaurant (reservations required; no lunch), volleyball, boating. MC, V. MAP. Closed mid-Oct.–mid-May. One wk minimum stay in July and Aug.*

LODGING

$–$$ **Captain's Quarters Inn & Motel.** Accommodations, as plain and unadorned as Stonington itself, are in the middle of town, a two-minute walk from the Isle au Haut mailboat. You have your choice of motel-type rooms and suites or efficiencies, and you can take your breakfast muffins and coffee to the sunny deck overlooking the water. ☒ *Main St., Box 83, Stonington 04681,* ☎ *207/367–2420 or 800/942–2420. 13 units, 11 with bath. AE, D, MC, V.*

Isle au Haut

LODGING

$$$–$$$$ **The Keeper's House.** This converted lighthouse-keeper's house, set on a rock ledge surrounded by thick spruce forest, has its own special flavor. There is no electricity, but every guest receives a flashlight at registration; guests dine by candlelight on seafood or chicken and read in the evening by kerosene lantern. Trails link the historic inn with Acadia National Park's Isle au Haut trail network, and you can walk to the village—a collection of simple houses, a church, a tiny school, and a general store. The innkeepers are happy to pack lunches for anyone who wants to spend the day exploring the island. The five guest rooms are spacious, airy, and simply decorated with painted wood furniture and local crafts. A separate cottage, the Oil House, has no indoor plumbing. Access to the island is via the daily (except Sunday and holidays) mailboat from Stonington—a scenic, 40-minute trip. ☒ *Box 26, 04645,* ☎ *207/367–2261. 5 rooms share bath, 1 cottage. Dock, bicycles. AP, BYOB. No credit cards. No Sun. or holiday check-in. Closed Nov.–Apr.*

Islesboro

LODGING

$$$$ **Dark Harbor House.** The yellow-clapboard, neo-Georgian summer "cottage" of 1896 has a stately portico and a dramatic hilltop setting on the island of Islesboro. An elegant double staircase curves from the ground floor to the bedrooms, which are spacious, some with balconies, five with fireplaces, two with four-poster beds. The dining room, open to the public for dinner by reservation, emphasizes seafood. ☒ *Main Rd., Box 185, 04848,* ☎ *207/734–6669. 10 rooms with bath. Restaurant. MC, V. Closed mid-Oct.–mid-May.*

Lincolnville Beach

DINING

$–$$ **Chez Michel.** This unassuming restaurant, serving up a fine rabbit pâté, mussels marinière, steak au poivre, and poached salmon, might easily be on the Riviera instead of Lincolnville Beach. Chef Michel Hetuin creates bouillabaisse as deftly as he whips up New England fisherman chowder, and he welcomes special requests. ✕ *Rte. 1,* ☎ *207/789–5600. Reservations accepted for 6 or more. D, MC, V. Closed Nov.–mid-Apr.*

LODGING

$$$$ **Inn at Sunrise Point.** For luxury and location, you can't beat this ele-
★ gant B&B perched on the water's edge, with magnificent views over Penobscot Bay. Travel-writer Jerry Levitin built his dream getaway here. Three rooms in the main house and four cottages are simply, but tastefully decorated. Each room has a television and VCR, fireplace, terry-

cloth robes, and telephone. The cottages also have whirlpool tubs and private decks. A full breakfast is served in the solarium; guests take high tea in the paneled library with stone fireplace. 🏠 *Box 1344, Camden 04843,* ☎ *207/236–7716 or 800/435–6378. 7 rooms with bath.*

Rockland

DINING

$$ Jessica's. Perched on a hill at the extreme southern end of Rockland,
★ Jessica's occupies four cozy dining rooms in a tastefully renovated Victorian home. Billed as a European bistro, this restaurant lives up to its Continental label with creative entrées that include veal Zurich, paella, and pork Portofino; other specialties of the Swiss chef are focaccia with a selection of toppings and a half-dozen pastas and risottos. ✗ *2 S. Main St. (Rte. 73),* ☎ *207/596–0770. Reservations advised. D, MC, V. Closed Tues. in winter.*

LODGING

$$$–$$$$ Limerock Inn. The onetime commercial-fishing town of Rockland is coming back to life as one that caters to tourists. You can walk to the Farnsworth and the Shore Village museums from this magnificent Queen Anne–style Victorian, located on a quiet residential street. Meticulously decorated rooms include Island Cottage, with a whirlpool tub and doors that opens onto a private deck overlooking the backyard garden, and Grand Manan, which has a fireplace, whirlpool tub, and a four-poster king-size bed. 🏠 *98 Limerock St., 94841,* ☎ *207/594–2257 or 800/546–3762. 8 rooms with bath, 2 can be suites. Croquet, bicycles, boating. MC, V. Full breakfast included.*

Stockton Springs

LODGING

$–$$ Hichborn Inn. A Victorian Italianate on the National Register for Historic Places, this inn was originally the home of N.G. Hichborn, a prolific shipbuilder and politician and a cousin of Paul Revere. Small and romantic, the Hichborn is just north of Searsport, off Route 1, in a quiet neighborhood one door down from a classic white-steepled New England church. Public areas include a music room with a piano; a cheery sunporch with tables for two set for breakfast; and a dark and cozy parlor with maroon walls, a fireplace, and a tray of brandy, sherry, and cordials for self-service. Of the three guest rooms, one has a brass bed, one a sleigh bed, and the other an ornate, Victorian carved-walnut bed. Finishing touches include marble top dressers and robes. Your hosts, Nancy and Bruce Suppes, might serve fruit soup and Belgian waffles for breakfast. Eight friendly, protective ghosts have been spotted here over the years. 🏠 *Church St. (Box 115),* ☎ *207/567–4183. 2 rooms with bath, 1 room shares bath. No credit cards accepted. No Children. Full breakfast included.*

Tenants Harbor

DINING AND LODGING

$$–$$$ East Wind Inn & Meeting House. On Route 131, 10 miles off Route 1, and set on a knob of land overlooking the harbor and the islands, the East Wind offers simple hospitality, a wraparound porch, and unadorned but comfortable guest rooms, each furnished with an iron bedstead, flowered wallpaper, and heritage bedspread. The dinner menu features seafood supreme, prime rib, boiled lobster, and baked stuffed haddock. 🏠 *Rte. 131, Box 149, 04860,* ☎ *207/372–6366,* ℻ *207/372–6320. 23 rooms, 9 with bath; 3 suites. Restaurant (reservations advised; no lunch). Full breakfast included. AE, MC, V. Closed Feb.*

The Arts

Music

Bay Chamber Concerts (Rockport Opera House, Rockport, ☎ 207/236–2823) offers chamber music every Thursday night and some Friday nights during July and August; concerts are given once a month September through May. **Kneisel Hall Chamber Music Festival** (Kneisel Hall, Rte. 15, Blue Hill, ☎ 207/374–2811) has concerts on Sunday and Friday in summer.

Theater

The Belfast Maskers (Railroad Theater, Box 1017, Belfast, ☎ 207/338–9668) deserve their strong regional reputation. This group, which has received celebrity support from the likes of Ali McGraw and Liv Ullmann, presents both modern and classic works year-round.

Camden Civic Theatre (Camden Opera House, ☎ 207/236–7595), a community theater, specializes in musicals June through August. **Cold Comfort Productions** (Box 259, Castine, no ☎), a community theater, mounts plays in July and August.

Nightlife

Dennett's Wharf (Sea St., Castine, ☎ 207/326–9045) draws a crowd every lunchtime for a terrific view, and every evening for drinking and dancing. It's open from May through October. **Left Bank Bakery and Cafe** (Rte. 172, Blue Hill, ☎ 207/374–2201) rates a gold star for bringing top-notch musical talent from all over the country to sleepy Blue Hill. **Peter Ott's Tavern** (16 Bay View St., Camden, ☎ 207/236–4032) is a steakhouse with a lively bar scene. **Sea Dog Tavern & Brewery** (43 Mechanic St., Camden, ☎ 207/236–6863) is a popular brew pub offering locally made lagers and ales in a retrofitted woolen mill.

Penobscot Bay Essentials

Getting Around

BY CAR

Route 1 follows the west coast of Penobscot Bay, linking Rockland, Rockport, Camden, Belfast, and Searsport. On the east side of the bay, Route 175 (south from Route 1) takes you to Route 166A (for Castine) and Route 15 (for Blue Hill, Deer Isle, and Stonington). A car is essential for exploring the bay area.

Important Addresses and Numbers

EMERGENCIES

Blue Hill Memorial Hospital (Water St., Blue Hill, ☎ 207/374–2836). **Island Medical Center** (Airport Rd., Stonington, ☎ 207/367–2311). **Penobscot Bay Medical Center** (Rte. 1, Rockport, ☎ 207/596–8000). **Waldo County General Hospital** (56 Northport Ave., Belfast, ☎ 207/338–2500).

VISITOR INFORMATION

Belfast Area Chamber of Commerce (Box 58, Belfast 04915, ☎ 207/338–5900; Information booth: 31 Front St., ☉ Daily 10–6, May–Oct.). **Blue Hill Chamber of Commerce** (Box 520, Blue Hill 04614, no ☎). **Castine Town Office** (Emerson Hall, Court St., Castine 04421, ☎ 207/326–4502). **Deer Isle–Stonington Chamber of Commerce** (Box 459, Stonington 04681, ☎ 207/348–6124). **Rockland–Thomaston Area Chamber of Commerce** (Harbor Park, Box 508, Rockland 04841, ☎ 207/596–0376; ☉ Daily 8–5 in summer, weekdays 9–4 in winter). **Rockport-Camden-Lincolnville Chamber of Commerce** (Public Landing, Box 919, Camden 04843, ☎ 207/236–4404; ☉ Weekdays 9–5, Sat. 10–5, Sun. noon–4 in summer; weekdays 9–5, Sat. 10–4 in winter). **Searsport Chamber of Commerce** (East Main St., Searsport 04974, ☎ 207/548–6510).

ACADIA

East of Penobscot Bay, Acadia is the informal name for the area that includes Mount Desert Island (pronounced dessert) and its surroundings: Blue Hill Bay; Frenchman Bay; and Ellsworth, Hancock, and other mainland towns. Mount Desert, 13 miles across, is Maine's largest island, and it harbors most of Acadia National Park, Maine's principal tourist attraction with more than 4 million visitors a year. The 40,000 acres of woods and mountains, lake and shore, footpaths, carriage roads, and hiking trails that make up the park extend as well to other islands and some of the mainland. Outside the park, on Mount Desert's east shore, Bar Harbor has become a busy tourist town. An upper-class resort town of the 19th century, Bar Harbor serves park visitors with a variety of inns, motels, and restaurants.

Exploring

Numbers in the margin correspond to points of interest on the Acadia map.

❶ Coastal Route 1 passes through Ellsworth, where Route 3 turns south to Mount Desert Island and takes you into the busy town of **Bar Harbor.** Most of Bar Harbor's grand mansions were destroyed in a mammoth fire that devastated the island in 1947, but many of the surviving estates have been converted to attractive inns and restaurants. Motels abound, yet the town retains the beauty of a commanding location on Frenchman Bay. Shops, restaurants, and hotels are clustered along Main, Mt. Desert, and Cottage streets.

Bar Harbor Historical Society Museum, on the lower level of the Jesup Memorial Library, displays photographs of Bar Harbor from the days when it catered to the very rich. Other exhibits document the great fire of 1947. *34 Mt. Desert St., ☎ 207/288–4245. ☛ Free. ☉ Mid-June–mid-Oct., Mon.–Sat. 1–4 or by appointment.*

❷ The **Hulls Cove** approach to Acadia National Park is four miles northwest of Bar Harbor on Route 3. Even though it is often clogged with traffic in summer, the Park Loop Road provides the best introduction to Acadia National Park. At the start of the loop at Hulls Cove, the visitor center shows a free 15-minute orientation film. Also available at the center are books, maps of the hiking trails and carriage roads in the park, the schedule for naturalist-led tours, and cassettes for drive-it-yourself park tours.

❸ Follow the road to the small ticket booth, where you pay the $5-per-vehicle entrance fee. Take the next left to the parking area for **Sand Beach,** a small stretch of pink sand backed by the mountains of Acadia and the odd lump of rock known as The Beehive. The **Ocean Trail,** which parallels the Park Loop Road from Sand Beach to the Otter Point parking area, is a popular and easily accessible walk with some of the most spectacular scenery in Maine: huge slabs of pink granite heaped at the ocean's edge, ocean views unobstructed to the horizon, and **Thunder Hole,** a natural seaside cave into which the ocean rushes and roars.

❹ Those who want a mountaintop experience without the effort of hiking can drive to the summit of **Cadillac Mountain,** at 1,532 feet the highest point along the eastern seaboard. From the smooth, bald summit

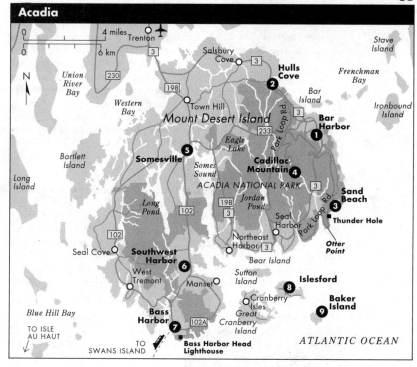

you have a 360-degree view of the ocean, islands, jagged coastline, and the woods and lakes of Acadia and its surroundings.

On completing the 27-mile Park Loop Road, you can continue your auto tour of the island by heading west on Route 233 for the villages on Somes Sound, a true fjord—the only one on the East Coast—which

5 almost bisects Mount Desert Island. **Somesville,** the oldest settlement on the island (1621), is a carefully preserved New England village of white-clapboard houses and churches, neat green lawns, and bits of blue water visible behind them.

6 Route 102 south from Somesville takes you to **Southwest Harbor,** which combines the rough, salty character of a working port with the refinements of a summer resort community. From the town's Main Street (Rte. 102), turn left onto Clark Point Road to reach the harbor.

TIME OUT At the end of Clark Point Road in Southwest Harbor, **Beal's Lobster Pier** serves lobsters, clams, and crab rolls in season at dockside picnic tables.

Those who want to tour more of the island can continue south on Route 102, following Route 102A where the road forks, and passing through the communities of Manset and Seawall. The Bass Harbor Head light-house, which clings to a cliff at the eastern entrance to Blue Hill Bay,

7 was built in 1858. The tiny lobstering village of **Bass Harbor** has cot-tages for rent, inns, a restaurant, a gift shop, and the Maine State Ferry Service's car-and-passenger ferry to Swans Island. ☎ *207/244–3254, 5 daily runs June–Nov., fewer trips rest of yr.*

Island Excursions

Off the southeast shore of Mount Desert Island at the entrance to Somes Sound, the five **Cranberry Isles**—Great Cranberry, Islesford (or Little Cranberry), Baker Island, Sutton Island, and Bear Island—escape the hubbub that engulfs Acadia National Park in summer. Great Cranberry and Islesford are served by the **Beal & Bunker passenger ferry** (☎ 207/ 244–3575) from Northeast Harbor, and by **Cranberry Cove Boating Company** (☎ 207/244–5882) from Southwest Harbor. Baker Island is reached by the summer cruise boats of the **Islesford Ferry Company** (☎ 207/276–3717) from Northeast Harbor; Sutton and Bear islands are privately owned.

❽ **Islesford** comes closest to having a village: a collection of houses, a church, a fishermen's co-op, a market, and a post office near the ferry dock. The **Islesford Historical Museum,** run by Acadia National Park, has displays of tools, documents relating to the island's history, and books and manuscripts of the writer Rachel Field (1894–1942), who summered on Sutton Island. The simple **Islesford Dock Restaurant** (☎ 207/ 244–7446), overlooking the island's harbor, serves lunch and dinner mid-June to mid-September. *Islesford Historical Museum,* ☎ *207/288– 3338.* ☛ *Free.* ☉ *Mid-June–Labor Day, Tues.–Sat. 10:30–noon, 12:30– 4:30.*

❾ The 123-acre **Baker Island,** the most remote of the group, looks almost black from a distance because of its thick spruce forest. The Islesford Ferry cruise boat from Northeast Harbor offers a 4½-hour narrated tour, during which you are likely to see ospreys nesting on a sea stack off Sutton Island, harbor seals basking on ledges, and cormorants flying low over the water. Because Baker Island has no natural harbor, the tour boat ties up off-shore, and you take a fishing dory to get to shore.

What to See and Do with Children

Acadia Zoo has pastures, streams, and woods that shelter about 40 species of wild and domestic animals, including reindeer, wolves, monkeys, and a moose. A barn has been converted to a rain-forest habitat for monkeys, birds, reptiles, and other Amazon creatures. *Rte. 3, Trenton,* ☎ *207/667–3244.* ☛ *$5 adults, $4 senior citizens and children 3–12.* ☉ *May–Nov., daily 9:30–dusk.*

Mount Desert Oceanarium has exhibits in three locations on the fishing and sea life of the Gulf of Maine, as well as hands-on exhibits such as a "touch tank." *Clark Point Rd., Southwest Harbor,* ☎ *207/244– 7330; Rte. 3, Thomas Bay, Bar Harbor,* ☎ *207/288–5005; Lobster Hatchery at 1 Harbor Pl., Bar Harbor,* ☎ *207/288–2334. Call for admission fees (combination tickets available for all 3 sites).* ☉ *Mid-May–mid-Oct., Mon.–Sat. 9–5; hatchery open evenings July–Aug.*

Off the Beaten Path

Bartlett Maine Estate Winery offers tours, tastings, and gift packs. Wines are produced from locally grown apples, pears, blueberries, and other fruit. *Rte. 1, Gouldsboro, north of Bar Harbor (via Ellsworth),* ☎ *207/546–2408.* ☉ *June–mid-Oct., Tues.–Sat. 10–5, Sun. noon–5.*

Jackson Laboratory, a center for research in mammalian genetics, studies cancer, diabetes, heart disease, AIDS, muscular dystrophy, and other diseases. *Rte. 3, 3½ mi south of Bar Harbor,* ☎ *207/288–3371.* ☛ *Free audiovisual presentations, mid-June–mid-Sept., Tues. and Thurs. at 3.*

Shopping

Bar Harbor in summer is prime territory for browsing for gifts, T-shirts, and novelty items; for bargains, head for the outlets that line Route 3 in Ellsworth, which have good discounts on shoes, sportswear, cookware, and more.

Antiques

E. and L. Higgins (Bernard Rd., Bernard, ☎ 207/244–3983) has a good stock of wicker, along with pine and oak country furniture. **Marianne Clark Fine Antiques** (Main St., Southwest Harbor, ☎ 207/244–9247) has an eclectic array of formal and country furniture, American paintings, and accessories from the 18th and 19th centuries.

Books

Port in a Storm Bookstore (Main St., Somesville, ☎ 207/244–4114) is a book lover's nirvana on a rainy day (or even a sunny one) on Mount Desert Island.

Crafts

Acadia Shops (5 branches: inside the park at Cadillac Mountain summit; Thunder Hole on Ocean Dr.; Jordan Pond House on Park Loop Rd.; and 45 and 85 Main St., Bar Harbor) sell crafts and Maine foods and books. **Island Artisans** (99 Main St., Bar Harbor, ☎ 207/288–4214) is a crafts cooperative. **The Lone Moose–Fine Crafts** (78 West St., Bar Harbor, ☎ 207/288–4229) has ship models, art glass, and works in clay, pottery, wood, and fiberglass. The **Eclipse Gallery** (12 Mt. Desert St., Bar Harbor, ☎ 207/288–9048) represents the work of nearly 200 contemporary American artisans, carrying handblown glass, jewelry, and ceramics.

Sports and the Outdoors

Biking, Jogging, and Cross-Country Skiing

The network of carriage roads that wind through the woods and fields of Acadia National Park is ideal for biking and jogging when the ground is dry and for cross-country skiing in winter. The Hulls Cove Visitor Center has a carriage-road map.

Bikes can be rented at **Acadia Bike & Canoe** (48 Cottage St., Bar Harbor, ☎ 207/288–9605), **Bar Harbor Bicycle Shop** (141 Cottage St., ☎ 207/288–3886), and **Southwest Cycle** (Main St., Southwest Harbor, ☎ 207/244–5856).

Camping

The two campgrounds in Acadia National Park—**Blackwoods** (Rte. 3, ☎ 800/365–2267), open year-round, and **Seawall** (Rte. 102A, ☎ 207/244–3600), open late May to late September—fill up quickly during the summer season, even though they have a total of 530 campsites. Space at Seawall is allocated on a first-come, first-served basis, starting at 8 AM. Between mid-May and mid-October, reserve a Blackwoods site within eight weeks of a scheduled visit. No reservations are required off-season. Off Mount Desert Island, but convenient to it, the campground at **Lamoine State Park** (Rte. 84, Lamoine, ☎ 207/667–4778) is open mid-May–mid-October; the 55-acre park has a splendid front-row seat on Frenchman Bay.

Canoeing and Sea Kayaking

For canoe rentals and guided kayak tours, try **Acadia Bike & Canoe,** above, or **National Park Canoe Rentals** (137 Cottage St., Bar Harbor, ☎ 207/288–0342, or Pretty Marsh Rd., Somesville, at the head of Long Pond, ☎ 207/244–5854).

Carriage Rides

Wildwood Stables (Park Loop Rd., near Jordan Pond House, ☎ 207/ 276–3622) gives romantic tours in traditional horse-drawn carriages on the 51-mile network of carriage roads designed and built by philanthropist John D. Rockefeller, Jr. There are three two-hour trips and three one-hour trips daily, including a "tea-and-popover ride" that stops at Jordan Pond House (*see* Dining and Lodging, *below*) and a sunset ride to the summit of Day Mountain.

Cruises

BAR HARBOR

Acadian Whale Watcher (Golden Anchor Pier, West St., ☎ 207/288– 9794 or 800/421–3307) runs 3½-hour whale-watching cruises June–mid-October. *Chippewa* (Bar Harbor Inn Pier, ☎ 207/288–4585 or 207/288–2373) is a 65-foot classic motor vessel that cruises past islands and lighthouses three times a day (including sunset) in summer. **Frenchman Bay Company** (Harbor Place, ☎ 207/288–3322 or 800/508– 1499) operates the windjammer *Bay Lady,* the nature/sightseeing cruise vessel *Acadian,* and the 300-passenger *Whale Watcher* in summer. *Natalie Todd* (Bar Harbor Inn Pier, ☎ 207/288–4585 or 207/288–2373) offers two-hour cruises on a three-masted windjammer mid-May–mid-October.

BASS HARBOR

Bass Harbor Cruises (Bass Harbor Ferry Dock, ☎ 207/244–5365) operates two-hour nature cruises (with an Acadia naturalist) twice daily in summer.

NORTHEAST HARBOR

Blackjack (Town Dock, ☎ 207/276–5043 or 207/288–3056), a 33-foot Friendship sloop, makes four trips daily, mid-June–mid-October.

Hiking

Acadia National Park maintains nearly 200 miles of foot and carriage paths, ranging from easy strolls along flatlands to rigorous climbs that involve ladders and handholds on rock faces. Among the more rewarding hikes are the Precipice Trail to Champlain Mountain, the Great Head Loop, the Gorham Mountain Trail, and the path around Eagle Lake. The Hulls Cove Visitor Center has trail guides and maps.

Sailing and Boating

Harbor Boat Rentals (Harbor Pl., 1 West St., ☎ 207/288–3757) has 13- and 17-foot Boston whalers and other powerboats. **Manset Yacht Service** (Shore Rd., ☎ 207/244–4040) rents sailboats.

Dining and Lodging

Bar Harbor has the greatest concentration of accommodations on Mount Desert Island. Much of this lodging has been converted from elaborate 19th-century summer cottages. A number of fine restaurants are also tucked away in these old homes and inns. Dress is casual unless noted otherwise.

Bar Harbor

DINING

$$$ The Porcupine Grill. Named for a cluster of islets in Frenchman Bay, this two-story restaurant has earned culinary fame for its cornbread-stuffed pork chops, crabmeat terrine made with local goat cheese, salmon with citrus relish, fresh pastas, and a Caesar salad tossed with Reggiano Parmesan and fried shrimp. Soft green walls, antique furnishings, and Villeroy & Boch porcelain create an ambience that complements the cuisine. ✕ *123 Cottage St.,* ☎ *207/288–3884. Reservations advised. AE, MC, V. No lunch. Closed Mon.–Thurs. Jan.–June.*

$$–$$$
★ **George's.** Candles, flowers, and linens grace the tables in four small dining rooms in an old house. The menu shows a distinct Mediterranean influence in the phyllo-wrapped lobster; the lamb and wild game entrées are superb. Couples tend to linger in the romantic setting. ✕ *7 Stephen's La.,* ☎ *207/288–4505. Reservations advised. AE, D, DC, MC, V. No lunch. Closed late Oct.–mid-June.*

$$ **Jordan Pond House.** Oversize popovers (with homemade strawberry jam) and tea are a century-old tradition at this rustic restaurant in the park, where in fine weather you can sit on the terrace or the lawn and admire the views of Jordan Pond and the mountains. Teatime is 2:30 to 5:30. The dinner menu offers lobster stew, seafood thermidor, and fisherman's stew. ✕ *Park Loop Rd.,* ☎ *207/276–3316. Reserve a day ahead in summer. AE, D, MC, V. Closed late Oct.–May.*

LODGING

$$$$ **Holbrook House.** Built in 1876 as a summer home and originally known as Ashley Cottage, the lemon-yellow Holbrook House stands right on Mt. Desert Street, the main access route through Bar Harbor. The downstairs public rooms include a lovely, formal sitting room with bright, summery chintz on chairs and framing windows and a Duncan Phyfe sofa upholstered in white silk damask. The guest rooms and two separate cottages are all furnished with lovingly handled family pieces in the same refined taste as the public rooms. ☎ *74 Mt. Desert St., 04609,* ☎ *207/288–4970 or 800/695–1120. 10 rooms with bath in inn, 2 cottage suites. Croquet. Full breakfast and afternoon refreshments included. MC, V. Closed late-Oct.–May.*

$$$$
★ **Inn at Canoe Point.** Seclusion and privacy are bywords of this snug, 100-year-old Tudor-style house on the water at Hulls Cove, 2 miles from Bar Harbor and ¼ mile from Acadia National Park's Hulls Cove Visitor Center. The Master Suite, a large room with a fireplace, is a favorite for its size and for its French doors, which open onto a waterside deck. The inn's large living room has huge windows on the water, a granite fireplace, and a waterfront deck where a full breakfast is served on summer mornings. ☎ *Box 216, Rte. 3, 04609,* ☎ *207/288–9511. 3 rooms with bath, 2 suites. Full breakfast included. No credit cards.*

$$$–$$$$ **Cleftstone Manor.** Attention, lovers of Victoriana! This inn was made in high Victorian heaven expressly for you. Ignore the fact that it is set amid sterile motels just off Route 3, the road along which traffic roars into Bar Harbor. Inside this rambling brown house, a deeply plush mahogany-and-lace world awaits. The parlor is cool and richly furnished with red velvet and brocade-trim sofas with white doilies, grandfather and mantel clocks, and oil paintings hanging on powder-blue walls. Guest rooms are similarly ornate, and five rooms have fireplaces. ☎ *Rte. 3, Eden St., 04609,* ☎ *207/288–4951 or 800/962–9762. 14 rooms with bath, 2 suites. Full breakfast and afternoon and evening refreshments included. D, MC, V. Closed Nov.–late Apr.*

$$–$$$ **Wonder View Inn.** Although the rooms here are standard motel accommodations, with two double beds and nondescript furniture, this establishment is distinguished by its extensive grounds, an imposing view of Frenchman Bay, and a convenient location opposite the Bluenose Ferry Terminal. The woods muffle the sounds of traffic on Route 3. The gazebo-shaped dining room—the Rinehart Dining Pavilion—has picture windows overlooking the bay and is open to the public for breakfast and dinner. ☎ *Rte. 3, Box 25, 04609,* ☎ *207/288–3358 or 800/ 341–1553,* FAX *207/288–2005. 80 rooms with bath. Dining room, pool. AE, D, MC, V. Closed late Oct.–mid-May.*

Hancock

DINING AND LODGING

$$$–$$$$ **Le Domaine.** This inn, on 100 acres 9 miles east of Ellsworth, has seven
★   rooms done in French country style, with chintz and wicker, simple desks,
and window seats; five of them have balconies or porches over the gar-
dens. The elegant but not intimidating dining room has polished wood
floors, copper pots hanging from the mantel, and silver, crystal, and
linen on the tables; a screened-in dining area overlooks the gardens in
back. Owner Nicole Purslow, trained at Cordon Bleu in her native France,
prepares such specialties as *lapin pruneaux* (rabbit in a rich brown sauce),
sweetbreads with lemon and capers, and coquilles St. Jacques. ☎ *Rte.
1, Box 496, 04640,* ☎ *207/422–3395, 207/422–3916, or 800/554–
8498;* FAX *207/422–2316. 7 rooms with bath. Restaurant (reserva-
tions advised; no lunch; $$$), badminton, hiking, boating, fishing. AE,
D, MC, V. MAP. Closed Nov.–mid-May.*

Northeast Harbor

DINING AND LODGING

$$$–$$$$ **Asticou Inn.** This grand turn-of-the-century inn at the head of exclu-
sive Northeast Harbor serves a loyal clientele. Guest rooms in the main
building have a country feel, with bright fabrics, white lace curtains,
and white painted furniture. The more modern cottages scattered
around the grounds afford greater privacy; among them, the decks and
picture windows make the Topsider Cottages particularly attractive.
Also part of the inn is the Victorian-style Cranberry Lodge, across the
street. At night, guests trade Topsiders and polo shirts for jackets and
ties to dine in the stately formal dining room, which is open to the pub-
lic by reservation. A typical menu includes swordfish with orange
mustard glaze, lobster, shrimp scampi, and chicken in a lemon cream
and mushroom sauce. ☎ *Rte. 3, 04662,* ☎ *207/276–3344 or 800/258–
3373,* FAX *207/276–3373. 27 rooms with bath, 23 suites, 6 cottages.
Restaurant (reservations required; no lunch), pool, tennis courts. MAP
in summer. MC, V. Inn and restaurant closed mid-Sept.–mid-June;
cottages, lodge closed Jan.–Apr.*

Southwest Harbor

DINING AND LODGING

$$$$ **Claremont Hotel.** Built in 1884 and operated continuously as an inn,
the Claremont calls up memories of long, leisurely vacations of days
gone by. The yellow-clapboard structure commands a view of Somes
Sound, croquet is played on the lawn, and cocktails and lunch are served
at the Boat House in midsummer. The highlight of the summer season
is the annual Claremont Croquet Classic, held at the hotel the first week
in August. The main hotel received a complete updating in 1994, but
traditionalists will be hard pressed to notice any changes: A historic
preservationist oversaw the rewiring and replumbing. There are also
two guest houses on the property and 12 cottages, some with water
views. The large, elegant dining room, open to the public for break-
fast and dinner, is awash in light streaming through the picture win-
dows. The menu changes weekly and always includes fresh fish and at
least one vegetarian entrée. ☎ *Off Clark Point Rd., Box 137, 04679,*
☎ *207/244–5036 or 800/244–5036,* FAX *207/244–3512. 24 rooms with
bath, 12 cottages, 2 guest houses. Restaurant (reservations required;
jacket required for dinner; no lunch; $$), croquet, dock, boating, bicycles, tennis court. MAP. No credit cards. Hotel and restaurant closed
mid-Oct.–mid-June. Cottages closed Nov.–late May.*

LODGING

$$–$$$ **The Island House.** This sweet B&B on the quiet side of the island has simply decorated bedrooms in the main house as well as a carriage house suite, complete with sleeping loft and kitchenette. Rate includes full breakfast. ☒ *Box 1006, 04679,* ☎ *207/244–5180. 4 rooms share 3 baths, 1 suite. No credit cards.*

The Arts

Music

Arcady Music Festival (☎ 207/288–3151) schedules concerts (primarily classical) at a number of locations around Mount Desert Island, as well as at selected off-island sites, from mid-July through August. **Bar Harbor Festival** (59 Cottage St., Bar Harbor, ☎ 207/288–5744) programs recitals, jazz, chamber music, string orchestra, and pops concerts by up-and-coming young professionals from mid-July to mid-August. **Pierre Monteux School for Conductors and Orchestra Musicians** (Rte. 1, Hancock, ☎ 207/422–3931) presents public concerts by faculty and students during the term (late June–late July). Symphonic concerts are Sunday at 5 and chamber-music concerts are Wednesday at 8—all held in the Pierre Monteux Memorial Hall.

Theater

Acadia Repertory Company (Masonic Hall, Rte. 102, Somesville, ☎ 207/244–7260) mounts plays in July and August.

Nightlife

Acadia has relatively little nighttime activity. A lively boating crowd frequents the lounge at the **Moorings Restaurant** (Shore Rd. Manset, ☎ 207/244–7070), which is accessible by boat and car, and stays open until after midnight from mid-May through October.

Acadia Essentials

Getting Around

BY CAR

North of Bar Harbor, the scenic 27-mile Park Loop Road takes leave of Route 3 to circle the eastern quarter of Mount Desert Island, with one-way traffic from Sieur de Monts Spring to Seal Harbor and two-way traffic between Seal Harbor and Hulls Cove. Route 102, which serves the western half of Mount Desert, is reached from Route 3 just after it crosses onto the island or from Route 233 west from Bar Harbor. All of these island roads pass in, out, and through the precincts of Acadia National Park.

Guided Tours

Acadia Taxi and Tours (☎ 207/288–4020) conducts half-day historic and scenic tours of the area.

National Park Tours (☎ 207/288–3327) operates a 2½-hour bus tour of Acadia National Park, narrated by a local naturalist. The bus departs twice daily, May–October, across from Testa's Restaurant at Bayside Landing on Main Street in Bar Harbor.

Acadia Air (☎ 207/667–5534), on Route 3 in Trenton, between Ellsworth and Bar Harbor at Hancock County Airport, offers aircraft rentals and seven different aerial sightseeing itineraries, from spring through fall.

Important Addresses and Numbers

EMERGENCIES

Mount Desert Island Hospital (10 Wayman La., Bar Harbor, ☎ 207/288–5081). **Maine Coast Memorial Hospital** (50 Union St., Ellsworth, ☎ 207/667–5311). **Southwest Harbor Medical Center** (Herrick Rd., Southwest Harbor, ☎ 207/244–5513).

VISITOR INFORMATION

Acadia National Park (Box 177, Bar Harbor 04609, ☎ 207/288–3338; the Hulls Cove Visitor Center, off Rte. 3, at start of Park Loop Rd., is ☉ Daily 8–4:30, May–June and Sept.–Oct.; until 6 PM July and Aug.). **Bar Harbor Chamber of Commerce** (93 Cottage St., Box 158, Bar Harbor 04609, ☎ 207/288–3393, 207/288–5103, or 800/288–5103; ☉ Weekdays 8–5 in summer, weekdays 8–4:30 in winter). There's also an information office in **Bluenose Ferry Terminal** (Rte. 3, Eden St.; ☉ Daily 8 AM–11 PM July–early Oct.; daily 9–5 mid-May–July and early Oct.–mid-Oct.).

COASTAL MAINE ESSENTIALS

Arriving and Departing by Boat

Marine Atlantic (☎ 207/288–3395 or 800/341–7981) operates a car-ferry service year-round between Yarmouth (Nova Scotia) and Bar Harbor; **Prince of Fundy Cruises** (☎ 800/341–7540 or, in ME, 800/482–0955) operates a car ferry between Portland and Yarmouth (May–Oct.).

Dining

For most visitors, Maine means lobster. As a general rule, the closer you are to a working harbor, the fresher your lobster will be. Aficionados eschew ordering lobster in restaurants, preferring to eat them "in the rough" at classic lobster pounds, where you select your lobster swimming in a pool and enjoy it at a waterside picnic table. Shrimp, scallops, clams, mussels, and crab are also caught in the cold waters off Maine, and the better restaurants in Portland and the coastal resort towns prepare the shellfish in creative combinations with lobster, haddock, salmon, and swordfish. Blueberries are grown commercially in Maine, and Maine cooks use them generously in pancakes, muffins, jams, pies, and cobblers. Full country breakfasts of fruit, eggs, breakfast meats, pancakes, and muffins are commonly served at inns and bed-and-breakfasts.

CATEGORY	COST*
$$$$	over $35
$$$	$25–$35
$$	$15–$25
$	under $15

average cost of a three-course dinner, per person, excluding drinks, service, and 7% restaurant sales tax

Lodging

Bed-and-breakfasts and Victorian inns furnished with lace, chintz, and mahogany have joined the family-oriented motels of Ogunquit, Boothbay Harbor, Bar Harbor, and the Camden-Rockport region. Two world-class resorts with good health club and sports facilities are on the coast near Portland and on Penobscot Bay near Rockland. At many of Maine's larger hotels and inns with restaurants, Modified American Plan (includes breakfast and dinner) is either an option or required during the peak summer season.

CATEGORY	COST*
$$$$	over $100
$$$	$80–$100
$$	$60–$80
$	under $60

Prices are for a standard double room during peak season, excluding 7% lodging sales tax.

Visitor Information

Maine Publicity Bureau (325B Water St., Box 2300, Hallowell 04347, ☎ 207/623–0363 or, outside ME, 800/533–9595; FAX 207/623–0388).
Maine Innkeepers Association (305 Commercial St., Portland 04101, ☎ 207/773–7670) publishes a statewide lodging and dining guide.

4 New Brunswick

New Brunswick is where the great Canadian forest, sliced by sweeping river valleys and modern highways, meets the Atlantic. To the north and east, the gentle, warm Gulf Stream washes quiet beaches. Besides the seacoast, there are pure inland streams, pretty towns, and historic cities. The province's dual heritage (35% of its population is Acadian French) provides added spice.

NEW BRUNSWICK IS WHERE the great Canadian forest, sliced by sweeping river valleys and modern highways, meets the sea. It's an old place in New World terms, and the remains of a turbulent past are still in evidence in some of its quiet nooks. Near Moncton, for instance, bees gather nectar, and wild strawberries perfume the air of the grassy slopes of Fort Beauséjour, where, in 1755, one of the last battles for possession of Acadia took place—the English finally overcoming the French. The dual heritage of New Brunswick (35% of its population is Acadian French) provides added spice. If you decide to stay in both Acadian and Loyalist regions, a trip to New Brunswick can seem like two vacations in one.

By Colleen
Whitney
Thompson

Updated by
Ana Watts

More than half the province is surrounded by coastline—the rest nestles into Québec and Maine, creating slightly schizophrenic attitudes in border towns. The dramatic Bay of Fundy, which has the highest tides in the world, sweeps up the coast of Maine, around the enchanting Fundy Isles at the southern tip of New Brunswick and on up the province's rough and intriguing south coast. To the north and east, the gentle, warm Gulf Stream washes quiet beaches.

New Brunswick is still largely unsettled—85% of the province is forested lands. Inhabitants have chosen the easily accessible area around rivers, ocean, and lakes, leaving most of the interior to the pulp companies. For years this Cinderella province has been virtually ignored by tourists who whiz through to better-known Atlantic destinations. New Brunswick's residents can't seem to decide whether this makes them unhappy or not. Money is important in the economically depressed maritime area, where younger generations have traditionally left home for higher-paying jobs in Ontario and "the West." But no one wishes to lose the special characteristics of this still unspoiled province by the sea.

This attitude is a blessing in disguise to motorists who do leave the major highways to explore 2,240 kilometers (1,400 miles) of spectacular seacoast, pure inland streams, pretty towns, and historical cities. The custom of hospitality is so much a part of New Brunswick nature that tourists are perceived more as welcome visitors than paying guests. Even cities often retain a bit of naïveté. It makes for a charming vacation, but don't be deceived by ingenuous attitudes. Most residents are products of excellent school and university systems, generally travel widely, live in modern cities, and are well versed in world affairs.

EXPLORING

Our exploration of New Brunswick is broken down into four areas: a tour of the city of Fredericton, a tour of the Saint John Valley ending in the city of Saint John, a tour of the Fundy Coast, and a jaunt north to the sunny Acadian Peninsula.

Tour 1: Fredericton

Numbers in the margin correspond to points of interest on the New Brunswick and Fredericton maps.

The small inland city of **Fredericton** spreads itself on a broad point of land jutting into the Saint John River. Its predecessor, the early French settlement of St. Anne's Point, was established in 1642, during the reign of the French governor Villebon, who made his headquarters at the junction of the Nashwaak and the Saint John rivers. Settled by Loy-

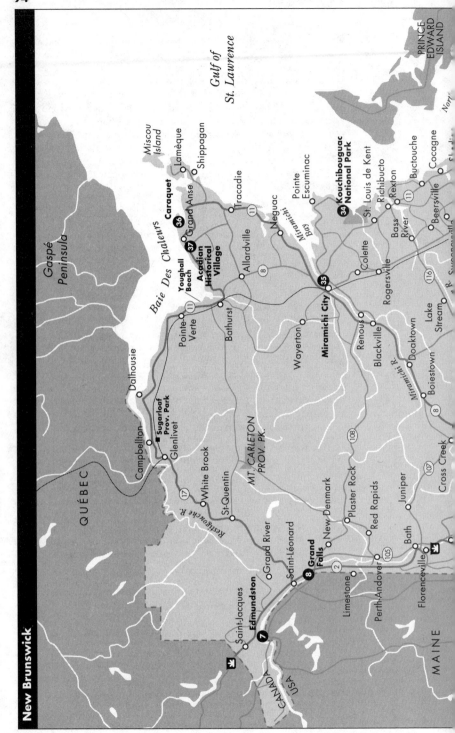

Gulf of
St. Lawrence

PRINCE
EDWARD
ISLAND

Gaspé
Peninsula

Baie Des Chaleurs

Miscou
Island

Lamèque

Shippagan

Caraquet

36 Grand Anse

37 Acadian
Historical
Village

Youghall
Beach

Tracadie

(11)

Neguac

Pointe
Escuminac

Miramichi
Bay

34 Kouchibouguac
National Park

St. Louis de Kent

Richibucto

Rexton

(11)

Buctouche

Cocagne

Beersville

Allardville

(8)

Bass
River

Colette

Rogersville

Lake
Stream

35 Miramichi City

Renous

Blackville

Doaktown

Boiestown

(116)

Wayerton

Bathurst

Pointe-
Verte

(11)

Dalhousie

Sugarloaf
Prov. Park

Glenlivet

Campbellton

QUÉBEC

White Brook

St-Quentin

(17)

MT. CARLETON
PROV. PK.

Miramichi R.

(8)

(108)

(107)

Cross Creek

Restigouche R.

Grand River

Saint-Léonard

New Denmark

Plaster Rock

Red Rapids

Juniper

Bath

Boiestown

8 Grand
Falls

(2)

Limestone

Perth-Andover

(105)

Florenceville

7 Edmundston

Saint-Jacques

CANADA
USA

MAINE

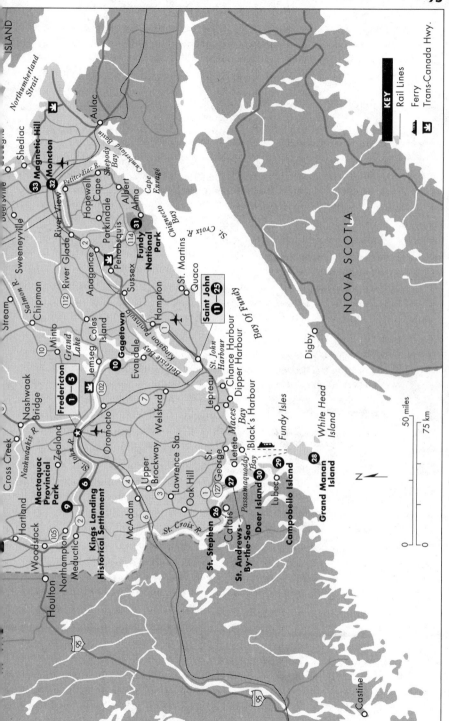

KEY

Rail Lines
Ferry
Trans-Canada Hwy.

ISLAND

Northumberland Strait

Shediac

Magnetic Hill

Moncton

33

32

Petitcodiac R.

River Glade

Sweeneyville

Beersville

River View

Hopewell Cape

Parkindale

Penobsquis

Anagance

Sussex

Shepody Bay

Cumberland Basin

Aulac

Albert

Alma

Cape Enrage

Fundy National Park

31

114

St. Martins

Quaco

Hampton

2

112

Salmon R.

Stream

Chipman

Minto

Grand Lake

Jemseg

Coles Island

10

Gagetown

10

Evandale

Belleisle Bay

Kingston Peninsula

St. John Harbour

Chance Harbour

Dipper Harbour

Lepreau

Saint John

11 — 25

Bay Of Fundy

1

Fredericton

1 — 5

Nashwaak

102

7

Oromocto

Welsford

Lawrence Sta.

Oak Hill

St.

St. George

Maces Bay

Olefete

Black's Harbour

Passamaquoddy Bay

Deer Island

30

Lubec

Campobello Island

Fundy Isles

White Head Island

Grand Manan Island

28

29

Digby

NOVA SCOTIA

St. Croix R.

Chignecto Bay

Nashwaaksis R.

Mactaquac Provincial Park

Zealand

St. John R.

Kings Landing Historical Settlement

9

6

2

4

McAdam

6

St. Croix R.

Upper Brockway

3

127

St. Stephen

26

Calais

St. Andrews-By-the-Sea

27

Cross Creek

Woodstock

Hartland

105

Northampton

Meductic

2

Houlton

95

95

Castine

N

0   50 miles

0   75 km

alists and named for Frederick, second son of George III, the city serves as the seat of government for New Brunswick's 728,500 residents. From the first town plan, the wealthy and scholarly Loyalists set out to create a gracious and beautiful place, and thus even before the establishment of the University of New Brunswick, in 1785, the town served as a center for "liberal arts and sciences."

Fredericton's streets are shaded by leafy plumes of ancient elms. Downtown Queen Street runs parallel with the river, and its blocks enclose historic sites and attractions. Most major sites are within walking distance of each other.

❶ The **Military Compound** extends two blocks along Queen Street, at the corner of Carleton Street. The buildings have been restored, and visitors are welcome to tour the Guard House and Soldiers' Barracks; soldiers from the British 15th Regiment will be your guide. Redcoats stand guard; in summer a changing-of-the-guard ceremony takes place in Officer's Square at 11 and 7. *Queen St. at Carleton St.,* ☎ *506/453–3747.* ☛ *Free.* ☼ *Early June–Labor Day, daily 10–6; Sept.–June, group tours by appointment.*

Within the Military Compound stands the John Thurston Clark Building—an outstanding example of Second Empire architecture. On the main floor is the **National Exhibition Centre.** You'll have fun with the scintillating displays of arts, crafts, history, science, and technology. Upstairs you'll find the **Sports Hall of Fame,** which celebrates the surprising array of locals who have made sports history, most notably Ron Turcotte, who won horse racing's Triple Crown on the immortal Secretariat. The Hall of Fame's collection of original charcoal portraits of honored members is the largest of its kind in Canada. *503 Queen St.,* ☎ *506/453–3747.* ☛ *Free.* ☼ *Both attractions: May–Labor Day, daily 10–6 or by appointment; Labor Day–Apr., Tues.–Sun. noon–5 or by appointment.*

❷ The Officer's Quarters houses the **York-Sunbury Museum,** a living picture of the community from the time when only natives inhabited the area, through the pioneer days, to the immediate past. It also contains the shellacked remains of one of Fredericton's legends, the puzzling Coleman Frog. This giant frog, allegedly discovered in nearby Killarney Lake by late hotelier Fred Coleman, supposedly weighed 42 pounds soaking wet at the time of its death (by a dynamite charge set by unorthodox fishermen). Coleman had the frog stuffed and displayed it for years in the lobby of his hotel. Take a look and judge for yourself—the frog just keeps on smiling. *Officer's Sq., Queen St.,* ☎ *506/455–6041.* ☛ *$1 adults, 50¢ senior citizens and students, $2.50 families.* ☼ *May–Labor Day, Mon.–Sat. 10–6 (in addition, July and Aug., Mon. and Fri. 10–9 and Sun. noon–6); Labor Day–mid-Oct., weekdays 9–5, Sat. noon–4; mid-Oct.–Apr., Mon., Wed., and Fri. 11–3 or by appointment.*

The late Lord Beaverbrook, former New Brunswick resident and multimillionaire British peer and newspaper magnate, showered gifts upon his native province. Walk east from Officer's Quarters, and just beyond the intersection of Queen and St. John streets you'll find the **Beaverbrook Art Gallery,** displaying works by many of New Brunswick's noted artists as well as internationally acclaimed painters. Salvador Dali's gigantic canvas *Santiago el Grande* is worth more than a passing glance. There are also canvases by Reynolds, Turner, Hogarth, Gainsborough, the Canadian Group of Seven, and even Andy Warhol. The gallery has the largest collection in any public institution of the works of Cornelius Krieghoff, famed Canadian landscape painter of the early 1800s. *703*

Queen St., ☎ *506/458–8545.* ☛ *$3 adults, $2 senior citizens, $1 students.* ⊙ *July and Aug., weekdays 9–6, weekends 10–5; Sept.–June, Tues.–Fri. 9–5, Sat. 10–5, Sun. noon–5.*

Across the street from the gallery sits the Playhouse (686 Queen St., ☎ 506/458–8344), a gift of the Beaverbrook and Dunn Foundation to the city and province. It is the home of the professional **Theatre New Brunswick,** whose major season runs from September through May.

❹ Directly across the street from the gallery is the 1880 **Provincial Legislature.** The interior of the Chamber, restored in 1988, reflects the taste of the late Victorians. The chandeliers are brass and the prisms are Waterford. The portraits of King George III and Queen Charlotte are replicas of paintings by Sir Joshua Reynolds. There is a free-standing staircase, and a volume of Audubon's *Birds of America* is on display. *Queen St.,* ☎ *506/453–2527.* ☛ *Free.* ⊙ *Legislature tours: early June–late Aug., daily 9–8; early Sept.–June, weekdays 9–4. Library: year-round, weekdays 8:15–5.*

❺ A bit farther along, at the intersection where Queen Street becomes Waterloo Row, you'll come to the **Christ Church Cathedral,** one of Fredericton's prides. Completed in 1853, the gray stone building is an excellent example of decorated Gothic architecture and the first new cathedral foundation built on British soil since the Norman Conquest. Inside you'll see a clock known as "Big Ben's little brother," the test-run for London's famous timepiece, designed by Lord Grimthorpe. Free tours are given June–August, daily 9–9.

Continue east on Waterloo Row (Rte. 102), turn right at University Avenue to the **University of New Brunswick** campus. Be prepared to climb—the buildings are scattered over a fairly steep hill. The college was established in 1785—ancient by Canadian standards—and was originally called the College of New Brunswick, and later Kings College. Its Old Arts Building is the oldest university structure still in use in the country.

Tour 2: The Saint John River Valley to Saint John

★ ❻ To understand New Brunswick's background and history, visit **Kings Landing Historical Settlement,** located about 30 kilometers (23 miles) west of Fredericton on the Trans-Canada Highway (Route 2). This reconstructed village—more than 60 buildings, including homes, inn, forge, store, church, school, working farms, and sawmill—illustrates life in the central Saint John River valley between 1790 and 1900. Winding country lanes, creaking wagons, old houses, and freshly baked bread pull you back a century or more. The costumed staff is friendly and informative. The Tap Room of Kings Head Inn is a congenial spot to try a draft of cold beer or a mug of frosty cider; the restaurant upstairs serves tasty, old-fashioned traveler's fare. After a hearty meal of King George III's roast beef or Mrs. Long's chicken-vegetable pie, drop by the General Store. It's the heart of the community and the genial storekeeper makes everyone feel welcome. *Box 522, Fredericton,* ☎ *506/363–5090.* ☛ *$7.50 adults, $6 senior citizens and students under 18, $4.50 ages 6–18, children under 6 free, $18 families. Other discounts and group rates available.* ⊙ *June–mid-Oct., daily 10–5.*

The Saint John River forms 120 kilometers (75 miles) of the border with Maine and rolls down to Saint John, New Brunswick's largest, and Canada's oldest, city. Gentle hills of rich farmland and the blue sweep of the water make this a pretty drive. The Trans-Canada High-

98

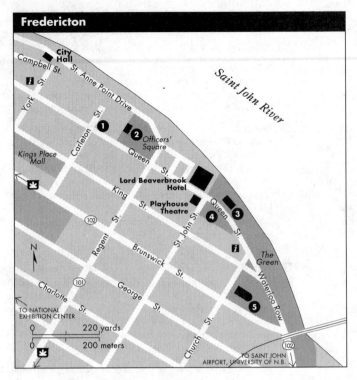

way (Route 2) follows the banks of the river for most of its winding, 403-kilometer (250-mile) course.

At the northern end of the valley, near the border with Québec, you will find yourself in the mythical Republic of Madawaska. In the early 1800s the narrow wedge of land was coveted by Québec on one side and New Brunswick on the other; the United States claimed it as well. Seeking to retain it for New Brunswick, Governor Sir Thomas Carleton found it easy to settle with Québec. He rolled dice all night with the governor of British North America at Québec, who happened to be his brother. Sir Thomas won at dawn—by one point. Settling with the Americans was more difficult. The border had always been disputed, and even the lumbermen engaged in combat. Finally, in 1842, the British flag was hoisted over Madawaska county. One old-timer, tired of being asked to which country he belonged, replied, "I am a citizen of the Republic of Madawaska." So began the republic, which exists today with its own flag (an independent eagle on a field of white) and a coat of arms.

➐ **Edmundston,** the unofficial capital of Madawaska, has always depended on the wealth of the deep forest around it. Even today, Edmundston looks to the Fraser Company pulp mills as the major source of employment. It was in these woods that the legend of Paul Bunyan was born. Tales spread to Maine and even to the West Coast. The Foire Brayonne festival, held annually during the last week of July, is proud to claim the title of the biggest festival outside of Québec's Winter Carnival. It is certainly one of the most lively and vibrant cultural events in New Brunswick, offering concerts by acclaimed artists as well as local musicians and entertainers who enliven the Arts & Crafts Square.

Nearby St. Jacques is home to New Brunswick's new Botanical Garden. Roses, rhododendrons, alpine flowers, and dozens of annuals and perennials bloom in the eight gardens while Mozart, Handel, Bach, or Vivaldi plays in the background. Two arboretums feature coniferous and deciduous trees and shrubs. *Main St.,* ☎ *506/739–6335.* ☛ *Adults $4.75, senior citizens and students $4.25, children 6–12 $2.25.* ☉ *Mid-May–mid-Oct., daily 9–dusk.*

8 About 50 kilometers (30 miles) downriver, at **Grand Falls,** the Saint John throws itself over a high cliff, squeezes through a narrow rocky gorge, and emerges as a wider river. The result is a magnificent cascade, whose force has worn strange round wells in the rocky bed—some as much as 16 feet in circumference and 30 feet deep. Take the Gorge Walk from the tourist information center($2 adults, $1 children, $5 families) where you'll see the holes and the magnificent stream up close. According to Indian legend, a young maiden named Malabeam led her Iroquois captors to their deaths over the foaming cataract rather than guide them to her village. Local history is depicted at the **Grand Falls Historical Museum.** *209 Sheriff St.,* ☎ *506/473–5265.* ☛ *Free.* ☉ *July and Aug., Mon.–Sat. 9–5, Sun. 2–5; Sept.–June, by appointment.*

Although Grand Falls is largely French-speaking, English becomes more prevalent as you move down the Saint John River valley. Stop in **Florenceville** for a look at the small but reputable **Andrew and Laura McCain Gallery** (McCain St., ☎ 506/392–5249), which has launched the career of many a New Brunswick artist.

The Trans-Canada Highway is intriguingly scenic, but if you're looking for less crowded highways and typical small communities, cross the river to Route 105 at Hartland, via the **longest covered bridge** in the world—1,282 feet in length.

If you prefer, stay on the Trans-Canada Highway until you reach the quiet hamlet of **Woodstock** (population 4,911). The town was named for a novel by Sir Walter Scott, and is most lively during its Old Home Week celebrations, in July. Built in 1883, the **Old Courthouse**—once a coach stop, a social hall, a political meeting place, and the seat of justice for the area—has been carefully restored.

TIME OUT Between Woodstock and Meductic, look for good German food at **Heino's Restaurant,** in the John Gyles Motel (junction Route 2 and Trans-Canada Highway, ☎ 506/328–6622).

9 Within the **Mactaquac Provincial Park** is Mactaquac Pond, whose existence is attributed to the building of the hydroelectric dam, which has caused the upper Saint John River to flood as far up as Woodstock. The park has wheelchair-accessible campsites. The park facilities include an 18-hole golf course, two beaches with lifeguards, and two marinas, supervised craft activities, and a dining room. *Rte. 105 at Mactaquac Dam,* ☎ *506/363–3011. 300 campsites; reservations advised in high season.* ☛ *$3.50 per vehicle in summer, free off-season.* ☉ *Mid-May–Thanksgiving for overnight camping; early Sept.–mid-May for day and evening activities.*

From Fredericton to Saint John you have a choice of two routes. Route 7 cuts away from the river to run straight south for its fast 109 kilometers (68 miles). Route 102 leads along the Saint John River through engaging communities. You don't have to decide until you hit **Oromocto,** the site of the Canadian Armed Forces Base, **Camp Gagetown** (not to be confused with the pretty town of Gagetown farther down river), the largest military base in Canada. Prince Charles completed his helicopter training here. An interesting military museum within the base is open to the public. *Building A5,* ☎ *506/422–2630.* ☛ *Free.* ☉ *July* *and Aug., weekdays 9–5, weekends and holidays noon–5; Sept.–June, weekdays 8:30–noon and 1–4.*

⑩ If you opt for Route 102 you can stop in **Gagetown,** one of New Brunswick's pleasant historic communities, bustling with artisans' studios and the summer sailors who tie up at the marina. The gingerbread-trimmed **Tilley House** takes you back to Canada's beginnings. Once the home of Sir Leonard Tilley, one of the Fathers of Confederation, it is now home of the Queens County Museum. *Front St.,* ☎ *506/488–2966.* ☛ *$1 adults, 25¢ students.* ☉ *Mid-June–mid-Sept., daily 10–5.*

From Gagetown you can ferry across the river to Jemseg and continue to **Grand Lake Provincial Park** (☎ 506/385–2919), which offers freshwater swimming off the sandy beaches of Grand Lake. At Evandale (farther south) you can ferry to Belleisle Bay and the beautiful **Kingston Peninsula,** with its mossy Loyalist graveyards and pretty churches.

⑪ As you travel south past farms, churches, and homes and public buildings, you'll begin to get a feeling for how old New Brunswick really is, and nowhere more so than in **Saint John.** It was the first incorporated city in Canada and has that weather-beaten quality common to so many antique seaport communities. Although sometimes termed a blue-collar town because so many of its residents work for Irving Oil, its genteel Loyalist heritage lingers; you sense it in the grand old buildings, the ladies' teas at the old Union Club, and the beautifully restored downtown harbor district.

The city has spawned many of the province's major artists—Jack Humphrey, Millar Brittain, Fred Ross—along with such Hollywood notables as Louis B. Mayer, Donald Sutherland, and Walter Pidgeon. There's also a large Irish population that emerges in a jubilant Irish Festival every March. In July, costumed residents reenact the landing of the Loyalists during the Loyalist City Festival.

In 1604, two Frenchmen, Samuel de Champlain and Sieur de Monts, landed here on Saint John the Baptist Day to trade with the natives. Nearly two centuries later, in May of 1785, 3,000 Loyalists escaping from the Revolutionary War poured off a fleet of ships to found a city amid the rocks and forests. From those beginnings, Saint John has emerged as a thriving industrial port.

Up until the early 1980s, the buildings around Saint John's waterfront huddled together in forlorn dilapidation, their facades crumbling and blurred by a century of grime. A surge of civic pride sparked a major renovation project that reclaimed these old warehouses as part of an enchanting waterfront development.

Numbers in the margin correspond to points of interest on the Downtown Saint John and Greater Saint John maps.

⑫ You can easily explore Saint John's town center and harbor area on foot. Get your bearings on **King Street,** the town's old main street, whose sidewalks are paved with red brick and lit with old-fashioned lamps.

⑬ King Street connects **Market Slip** on the waterfront with King Square at the center of town.

★ **⑭** Market Slip, where the Loyalists landed in 1783, and the adjoining **Market Square** feature historic displays, shops, restaurants, and cafés (some with outdoor dining in summer). Though the Market Square area is not as bustling as it once was, the **New Brunswick Museum** (*see below*) is scheduled to open a major exhibition center and discovery center here in the summer of 1996; this opening should boost the area's popularity.

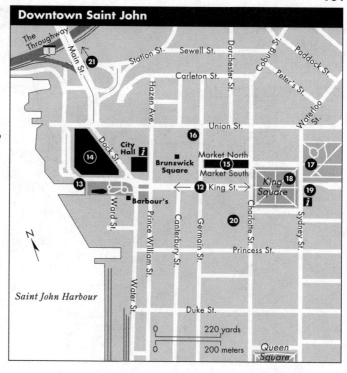

Downtown Saint John

Market Slip is the site of **Barbour's General Store** (☎ 506/658–2939), a fully stocked 19th-century shop redolent of the past. Inside, the scents of tobacco, pickles, smoked fish, and peppermint sticks mingle with the tangy, unforgettable aroma of dulse, the edible seaweed. Beside the store is a 19th-century red schoolhouse, now a tourist information center. Skywalks and underground passages lead from Market Square to City Hall, the Delta Hotel, and Brunswick Square, an adjoining shopping mall.

⑮ Stroll up King Street to Germain Street, turn left, and walk up to the block-long **Old City Market,** built in 1876, which offers a variety of temptations, including fresh-cooked lobster, great cheeses, dulse, and other inexpensive snacking along with much friendly chatter.

⑯ The imposing **Old Loyalist House,** built in 1810 by Daniel David Merritt, a wealthy Loyalist merchant, is distinguished by its authentic period furniture and eight fireplaces. *120 Union St., ☎ 506/652–3590.* ☛ *$2 adults, 25¢ children.* ⊙ *June–Sept., Mon.–Sat. 10–5, Sun. 2–5, or by appointment; Oct.–May, by appointment.*

⑰ Follow Union Street away from the harbor to Sydney Street and turn
⑱ right to visit the **Old Loyalist Burial Grounds.** At one corner, in adjacent **King Square,** you'll find a strange mass of metal on the ground. It is actually a great lump of melted stock from a neighboring hardware store that was demolished in Saint John's Great Fire of 1877, in which hundreds of buildings were destroyed.

⑲ At the corner of King and Sydney streets is the **Old Courthouse.** Its spiral staircase, built of tons of unsupported stone, ascends seemingly by miracle for three stories.

102

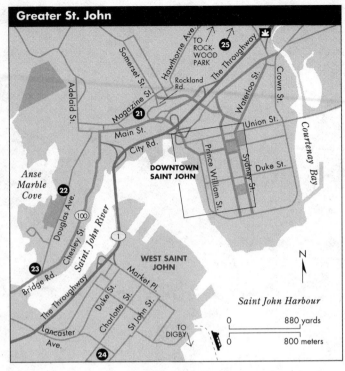

Greater St. John

Walk around the south side of King Square to visit **Trinity Church** (115 Charlotte St., ☎ 506/693–8558), which dates from 1877, when it was rebuilt after the Great Fire. Inside, over the west door, note the coat of arms—a symbol of the monarchy—rescued from the council chamber of the colony at Massachusetts Bay. The coat of arms was deemed a worthy refugee and given a place of honor in the church.

If you have a car, drive north from downtown on Prince William Street to Main Street; in a park on your right you'll find **Fort Howe** (Rockland Road and Magazine Street). The reconstructed fortress sits atop a cliff overlooking the harbor and affords fine views from its walls. It is near the site of Fort LaTour, a French stronghold resolutely defended by Madame LaTour from her absent husband's fur-trading rival. Finally surrendering on the condition that the lives of her men would be spared, the unfortunate woman was betrayed and forced to watch them all put to death. She died shortly after, of a broken heart it is said—a romantic fate befitting her former profession as star of the Paris stage.

Main Street soon crosses Douglas Avenue; turn left to reach two of the city's most notable attractions. First is the **New Brunswick Museum,** Canada's oldest continuing museum, with a hands-on family Discovery Centre, a library and archives, three floors of galleries, and a gift shop. Ongoing exhibits of fine and decorative arts, marine history, and natural sciences bring the province's history to life. There are also exhibits of exotic artifacts and specimens collected around the world since the early 1800s. A major expansion of exhibition and public facilities is scheduled to open in Market Square (*see above*) in 1996 ; a museum gift shop is already there. *277 Douglas Ave., ☎ 506/643–2300. ☛ $3.25 adults and senior citizens, $1.25 students and children over 4, $8 families. Group rates and tours can be arranged. ☉ Mid-May–Labor Day,* *daily 10–5; Sept.–May, Mon.–Thursday 10–5, Fri. 10 AM–9 PM, weekends noon–5.*

㉓ Continue on Douglas Avenue to reach the **Reversing Falls Rapids,** touted by tourist brochures as a sight no one should miss. Actually, you *should* see it, though less for its beauty than its interest: Twice daily, the strong Fundy Tides rise faster than the river can empty, and the tide water attempts to push the river water back upstream. When the tide ebbs, the river once again pours over the rock ledges and the rapids appear to reverse themselves. To learn more about the phenomenon, continue down Douglas Avenue and cross the river to the Reversing Falls Tourist Bureau and see their excellent free film. A pulp mill on the bank is less scenic, and the stench it occasionally sends out is one of the less-than-charming parts of a visit.

㉔ Cross the river on Bridge Road to **West Saint John.** Make a left on Lancaster Avenue at Simms Corner and proceed to Charlotte Street, where you can't miss the **Carleton Martello Tower.** Like Fort Howe, this is a great place to survey the harbor. The tower was built during the war of 1812 as a precaution against American attack. The guides will tell you about the spartan life of a soldier living in the stone fort and an audio-visual presentation outlines its role in the defense of Saint John during World War II. *Charlotte Extension W,* ☏ *506/636–4011.* ☛ *Free.* ☉ *June–mid-Oct., daily 9–5.*

㉕ **Cherry Brook Zoo** houses Siberian tigers, wildebeests, and other exotic species. *RR1 Sandy Point Rd.,* ☏ *506/634–1440.* ☛ *$4 adults, $3.40 senior citizens, $3 children ages 6–18, $2 children ages 3–5.* ☉ *Daily 10–dusk. Tour rates available.*

Tour 3: The Fundy Coast

Numbers in the margin correspond to points of interest on the New Brunswick map.

Bordering the chilly and powerful tidal Bay of Fundy is some of New Brunswick's loveliest coastline. A tour of the region will take you from the border town of St. Stephen, through tiny fishing villages and past rocky coves, to Fundy National Park, where the world's most extreme tides rise and fall twice daily.

㉖ **St. Stephen,** on the Maine border, is a mecca for chocoholics, who converge on the small town during the Chocolate Festival held the first week in August. "Choctails," chocolate puddings and cakes, and even complete chocolate meals should come as no surprise when you realize that it was here that the chocolate bar was invented. Sample Ganong's famed, hand-dipped chocolates at the factory store, the **Ganong Chocolatier.** *73 Milltown Blvd.,* ☏ *506/465–5611.* ☉ *July and Aug., weekdays 9–8, Sat. 9–5, Sun. noon–5; Sept.–Dec., daily 9–5; Jan.–mid-May, Mon.–Sat. 9–5.*

A small side trip along Ledge Road will take you to **Crocker Hill Studios,** on the banks of the St. Croix River. Walk down the garden path to the artists' studio with its paintings and carved decoys. It is surrounded by a fragrant, tranquil herb garden. Relax in one of the comfortable garden benches and watch the osprey and eagles soar over the river, and seals make their way upstream on the incoming tide. ☏ *506/466–4251.* ☛ *$3 adults, $2 children under 16.* ☉ *June–Sept., daily 10–5; Oct.–June by appointment.*

㉗ Take Route 127 off Route 1 to **St. Andrews-by-the-Sea,** one of North America's prettiest and least-spoiled resort towns. Long the summer place of the affluent (mansions ring the town), St. Andrews retains its year-round population of fishermen, and little has changed in the past two centuries. Of the town's 550 buildings, 280 were erected before 1880; 14 have survived from the 1700s. Some Loyalists brought their homes with them piece by piece from Castine, Maine, across the bay, when the war didn't go their way.

Pick up a walking-tour map at the tourist information center on Water Street and follow it through the pleasant streets. Particular gems are the **Court House** and **Greenock Church.** The church owes its existence to a remark someone made at an 1822 dinner party about the "poor" Presbyterians not having a church of their own. Captain Christopher Scott, who took exception to the slur, spared no expense on the building, which is decorated with a carving of a green oak tree in honor of Scott's birthplace, Greenock, Scotland. Also along Water Street are numerous antiques shops and artists' studios. The porch of the **Shiretown Inn** (218 Water St., ☎ 506/529–8877) is a perfect place to relax with a snack.

The **Ross Memorial Museum** has a fine antiques collection. *188 Montague St., ☎ 506/529–1824. ☛ Free. ☺ Late May–June and early October, Mon.–Sat. 10–4:30; July–Sept., Mon.–Sat. 10–4:30, Sun. 1:30–4:30; shoulder seasons, Tues.–Sat. 10–4:30.*

A drive up Joe's Point Road takes you to the **Huntsman Aquarium and Museum,** which houses marine life and displays. *Brandy Cove Rd., ☎ 506/529–1202. ☛ $4 adults, $3.50 senior citizens, $2.75 children 4– 17, $10.70 families. ☺ Late May–mid-Oct., Tues.–Sat. 10–4:30; July and Aug., Tues.–Sat. 10–4:30, Sun. 1:30–4:30.*

Back on Route 1 is **St. George,** a pretty town with some excellent bed-and-breakfasts, one of the oldest Protestant graveyards in Canada, and a fish ladder running up the side of a dam.

The Fundy Isles—Grand Manan Island, Deer Island, and Campobello— are havens of peace that have lured harried mainlanders for generations. ㉘ **Grand Manan Island,** largest of the three, is also farthest away (about two hours by car-ferry from Black's Harbour); you might see spouting whales, sunning seals, or a rare puffin on the way. Circular herring weirs dot the coastal waters, and fish sheds and smokehouses lie beside long wharfs that reach out to bobbing fishing boats. Place names are romantic—Swallowtail, Southern Head, Seven Days Work, and Dark Harbour. It's easy to get around—only about 32 kilometers (20 miles) of road lead from the lighthouse at Southern Head to the one at Northern Head. Grand Manan attracted John James Audubon, that living encyclopedia of birds, in 1831. The puffin is the island's symbol. Whale-watching expeditions can be booked at the Marathon Hotel and the Compass Rose, and scuba diving to old wrecks is popular.

★ ㉙ Connected to Lubec, Maine, by an international bridge, **Campobello Island** may be approached from the other side by toll ferry from Deer Island. Neatly manicured, preening itself in the bay, Campobello Island has always had a special appeal to the wealthy and the famous. It was here that the Roosevelt family spent their summers. The **home of Franklin Delano Roosevelt,** former president of the United States, is now maintained as a lovely museum in his honor. Located in the center of Roosevelt International Park, a joint project of the Canadian and American governments, President Roosevelt's home was also the setting for the movie *Sunrise at Campobello. Roosevelt Park Rd., ☎ 506/ 752–2922. ☛ Free. ☺ House: late May–mid-Oct., daily 10–6; grounds: year-round.*

The island's **Herring Cove Provincial Park** has camping facilities and a nine-hole golf course. *Welshpool,* ☎ *506/752-7010, .*

30 An easy, 20-minute, free ferry ride from Letete near St. George brings you to the relaxing **Deer Island.** You'll enjoy exploring the fishing wharves, such as those at **Chocolate Cove.** You can walk through a small nature park at **Deer Point** while waiting for the toll ferry to nearby Campobello Island. If you listen carefully, you may be able to hear the sighing and snorting of "the Old Sow," the second largest whirlpool in the world. If you can't hear it, you'll be able to see it, just a few feet offshore. Exploring the island takes only a few hours; it's 12 kilometers (7½ miles) long, varying in width from almost 5 kilometers (3 miles) to a few hundred feet at some points.

After returning from the Fundy Isles to the mainland, proceed east along coastal Route 1. If you have the time, dip down to the peaceful, hidden fishing villages of **Maces Bay, Dipper Harbour,** and **Chance Harbour,** all much the same as they have been for centuries. At Dipper Harbour, you can rent sea kayaks and canoes, arrange for whale-watching and deep-sea fishing (Eastern Outdoors Marine, ☎ 506/634–1530 or 800/56–KAYAK), or buy a lobster roll to munch on while strolling the long sun-warmed wharf. Farther up the coast is **St. Martins,** with a rich shipbuilding heritage, whispering caves, miles of beaches, spectacular tides, and a cluster of covered bridges.

★ **31** Drive east through Saint John along a scenic stretch of Route 1 to Route 114, which angles south to the 206-square-kilometer (80-square-mile) **Fundy National Park.** Stand on a sandstone ledge above a dark-sand beach and watch the bay's phenomenal tide rise or fall. *Box 40, Alma, E0A 1B0,* ☎ *506/887–6000.* ☛ *$6 per car in summer; free rest of the year.*

Alma is the small seaside town that services the national park. Here you'll find great lobster and the local specialty, sticky buns. Past Alma, the coast road (Route 114) to Moncton winds by covered bridges and along rocky coasts, past such photogenic spots as the wild driftwood-cluttered beach at **Cape Enragé** and **Hopewell Cape,** home of the famous Giant Flowerpots—rock formations carved by the Fundy Tides.

Tour 4: Moncton and the Acadian Peninsula

32 A friendly town, often called the Gateway to Acadia because of its mix of English and French and its proximity to the Acadian shore, **Moncton** has a pretty downtown where wisely placed malls do a booming business.

This city has long touted two natural attractions, the Tidal Bore and the Magnetic Hill. You may be disappointed if you've read too much tourist hype. In days gone by, before the harbor mouth filled with silt, the **Tidal Bore** was indeed an incredible sight, a high wall of water that surged in through the narrow opening of the river to fill red mud banks to the brim. It still moves up the river, and the moving wave is worth waiting for, but it's nowhere near as lofty as it used to be, except sometimes in the spring when the tides are very high. Bore Park on Main Street is the best vantage point; viewing times are posted there.

★ **33** **Magnetic Hill,** north of town just off the Trans-Canada Highway, creates a bizarre optical illusion. If you park your car in neutral at the designated spot, you'll seem to be coasting up hill without power. An excellent family water-theme park, **Magic Mountain,** is adjacent to the hill. *Magnetic Hill,* ☎ *506/857–9283.* ☛ *$17.25 adults, $10.50 afternoon; $11.75 senior citizens and children under 12, $9.50 afternoon;*

$53.25 for a family of 4 for a full day. ☉ *Mid-June–July and mid-Aug.–Labor Day, daily 10–6; July–mid-Aug., daily 10–8.*

Among Moncton's notable man-made attractions is the **Acadian Museum,** at the University of Moncton, whose remarkable collection of artifacts reflects 300 years of Acadian life in New Brunswick. *Clement Cormier Bldg., Univ. of Moncton,* ☎ *506/858–4088.* ☛ *Free.* ☉ *June–Sept., weekdays 10–5, weekends 1–5; Oct.–May, Tues.–Fri. 1–4:30, weekends 1–4.*

Turn northeast along the coast from Moncton on Route 11 to the salty shores of such unique Acadian communities as **Shediac, Cocagne, Buctouche,** and **Rexton,** where you'll find warm sand dunes, lobster feeds, lighthouses, weathered wharves, and sea-stained churches. The friendliness of the Acadians makes this trip a joy, and the white, dune-edged beaches of **Kouchibouguac National Park** are among the finest on the continent. *Off Rte. 11, Kent County,* ☎ *506/876–2443. 249 campsites; reservations not accepted.* ☛ *$6 per vehicle, $4.50 senior citizens. 1-day, 4-day, and season passes available.*

★ ㉞

Route 11 continues north to the Miramichi River and the fabled **Miramichi region** of lumberjacks, fishermen, and "come all ye's." Celebrated for its salmon rivers and the ebullient nature of its residents (Scottish, English, Irish, and a smattering of French and Indian), this is a land of stories, folklore, and lumber kings. Sturdy wood homes dot the banks of Miramichi Bay at **Miramichi City** (where the politician and British media mogul Lord Beaverbrook grew up and is buried). At **Doaktown** (south of Miramichi City on Route 8), the **Miramichi Salmon Museum** (☎ 506/365–7787) provides a look at the endangered Atlantic salmon and at life in noted fishing camps along the rivers.

㉟

The **Woodmen's Museum** of Boiestown (in the exact center of the province), with artifacts that date from the 1700s to the present, is housed in what looks like two giant logs set on more than 60 acres of land. The museum portrays a lumberman's life through its displays, but its tranquil grounds are excuse enough to visit. Picnic facilities and camping sites are available. *Rte. 8, Boiestown,* ☎ *506/369–7214.* ☛ *$5 adults, $4 senior citizens, $2 children, $12 families.* ☉ *May–Sept., daily 9–5.*

㊱

Return to Miramichi City and swing north and east on Route 11 to **Caraquet,** on the Acadian Peninsula. The town is perched along the Baie des Chaleurs, with Québec's Gaspé Peninsula beckoning across the inlet.

★ ㊲

The pièce de résistance of the Acadian Peninsula is, without doubt, the **Acadian Historical Village,** 10 kilometers (6 miles) west of Caraquet on Route 11, near Grand Anse. As Kings Landing (near Fredericton) depicts the early English settlement, this village re-creates an early Acadian community between 1780 and 1890. Summer days are wonderfully peaceful: the chapel bell tolls, ducks waddle and quack under a footbridge, wagons creak, and the smell of hearty cooking wafts from cottage doors. Costumed staff act as guides, and a restaurant serves old-Acadian dishes. ☎ *506/727–3467.* ☛ *$8 adults, $4.50 children under 18, $6 students over 18, $6.50 senior citizens, $20 families (2 adults and 3 children).* ☉ *June–Labor Day, daily 10–6; Sept., daily 10–5.*

SHOPPING

New Brunswick is famous for its crafts, and the province's directory of craftspeople and crafts shops provides comprehensive listings of potters, weavers, glassblowers, jewelers, and carvers throughout the province. Get a copy from **Tourism New Brunswick** (Box 12345, Fredericton, E3B 5C3, ☎ 800/561–0123).

Fredericton

Mammoth crafts markets are held occasionally in town and every Labor Day weekend in Mactaquac Park. The **New Brunswick Craft Centre** (103 Church Street., ☎ 506/450–8393) offers crafts (pottery, blown glass, pressed flowers, metal flowers, turned wood, leather, and quilts) made by members of the New Brunswick Craft Council. **Aitkens Pewter** (81 Regent St., ☎ 506/453–9474) offers beautiful pewter goblets, belt buckles, and jewelry. **Mulhouse Country Classics,** (across the Princess Margaret Bridge, on the Trans-Canada Highway (Route 2), ☎ 506/459–8859) is a gem for crafts, Tilley Endurable clothing, and handmade furniture.

Excellent men's shoes can be bought at **Hartt's Shoe Factory** (401 York St., ☎ 506/458–8358). **The Linen Closet** (397 King St., ☎ 506/450–8393) sells lace, exquisite bedding, and Victorian nightgowns.

Gagetown

Flo Grieg's (Front St., ☎ 506/488–2074) carries superior pottery. **Claremont House B&B** (Tilley Rd., ☎ 506/488–2825) displays unusual batik items and copper engravings. **Loomcrofters** (Loomcroft Ln., off Main St., ☎ 506/488–2400) is a good choice for handwoven items.

Moncton

Five spacious malls and numerous pockets of shops in downtown Moncton make it one of the best places to shop in New Brunswick. Among the crafts to look for are the yarn portraits of La Sagouine, "the old sage" of Buctouche. The sayings of the old Acadian woman as she does her daily chores were made famous in Antonine Maillet's novel *La Sagouine.*

Saint-Andrews-by-the-Sea

This "veddy British" town has many places to buy English and New Brunswick woolens, English bone china, and marvelous wool yarn. **The Sea Captain's Loft** (Water St., ☎ 506/529–3190) specializes in these fine gifts. **Cottage Craft** (Town Sq., ☎ 506/529–3190) employs knitters year-round to make mittens and sweaters from their specially dyed wool. **Tom Smith's Studio** (Water St., ☎ 506/529–4234) is highly regarded for oriental Raku pottery.

Saint John

The little antiques stores and crafts shops sprinkled around the downtown area provide the best shopping in Saint John. **Prince William Street** provides interesting browsing in antiques shops and crafts boutiques. **House of Tara** (72 Prince William St., ☎ 506/634–8272) is wonderful for fine Irish linens and woolens. **Brunswick Square** (King and Germain Sts., ☎ 506/658–1000) has many top-quality boutiques. **Old City Market,** between Charlotte and Germain streets, bustles Monday–Saturday and always stocks delicious local specialties, such as maple syrup and lobster.

Saint-Léonard

The studio and store of the **Madawaska Weavers** (Main St., ☎ 506/423–6341) has handwoven items known the world over. Handsome skirts, stoles, and ties are some of the items for sale.

SPORTS AND THE OUTDOORS

Bicycling

Byroads, lanes, and rolling secondary highways run through small towns, along the ocean, and into the forest. Set out on your own, or try a guided adventure with a specialist tour operator, such as **Covered Bridge Bicycle Tours** (Dept. F, Box 693, Main Post Office, Saint John, E2L 4B3, ☎ 506/849–9028). B&Bs frequently have bicycles for hire and Tourism New Brunswick has listings and free cycling maps (*See* Important Addresses and Numbers *in* New Brunswick Essentials, *below*). Information on competitive cycling and races is available from **Velo New Brunswick** (457 Chartersville Rd., Dieppe, E1A 5H1).

Dogsledding

Miramichi Four Seasons Outfitters (*see below*) offers custom packages for all levels.

Fishing

Dotted with freshwater lakes, crisscrossed with fish-laden rivers, and bordered by 1,129 kilometers (700 miles) of seacoast, this province is one of Canada's natural treasures. Sports people are drawn by the excellent bass fishing and such world-famous salmon rivers as the Miramichi, the Restigouche, and the Nashwaak. Commercial fishermen often take visitors line fishing for groundfish. A freshwater fishing license for out-of-province visitors costs $30 for the season, $20 for 7 days, or $15 for 3 days and allows you to fish without a guide and for everything but salmon. For more information, call **New Brunswick Fish and Wildlife** (☎ 506/453–2440).

Golf

There are 36 excellent golf courses in New Brunswick. Many, such as the **Algonquin Golf Club** (☎ 506/529–3062) in St. Andrews-By-the-Sea and the **Gowan Brae Golf and Country Club** (☎ 506/546–2707) in Bathurst, provide sparkling views of the sea. The **Fundy National Park Golf Club** (☎ 506/887–2970) at Alma is nestled near cliffs overlooking the restless Bay of Fundy; deer grazing on the course are one of its hazards. Greens fees run about $20–$25, $15 for some nine-hole courses; visitors are generally welcome. For a list of golf courses, contact Tourism New Brunswick (*See* Important Addresses and Numbers *in* New Brunswick Essentials, *below*).

Hiking

Rocky coastline and inland highland trails offer hiking opportunities for both experienced and casual trekkers. **Miramichi Four Seasons Outfitters** (Box 705, R.R. 2, Miramichi, E1V 3L9, ☎ 506/622–0089) offers guided hiking tours. For general trail information, contact Eric Hadley at the **New Brunswick Trails Council** (c/o Department of Natural Resources and Energy, Box 6000, Fredericton, E3B 5H1, ☎ 506/453–2383).

Skiing

CROSS-COUNTRY

A perfect province for cross-country skiing, New Brunswick offers groomed trails at such provincial and national parks as Mactaquac Provincial Park near Fredericton, Fundy National Park in Alma, and Kouchibouguac National Park between Moncton and Bathurst. Many communities and small hotels offer groomed trails, but it's also possible to set off on your own in almost every section of the province.

DOWNHILL

New Brunswick downhill ski areas usually operate from mid-December through April. They include **Crabbe Mountain Winter Park** (☎ 506/463–8311) in Lower Hainesville (near Fredericton); **Sugarloaf Provincial Park** (☎ 506/789–2366) in Campbellton, northern New Brunswick; **Mont Farlagne** (☎ 506/735–8401) in Saint-Jacques, near Edmundston; **Poley Mountain Ski Area** (☎ 506/433–3230) in Sussex, north of Saint John; and **Silverwood Winter Park** (☎ 506/450–3380) in Fredericton.

Tennis

Courts are available in most city and town parks. Most are free. Many resorts and hotels have courts, as well.

Water Sports

CANOEING AND KAYAKING

Kayaking along the coasts of Fundy and Chaleur has become very popular. A list of canoe and kayak liveries is available from Tourism New Brunswick (*See* Important Addresses and Numbers *in* New Brunswick Essentials, *below*). **Eastern Outdoors** (Brunswick Sq., Saint John, ☎ 506/634–1530 or 800/56–KAYAK) offers single and double kayaks, lessons, tours, and white-water rafting on the world-famous Reversing Falls Rapids.

ROWING

Shells can be rented at the **Aquatic Center** (☎ 506/458–5513) in Fredericton.

SAILING

Sailboats can be chartered from many companies, including **Fundy Yacht Sales and Charter** (Rte. 2, Dipper Harbour, Lepreau, E0G 2H0, ☎ 506/634–1530 or 800/56–KAYAK).

Whale-Watching

One New Brunswick experience that is difficult to forget is the sighting of a huge humpback, right whale, finback, or minke. Whale-watching tours are available from **Ocean Search** (Marathon Inn, North Head, Grand Manan Island, ☎ 506/662–8488). **Cline Marine Tours** (☎ 506/529–2287) in St. Andrews-By-the-Sea and on Deer Island offers scenic and whale-watching tours. **Chaleur Phantom** (☎ 506/684–4722) in Dalhousie combines scenic tours, focusing on marine life in the calmer waters around the islands, with deep-sea fishing excursions.

DINING AND LODGING

Dining

Although there are not a lot of choices for fine dining in New Brunswick, a few good restaurants exist, and families will find plenty of quality food in many outlets. A number of gourmet restaurants have popped up in Saint John in recent years—so there is hope that dining throughout the province will follow suit.

In the spring, once the ice has left streams and rivers, a provincial delicacy—the fiddlehead fern—is picked from the shores. Eaten as a vegetable (boiled, drenched with lemon, butter, salt, and pepper), fiddleheads have something of an artichoke taste and go well with spring's bony fish, shad, and gaspereaux. Silver salmon, once a spring staple when set nets were allowed, is still available but quite costly. Most salmon served in restaurants is farm-reared. Lobster, a favorite maritime dish, is available in most restaurants, but is not always cheap. The custom of the residents is to buy it fresh from the fishermen or shore outlets and devour it in huge quantities. Because of the cool waters, shellfish is especially tasty. Look for oysters, scallops, clams, crab, and mussels. And be sure to try the purple seaweed called dulse, which the natives eat like potato chips. To be truly authentic, accompany any New Brunswick–style feast with hearty Moosehead beer, brewed in Saint John and one of the province's well-known exports.

Jeans and shorts are acceptable everywhere except at the expensive and very expensive listings, where jackets and ties are occasionally required. Unless noted, no reservations are needed.

CATEGORY	COST*
$$$	$20–$40
$$	$10–$20
$	under $10

per person, excluding drinks, service, and 11% sales tax

Lodging

New Brunswick has a number of officially designated Heritage Inns— historically significant establishments built in the last century. Their accommodations run the gamut from elegant to homey; many have antique china and furnishings or other charming touches.

Hotels and motels in and around Saint John and Fredericton are adequate and friendly. Accommodations in Saint John are at a premium in summer, so reserve ahead to ensure a place to stay.

CATEGORY	COST*
$$$	over $60
$$	$45–$60
$	under $45

All prices are for a standard double room, excluding 10% service charge.

Campbellton

DINING AND LODGING

$$$ **Aylesford Inn.** Truly a find, this friendly inn housed in a Victorian man-
★ sion near the Québec border and Sugarloaf Provincial Park has guest rooms handsomely furnished with Eastlake and Canadian-pine antiques. Large gardens and verandas offer views of the Restigouche River. Excellent dinners are served to guests (quail and frogs' legs are featured entrées), and full breakfasts are included in the room rate. Nonguests are welcome for afternoon tea. ⊞ *8 MacMillan Ave., E3N 1E9, ☎ 506/ 759–7672. 6 rooms. Dining room, croquet. AE, MC, V.*

Campobello Island

LODGING

$$ **Lupine Lodge.** Originally a vacation home built by the Adams family (friends of the Roosevelts) around the turn of the century, these three attractive log buildings set on a bluff overlooking the Bay of Fundy have been converted into a modern guest lodge. Nature trails connect it to Herring Cove Provincial Park. Two of the cabins comprise the guest rooms; the third houses the dining room, which specializes in simple but well-prepared local seafood. ⊞ *Box 2, Welshpool, E0G 3H0, ☎ 506/752–2255. 10 rooms, 1 suite. Restaurant, lounge. MC, V.*

$$ **Owen House.** Mellow with history, this 200-year-old home was built
★ by Admiral Owen, who fancied himself ruler of the island. Its gracious old rooms have hosted such luminaries as actress Greer Garson, who stayed here (in a room with a fireplace in the bathroom) when filming *Sunrise at Campobello*. Breakfasts are wonderful—pancakes come topped with local berries. ⊞ *Welshpool, E0G 3H0, ☎ 506/752– 2555. 9 rooms. V.*

Caraquet

DINING AND LODGING

$–$$ **Hotel Paulin.** The word *quaint* really fits this property. The pretty rooms were redecorated in 1993. Each has its own unique look, with old pine dressers and brass beds, and the colors are as bright and cheerful as the seaside town. About half the rooms have private baths—the remainder share. An excellent small dining room specializes in fresh fish cooked to perfection. ⊡ *143 blvd. St.-Pierre W, E1W 1B6* ☎ *506/727–9981. 9 rooms, 1 suite. Dining room. MC, V.*

Deer Island

DINING AND LODGING

$$ **45th Parallel Motel and Restaurant.** Deer Island has only one motel—fortunately, it's clean and comfortable. A full breakfast is complimentary, and everything from lobster to pizza is available at the informal restaurant. Three of the rooms have kitchenettes. Pets are welcome. ⊡ *Fairhaven, E0G 1R0,* ☎ *506/747–2231. 10 rooms. Restaurant. AE, MC, V.*

LODGING

$$ **West Isles World B&B.** This white frame house overlooks the cove and offers three snug rooms with an informal country feel; the big upstairs bedroom has a water view. A full breakfast is included in the room rate. One room has a private bath, the other two share. The owners will arrange whale-watching cruises for you. ⊡ *Lord's Cove, E0G 2J0,* ☎ *506/747–2946. 3 rooms. No credit cards.*

Fredericton

DINING

$$ **Luna Steakhouse.** Specialties include huge Caesar salads, garlic bread, escargots, brochettes, and Italian food. In fine weather you can dine on an outdoor terrace. Inside, the stucco walls and dark arches make a cozy environment. ✕ *168 Dundonald St.,* ☎ *506/455–4020. AE, DC, MC, V.*

$–$$ **Bar B Q Barn.** Special children's menus and barbecued ribs and chicken are the standards; the blackboard lists plenty of other daily dinner specials, such as salmon, scallops, and chili. This popular spot has a convenient downtown location, and is great for winding down; the bar serves fine martinis. ✕ *540 Queen St.,* ☎ *506/455–2742. AE, DC, MC, V.*

$ **Pink Pearl.** This restaurant features tasty Cantonese food, with exceptional wontons and weekend buffets. There's nothing fancy here, but you can count on good food and good value. ✕ *343 Queen St.,* ☎ *506/450–8997. MC, V.*

LODGING

$$$ **Auberge Wandlyn Inn.** Just off the Trans-Canada Highway, this hotel is away from the downtown area but close to three shopping malls, many restaurants, and theaters. The guest rooms are no-frills motelese, but the family-oriented dining room (children are welcomed) was completely redecorated in 1993 so it's bright and cheerful. There's a cozy bar. ⊡ *58 Prospect St. W, Box 214, E3B 4Y9,* ☎ *506/452–8937 or 800/561–0000 (eastern Canada), 800/561–0006 (U.S.),* ℻ *506/452–7658. 101 rooms. Restaurant, bar, indoor and outdoor pools, hot tub, sauna. AE, DC, MC, V.*

$$$ **Howard Johnson Motor Lodge.** This HoJo's is on the north side of the river and at the north end of the Princess Margaret Bridge. It has a terrace bar in a pleasant interior courtyard overlooked by the balconies of many of the rooms. Guest-room decor is standard for the chain. ⊡ *Trans-Canada Hwy., Box 1414, E3B 5E3,* ☎ *506/472–0480 or 800/596–4656,* ℻ *506/472–0170. 116 rooms. Restaurant, bar, indoor pool, tennis courts, exercise room. AE, DC, MC, V.*

$$$ **Lord Beaverbrook Hotel.** A central location is this modern, seven-story hotel's main attraction. Some rooms have Jacuzzis or minibars. The food in the main dining room is forgettable, but there is a lively bar. ⌨ *659 Queen St., E3B 5A6,* ☎ *506/455–3371 or 800/561–7666,* FAX *506/455–1441. 163 rooms. 2 restaurants, bar, no-smoking rooms, indoor pool. AE, DC, MC, V.*

$$$ Sheraton Inn Fredericton. Within walking distance of downtown, this big, fairly new hotel with elegant country decor offers sunset views over the river from the restaurant and many of the modern rooms. The restaurant has a pleasant outdoor terrace. The gift shop carries top-notch crafts. ⌨ *225 Woodstock Rd., E3B 2H8,* ☎ *506/457–7000 or 800/325–3535,* FAX *506/457–4000. 223 rooms. Restaurant, bar, minibars, indoor and outdoor pools, sauna, hot tub, exercise room. AE, DC, MC, V.*

$$–$$$ Carriage House Inn. This Heritage mansion has lovely bedrooms furnished with Victorian antiques. Homemade breakfast, complete with homemade maple syrup for the fluffy pancakes, is served in the solarium. Half of the rooms have private baths. ⌨ *230 University Ave., E3B 4H7,* ☎ *506/452–9924 or 800/267–6068,* FAX *506/458–0799. 10 rooms. MC, V.*

Grand Manan Island
LODGING

$$–$$$ Marathon Inn. Perched on a hill overlooking the harbor, this gracious mansion built by a sea captain offers guest rooms furnished with antiques. About half the rooms have private baths, the others share. Whale- and bird-watching cruises can be arranged for those wishing to explore. The restaurant specializes in seafood. ⌨ *Box 129, North Head, E0G 2M0,* ☎ *506/662–8488. 28 rooms. Restaurant, 2 lounges, pool, 2 tennis courts. MC, V.*

$$ Compass Rose. Lovely guest rooms, with comfortable turn-of-the-century furnishings, are available in the two old houses that have been combined into this small, English-style country inn. All the rooms share baths. It is conveniently near the ferry landing, and whale-watching tours can be arranged. A full English breakfast is included in the room rate. Morning and afternoon teas, lunch, and dinner are also served. ⌨ *North Head, E0G 2M0,* ☎ *506/662–8570. 8 rooms. Dining room. MC, V.*

Ludlow
LODGING

$$$ Pond's Chalet Resort. You'll get a traditional fishing-camp experience here, in a lodge and chalets set among trees overlooking a salmon river. The accommodations are comfortable but not luxurious. The dining room in the lodge turns out reliable but undistinguished food. ⌨ *Ludlow (near Boiestown), E0C 1N0,* ☎ *506/369–2612,* FAX *506/369–2293. 10 rooms in lodge, 14 cabins. Bar, dining room. AE, DC, MC, V.*

Miramichi Country
DINING AND LODGING

$$–$$$ Wharf Inn. Here in Miramichi country, the staff is friendly and the restaurant serves excellent salmon dinners. This low-rise modern building has two wings; guest rooms in the executive wing have extra amenities. ⌨ *Jane St.,* ☎ *506/622–0302,* FAX *506/622–0354. 70 rooms. Restaurant, bar, patio lounge, no-smoking rooms, indoor pool. AE, DC, MC, V.*

Moncton
DINING

$$ Cy's Seafood Restaurant. This favorite for seafood, decorated in dark
★   wood and brass, has been serving generous portions for decades. Though renowned for its seafood casserole, the restaurant also offers reliable

scallop, shrimp, and lobster dishes. You can see the Tidal Bore from the windows. ✗ *170 Main St.,* ☎ *506/857–0032. AE, DC, MC, V.*

$$ Fisherman's Paradise. In spite of the enormous dining area, which seats more than 350 people, this restaurant serves memorable à la carte seafood dishes in an atmosphere of candlelight and wood furnishings. The children's menu and such down-home specials as lobster-bake make this a good spot for families. ✗ *375 Dieppe Blvd.,* ☎ *506/859–4388. AE, DC, MC, V.*

LODGING

$$$ Best Western Crystal Palace. Moncton's newest hotel has theme rooms (want to be Ali Baba or Elvis for a night?) and, for families, an indoor pool and a miniature wonderland of rides, midway stalls, and coin games. Champlain Mall is just across the parking lot. ☎ *499 Paul St.,* ☎ *506/858–8584 or 800/528–1234,* FAX *506/858–5486. 115 rooms. Restaurant, indoor pool. AE, D, DC, MC, V.*

$$$ Hotel Beausejour. Moncton's finest hotel is conveniently located down-
★ town. The friendly greeting in the elegant lobby is matched by the friendly service. The decor of the guest rooms and executive suites echoes the city's Loyalist and Acadian roots. L'Auberge, the main hotel restaurant, has a distinct Acadian flavor. The Windjammer dining room is more formal, modeled after the opulent luxury liners of the turn of the century, and reservations are required. ☎ *750 Main St.,* ☎ *506/854–4344 or 800/441–1414 (Canada or U.S.), 800/561–2328 (Maritimes and Québec);* FAX *506/858–0957. 314 rooms. 2 restaurants, bar, café, pool. AE, DC, MC, V.*

Sackville
LODGING

$$–$$$ Marshlands Inn. In this white clapboard inn, a welcoming double liv-
★ ing room with fireplace sets the informal, country atmosphere. Bed-rooms are furnished with sleigh beds or four-posters, but some also have such modern touches as air-conditioning and in-room telephones. Most rooms also have private baths, four share. ☎ *Box 1440, E0A 3C0,* ☎ *506/536–0170,* FAX *506/536–0721. 21 rooms. Restaurant. AE, DC, MC, V.*

St. Andrews-by-the-Sea
DINING

$$–$$$ L'Europe. You may be amused by the cheerful decor in this intimate restaurant, in particular the whimsical objets d'art reflecting the tastes of the German owners. The food is European—some French, Swiss, German dishes, and so on, with particular attention given to seafood. All meals are served with delicious homemade Black Forest bread and pâté. ✗ *48 King St.,* ☎ *506/529–3818. Reservations advised. V. Closed Mon. and Oct.–early May. No lunch.*

LODGING

$$$ The Algonquin Resort. The wraparound veranda of this grand old hotel overlooks wide lawns and the bellmen wear kilts, setting a mood of relaxed elegance. A recent expansion added 50 rooms and three suites to the property; the rooms in the newer addition are larger than those in the original hotel, and have air-conditioning, two queen-size beds, and kitchenettes with microwave, refrigerator, coffeemaker, and toaster. The suites have huge fireplaces. Rooms in the original hotel were renovated, and all now have TVs. The dining room is noted for its buffets. In good weather, meals are served on the veranda. ☎ *Rte. 127, E0G 2X0,* ☎ *506/529–8823 or 800/563–4299,* FAX *506/529–4194. 250 rooms. 2 restaurants, 2 bars, pool, 2 golf courses, tennis. AE, DC, MC, V. Closed winter.*

St. George

LODGING

$$–$$$ **Granite Town Hotel.** Although this hotel was built in 1991, it has an old-country-inn feeling to it. The decor is subtle, with pine and washed-birch woodwork prominent. Light blues and pinks dominate in the rooms. The scenery is pleasant: one side of the building overlooks an apple orchard, the other sits just atop the bank of the Maguadavic River. A Continental breakfast is available but is not included in the room rate; there is a barbecue available for summertime use. Two of the rooms have Jacuzzis. ☎ *15 Main St., E0G 2Y0,* ☎ *506/755–6415,* FAX *506/755–6009. 32 rooms. Restaurant, bar, boating, bicycles, laundry. AE, D, DC, MC, V.*

Saint John

DINING

$$$ **Top of the Town.** With a spectacular view of the harbor and city, this dining room at Keddy's Fort Howe Hotel offers a sophisticated menu. Local seafood is abundant and creatively prepared; Fundy scallops are a specialty, and the Maritime Mix—mussels, herring, and lobster—is the favorite of true seafood lovers. The poached salmon served cold with a tangy dip is delightful. There is live dinner music nightly, except Sunday. ✕ *Main and Portland Sts.,* ☎ *506/657–7320. Reservations advised. AE, DC, MC, V.*

$$$ **Turn of the Tide.** This large hotel dining room is decorated with antiques and has terrific views of the harbor. Although the dining is pleasant at all times, the best meal of the week is the Sunday buffet, with a long table full of dishes from the exotic to the tried-and-true. ✕ *Saint John Hilton, 1 Market Sq.,* ☎ *506/693–8484. Reservations advised. AE, DC, MC, V. No lunch Sat.*

$$ **Mexicali Rosa's.** For a franchise, this restaurant has a lot of character. The decor is essentially Santa Fe–style, with adobe arches and so forth. The specialty is California-Mexican food, which is heavy on sauces, as opposed to Tex-Mex, which concentrates more on meats. Guests waiting to be seated can order a fine margarita in the large lounge. The chimichangas are with good reason the most popular dish. ✕ *88 Prince William St.,* ☎ *506/652–5252. AE, DC, MC, V.*

$–$$ **Grannan's.** Seafood brochette with scallops, shrimp, and lobster tail,
★ sautéed at your table in a white-wine and mushroom sauce, and a "Captain's Platter" for two, with salmon, halibut, scallops, lobster, jumbo shrimp, oysters, and steamed clams and mussels, are two of the specials in this nautically decorated restaurant. The desserts, including bananas Foster flambéed at your table, are memorable. Dining spills over onto the sidewalk in summer, and there are three lively bars connected to the restaurant. ✕ *Market Sq.,* ☎ *506/634–1555. AE, DC, MC, V. No lunch Sun.*

$–$$ **Incredible Edibles.** Here you can enjoy down-to-earth food—biscuits, garlic-laden hummus, salads, pastas, and desserts—in cozy rooms or, in summer, on the outdoor terrace. The menu also includes beef and chicken dishes. You'll get a good cup of coffee here, too. ✕ *42 Princess St.,* ☎ *506/633–7554. AE, DC, MC, V. Closed Sun.*

LODGING

$$$ **Saint John Hilton.** Part of the Market Square complex, this Hilton is furnished in Loyalist decor; guest rooms overlook the harbor or the town. Mellow antiques furnish corners of the Turn of the Tide dining room (*see* Dining, *above*) and the medieval-style Great Hall, which hosts banquets. A pedestrian walkway system connects this 12-story property to uptown shops, restaurants, bars, a library, and a civic center for concerts and sporting events. ☎ *1 Market Sq., E2L 4Z6,* ☎ *506/*

693–8484 or 800/561–8282, FAX 506/657–6610. 197 rooms. Restaurant, bar, pool. AE, DC, MC, V.

$$$ **Shadow Lawn Country Inn.** This charming village inn is located in an
★ affluent suburb, with tree-lined streets and palatial houses, 10 minutes
from Saint John. Tennis, golf, horseback riding, and a yacht club are
nearby. The inn has nine old-fashioned bedrooms, some with fireplaces.
Besides being open during breakfast (for guests, included in the room
rate), the dining room is open to the public for dinner; reservations are
recommended. Specialties include salmon Florentine and chicken Grand
Marnier. ☎ *Box 41, Rothesay Rd., E2E 5A3,* ☎ *506/847–7539,* FAX
506/849–9238. 9 rooms. Restaurant. AE, DC, MC, V.

Shediac
DINING AND LODGING

$$–$$$ **Chez Françoise.** This lovely old mansion with a wraparound veranda
★ has been decorated in Victorian style, with hardwood floors and an-
tiques. There are 10 guest rooms (six with private baths) in this house;
another building across the street houses an additional 10 (four with
baths). Front rooms in the main house have water views. The dining
room, open to the public for dinner, serves excellent traditional French
cuisine with an emphasis on seafood. ☎ *93 Main St.,* ☎ *506/532–4233.
20 rooms. Restaurant, bar. AE, DC, MC, V. Closed Jan.–May 1.*

THE ARTS AND NIGHTLIFE

The Arts

Theatre New Brunswick performs in the Playhouse in Fredericton (686
Queen St., ☎ 506/458–8344) and tours the province. Top musical
groups, noted professional singers, and other performers usually ap-
pear at the **Aitken Center** (☎ 506/453–5054) on the University of New
Brunswick campus near Fredericton, at **Colosseum** (☎ 506/857–4100)
in Moncton, and at **Harbour Station** in Saint John.

Beaverbrook Art Gallery (☎ 506/458–8545) in Fredericton is the
province's major gallery, but art exhibitions are also held at the **Aitken
Bicentennial Exhibition Center** (ABEC) in Saint John, at **Moncton City
Hall,** and at the University of Moncton's **Acadian Museum.**

Nightlife

Fredericton

Fredericton's nightlife is livelier than that of most cities, with lots of
live music in downtown pubs, especially on the weekends. Just wan-
der down **King Street** until you hear your kind of music. **Dolan's Pub**
(Piper's Lane/349 King St., ☎ 506/454–7474) is a bit of the "auld sod,"
with Celtic and folk-style entertainment. **The Exchange** (Piper's Lane/349
King St., ☎ 506/459–2911) is a mecca for jazz and blues lovers. **The
Lunar Rogue** (625 King St., ☎ 506/450–2065) has Maritime enter-
tainment in an old world pub atmosphere.

Moncton

Downtown here really rocks at night. **Ziggy's** (730 Main St., ☎ 506/
858–8844) offers dance and party music and lots of fun promotions.
Club Cosmopolitain (700 Main St., ☎ 506/857–9117) is open Wednes-
day through Sunday for rockin' 'n' rollin'. **Chevy's** (939 Mountain Rd.,
☎ 506/858–5861) boasts Moncton's biggest dance floor.

Saint John

Taverns and lounges, usually with music of some kind, provide a lively nightlife here. **O'Leary's Pub** (46 Princess St., ☎ 506/634–7135) is in the middle of the Trinity Royal Preservation Area and specializes in old-time Irish fun complete with Celtic performers. **Sherlock's** (7 Market Sq., ☎ 506/633–7470) is next to Loyalist Plaza outside Market Square. The scene really heats up here after midnight with lots of contemporary and retro music spun by a DJ. **Grannan's and Spirits** (1 Market Sq., ☎ 506/634–1555) are two of the many lively Market Square nightclubs. These high-powered nightspots are colorful.

NEW BRUNSWICK ESSENTIALS

Arriving and Departing

By Car Ferry

There are car ferries from Prince Edward Island and Nova Scotia. **Marine Atlantic** (☎ 902/794–5700) has a car-and-passenger ferry from Digby, Nova Scotia, which takes 2½ hours. For reservations in the United States, call 800/341–7981. The trip from Prince Edward Island takes 30–45 minutes; reservations are not required.

By Plane

Canadian Airlines International operates through **Air Atlantic** (☎ 800/665–1177 in Canada, ☎ 800/426–7000 in U.S.) in Saint John, Fredericton, Moncton, Charlo, and Miramichi, and serves the Atlantic provinces, Montréal, Ottawa, and Boston. **Air Canada** and its regional carrier **Air Nova** (☎ 800/776–3000 in U.S., ☎ 800/563–5151 in Canada) serve New Brunswick in Saint John, Moncton, Fredericton, Bathurst, and Saint-Léonard, and fly to the Atlantic provinces from Montréal, Toronto, and Boston.

By Train

VIA Rail offers passenger service three times a week from Moncton to Montréal and Halifax. Bus connections are available to Prince Edward Island and Newfoundland from Moncton.

Getting Around

By Bus

SMT (☎ 506/859–5100) runs buses within the province and connects with most major bus lines.

By Car

New Brunswick has an excellent highway system with numerous facilities. The only map you'll need is the one available at the tourist information centers listed below. Major entry points are at St. Stephen, Houlton, Edmundston, and Cape Tormentine from Prince Edward Island, and Aulac from Nova Scotia.

Guided Tours

Boat Tours

Harbor tours are offered in Saint John by **Partridge Island Tours** (☎ 506/693–2598) and **DMK Marine Tours** (☎ 506/635–4150, FAX 506/635–8714).

City Tours

Heritage Tour Guide Service (☎ 506/459–5950) provides guides for bus tours of Fredericton.

The **Calithumpians** theater company in Fredericton offers guides dressed in 18th-century costume for free historical walks from City Hall (☎ 506/457–1975).

In Saint John, free guided walking tours begin in Market Square at Barbour's General Store. For information call the Saint John Tourist and Convention Center (☎ 506/658–2990).

Special-Interest

More than 240 species of seabirds nest on Grand Manan Island, and this island is a paradise for painters, nature photographers, and hikers, not to mention whale-watchers. Any of these activities can be arranged by calling **Tourism New Brunswick** (*see below*). **Covered Bridge Bicycle Tours** (☎ 506/849–9028), based in Saint John, offers bike tours.

Important Addresses and Numbers

Emergencies

Dial 911 for medical emergencies and police in New Brunswick cities and their surrounding areas. For other areas, find emergency numbers inside the front cover of the local telephone directory. A universal 911 emergency program is scheduled to come on line in May of 1996; when it is instituted, 911 will access emergency service from anywhere in the province.

Hospitals

Dr. Everett Chalmers Hospital (Priestman St., Fredericton, ☎ 506/452–5400); **Moncton City Hospital** (135 MacBeath Ave., Moncton, ☎ 506/857–5111); **Dr. Georges Dumont Hospital** (330 Archibald St., Moncton, ☎ 506/862–4000); **Saint John Regional Hospital** (Tucker Park Rd., Saint John, ☎ 506/648–6000); **Chaleur Regional Hospital** (1750 Sunset Dr., Bathurst, ☎ 506/548–8961); **Campbellton Regional Hospital** (189 Lilly Lake Rd., Campbellton, ☎ 506/789–5000); **Edmundston Regional Hospital** (275 Hébert Blvd., ☎ 506/739–2200); **Miramichi Hospital** (673 King George Hwy., Miramichi, ☎ 506/627–7000).

Visitor Information

Tourism New Brunswick (Box 12345, Fredericton, E3B 5C3, ☎ 506/453–2170 or 800/561–0123) can provide information on the seven provincial tourist bureaus. Also helpful are information services of the cities of **Bathurst** (☎ 506/548–0410), **Campbellton** (☎ 506/789–2367), **Fredericton** (☎ 506/452–9508), **Moncton** (☎ 506/853–3590), and **Saint John** (☎ 506/658–2990).

5 Prince Edward Island

In the Gulf of St. Lawrence north of Nova Scotia and New Brunswick, Prince Edward Island seems too good to be true, with its crisply painted farmhouses, manicured green fields rolling down to sandy beaches, the warmest ocean water north of Florida, lobster boats in trim little harbors, and a vest-pocket capital city, Charlottetown, packed with architectural heritage.

PRINCE EDWARD ISLAND SEEMS too good to be true, with its crisply painted farmhouses, manicured green fields rolling down to sandy beaches, the warmest ocean water north of Florida, lobster boats in trim little harbors, and a vest-pocket capital city packed with architectural heritage.

When you experience PEI, you'll understand instantly that it was no accident that Lucy Maud Montgomery's novel of youth and innocence, *Anne of Green Gables,* was framed against this land. What may have been unexpected, however, was how the story burst on the world in 1908 and is still selling untold thousands of copies every year. After potatoes and lobsters, Anne is the island's most important product.

Anne is everywhere on the island: At the Confederation Centre of the Arts in Charlottetown you can often peruse Montgomery's original hand-written manuscript; even on cars throughout the province you'll see the freckled redhead, as the government stamped her face on the province's license plates. But Anne's fame stretches beyond PEI and Cavendish—fondly referred to as Anne's land. She attracts international attention, especially from the Japanese, with whom she is hugely popular.

Those visitors who have come because of Anne usually leave having fallen in love with her island. Outside the tourist mecca of Cavendish, the island seems like an oasis of peace in a world of turmoil. Here you'll find fishing ports, crossroads villages, small family farms. You can choose full-service resorts and gourmet restaurants, or bed-and-breakfasts and lobster suppers. You can opt for a farm vacation or take a deep-sea fishing cruise.

Visitors often tour the island in a loop: They take the ferry from New Brunswick to Bordon, see Anne country and the PEI National Park, and depart by ferry from Wood Island to Nova Scotia. This is a good strategy; but, to more deeply experience the island's character, stray to the wooded hills of the east—to compact, bustling Montague, strad-dling its river; or to the estuarine maze of Murray Harbour. Or go west to superb, almost-private beaches, the Acadian parishes of Egmont Bay and Tignish, and the silver-fox country around Summerside. Even if you're in a rush, it won't take long to get off the beaten path: In most places you can cross the island, north to south, in half an hour or so.

PEI is ringed by beaches, and few of them are heavily used. Ask a dozen islanders to recommend their favorites. Bothwell Beach, near Souris, says one—miles of singing sands, utterly deserted. West Point, says a second—lifeguards, restaurant nearby, showers at the provincial park. Greenwich, near St. Peter's Bay, another suggests—a half-hour walk through mag-nificent wandering dunes brings you to an endless empty beach.

When you're back in Charlottetown see the musical *Anne of Green Gables.* Have dinner first—there are great little places within a few blocks of the theater.

EXPLORING

The tours here divide Prince Edward Island into central Queens County, Kings County in the east, and Prince County at the western end of the island. Tour 1 is primarily a walking tour, and Tours 2, 3, and 4 fol-low the major scenic highways—Blue Heron Drive, Kings Byway, and Lady Slipper Drive. There are plenty of chances to get out of the car, go fishing, hit the beach, photograph wild flowers, or just watch the sea roll in.

Tour 1: Charlottetown

Sheltered on an arm of the Northumberland Strait, Prince Edward Island's first city is named for the stylish consort of King George III. Charlottetown, the largest community on the island, is a small city (population 30,000) with generous, gingerbread-clad Victorian houses and tree-shaded squares. It is often called "the Cradle of Confederation," a reference to the 1864 conference held here that led to the union of Nova Scotia, New Brunswick, Ontario, and Québec in 1867, and eventually, to Canada itself.

Charlottetown's main activities center on government, tourism, and private commerce. While new suburbs were springing up around it, the core of Charlottetown remained unchanged, and the waterfront has been restored to recapture the flavor of earlier eras. Today the waterfront includes the Prince Edward Hotel, several informal restaurants, handcraft and retail shops, and a marked walking path. You can easily explore the downtown on foot in a couple of hours. Irene Rogers's *Charlottetown: The Life in Its Buildings* gives much detail about the architecture and history of downtown Charlottetown.

Numbers in the margin correspond to points of interest on the Prince Edward Island and Charlottetown maps.

❶
❷ **Charlottetown**'s historic redbrick core is the setting for the modern, concrete **Confederation Centre of the Arts,** opened in 1964 as a tribute to the Fathers of Confederation. The Confederation Centre houses a 1,100-seat theater, a memorial hall, a gift shop featuring Canadian crafts, an art gallery and museum, and restaurant and catering facilities. From June to September the center's **Charlottetown Festival** offers excellent professional theater, including the annual musical adaptation of *Anne of Green Gables. Queen St., bet. Grafton and Richmond Sts.,* ☎ *902/ 628–1864; box office 902/566–1267;* FAX *902/566–4648.* ⊙ *Sept.–June, daily 9–5; June–Sept. hrs are extended.*

★ ❸ Next door, on Richmond Street, is the Georgian-style **Province House National Historic Site,** the meeting place of the provincial legislature. The three-story sandstone building, completed in 1847, contains the Confederation Chamber, where representatives of the 19th-century provinces met to discuss creating a union. The room, restored to its 1864 condition, and the legislative chamber are open to the public. Displays and a slide presentation portray the historic meeting. *Richmond St.,* ☎ *902/566–7626.* ☛ *Free.* ⊙ *Weekdays 9–5; July–Aug., daily 9–8. Reservations preferred for large groups. Note: When legislature is in session, certain rooms are closed to the public.*

❹
❺ Two churches near Province House are noteworthy. **St. Paul's Anglican Church** (east of Province House) was erected in 1747, making it the oldest Protestant church on the island. **St. Dunstan's Basilica,** south of Province House on Great George Street, is the seat of the Roman Catholic diocese on the island. Known for its twin Gothic spires and fine Italian carvings, it is one of Canada's largest churches.

TIME OUT **Off Broadway,** located in a historic building just blocks from the waterfront, is a cozy spot for lunch, late-afternoon tea, or a full meal. Try their broccoli pie or a decadently delightful dessert. *125 Sydney St.,* ☎ *902/ 566–4620. AE, MC, V.*

❻ A few blocks northeast of Province House, on Rochford Square, is **St. Peter's Cathedral.** All Saints Chapel contains murals by Robert Harris, the famous Canadian portrait painter. The chapel was designed in 1888

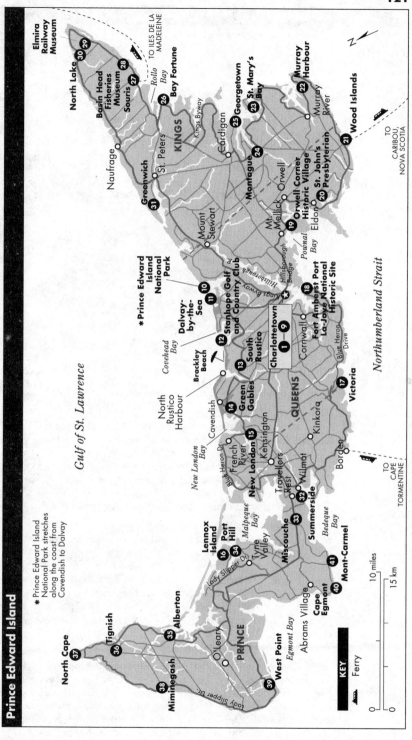

Prince Edward Island

Elmira Railway Museum

Basin Head Fisheries Museum

North Lake

Souris

Bay Fortune

Greenwich

St. Peters

KINGS

Kings Byway

Cardigan

Georgetown

St. Mary's Bay

Murray Harbour

Murray River

Wood Islands

TO ILES DE LA MADELEINE

Rollo Bay

Naufrage

Montague

Orwell

Orwell Corner Historic Village

St. John's Presbyterian

Eldon

Pownal Bay

Mt. Mellick

Mount Stewart

Kings Byway

Hillsborough Bridge

Hillsborough R.

Fort Amherst Port La-Joye National Historic Site

Charlottetown

Cornwall

Blue Heron Drive

QUEENS

Victoria

Kinkora

Borden

TO CARIBOU, NOVA SCOTIA

Northumberland Strait

TO CAPE TORMENTINE

Prince Edward Island National Park

Stanhope Golf and Country Club

Dalvay-the-Sea

Brackley Beach

South Rustico

Green Gables

Covehead Bay

North Rustico Harbour

Cavendish

New London Bay

French River

New London

Kensington

Travellers Rest

Wilmot

Summerside

Bedeque Bay

Miscouche

Tyne Valley

Malpeque Bay

Lennox Island

Port Hill

Lady Slipper Dr.

Mont-Carmel

Cape Egmont

Egmont Bay

Abrams Village

West Point

PRINCE

O'Leary

Alberton

Tignish

North Cape

Mimenegash

Lady Slipper Dr.

Gulf of St. Lawrence

* Prince Edward Island National Park stretches along the coast from Cavendish to Dalvay

KEY
Ferry

10 miles
15 km

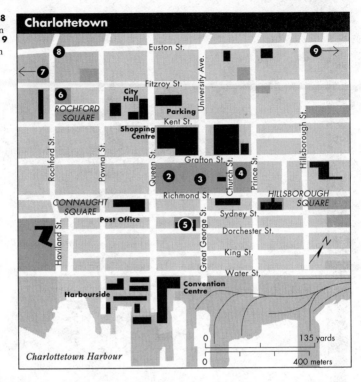

Charlottetown Harbour

by his brother W. C. "Willy" Harris, the most celebrated of the island's architects, and the designer of many historic homes and buildings.

7 At the southern tip of the city is the beautiful 40-acre **Victoria Park,** overlooking Charlottetown Harbour, a perfect place to stroll, picnic, or watch a baseball game. Next to the park, on a hill between groves of white birches, is the white colonial Government House, built in 1835 as the official residence of the province's lieutenant-governors. Call the City of Charlottetown Parks and Recreation office (☎ 902/368–1025) for more information. *Entrance at Lower Kent St. Park open daily sunrise–sunset.*

8 Near the park entrance, **Beaconsfield Historic House,** a gracious Victorian mansion, welcomes visitors. Designed by architect W. C. Harris and built in 1877, this is one of the island's finest residential buildings. On site are a gift shop and bookstore. During summer afternoons, tea and scones are served on the veranda. Special events such as theatrical and musical performances, socials, and lectures are held regularly. *2 Kent St.,* ☎ *902/368–6600.* ☛ *$2.50 adults, children free; group rates available.* ☺ *June–Labor Day, daily 10–5; Labor Day–June, Tues.–Sun., 1–5.*

9 At the eastern end of the city is the **Charlottetown Driving Park** on Kensington Road, home of a sport that is dear to the hearts of islanders—harness racing. Standardbred horses are raised on farms throughout the island, and harness racing on the ice and on country tracks has been popular for generations. In fact, there are more horses per capita on the island than in any other province of Canada. *Kensington Rd.,* ☎ *902/892–6823.* ☛ *$2 adults, 50¢ children. Year-round races held once a wk Jan.–May; three nights a wk in June, July, and most of Aug.; and twice daily (except Sun.) during Old Home Week in mid-Aug.*

Tour 2: Blue Heron Drive

Circling the island's center segment and roughly outlining Queens County, Blue Heron Drive is 190 kilometers (114 miles) long. It takes its name from the great blue heron, a stately water bird that migrates to Prince Edward Island every spring to nest in the shallow bays and marshes. You are likely to see several herons along the route. The highway marker is a white square with a blue border and a blue heron in the center.

From Charlottetown, Blue Heron Drive follows Route 15 north to the north shore, then winds along Route 6 through the north-shore fishing villages, the spectacular white sand beaches of Prince Edward Island National Park and Cabot Provincial Park, through the Anne of Green Gables country, and finally along the south shore with its red sandstone seascapes and historic sites. This drive circles some of the island's most beautiful landscapes and best beaches, but its north section around picturesque Cavendish and the Green Gables farmhouse is also cluttered with tourist traps. If you're looking for unspoiled beauty, you'll have to look beyond the fast-food outlets, tacky gift shops, and expensive carnival-type attractions and try to keep in your mind's eye the island's simpler days.

⑩ Prince Edward Island National Park stretches for about 40 kilometers (25 miles) along the north shore of the island on the Gulf of St. Lawrence. The park is blessed with nature's broadest brush strokes— sky and sea meet red sandstone cliffs, rolling dunes, and long stretches of sand. Beaches invite you to swim, picnic, or take a quiet walk. Trails lead through woodlands and along streams and ponds. Among more than 200 species of birds are the northern phalarope, Swainson's thrush, and the endangered piping plover. The park **visitor centers** in Cavendish and Brackley provide information on activities and events in the national park. The 56-acre campground has toilets, showers, electrical hookups, and a coin laundry. *24 km (15 mi) north of Charlottetown,* ☎ *902/672–6350.* ☛ *Summer admission.* ☉ *Park open daily; visitor center June–Oct., daily 10–6.*

⑪ At the eastern end of the national park is **Dalvay-by-the-Sea,** built in the 1890s as a summer home by an oil magnate. The park now operates the hotel as a resort lodge (*see* Lodging, *below*).

TIME OUT Three grand old hotels gracing the eastern end of the park all provide pleasant spots for a quiet break. At **Shaw's Hotel, Stanhope-by-the-Sea,** and **Dalvay-by-the-Sea** you can get good food in an extra special setting. Or go down to the wharf in Covehead, where you can get fresh seafood straight from the boat. Take it home or eat it on the spot: Fishermen will cook it to your liking.

⑫ A few kilometers west of Dalvay, off Route 6, along beautiful Covehead Bay, is the **Stanhope Golf and Country Club.** The 18-hole course is among the island's longest, most challenging, and most scenic.

⑬ Moving west, you pass Brackley Beach and then come to **South Rustico,** on Route 243. Rustico is an Acadian French district, one of several on the island. South Rustico sits on a peninsula on Rustico Bay, with a collection of Victorian houses gathered around a dainty church. One, Barachois Inn, has been lovingly restored as a bed-and-breakfast of high reputation. One of Canada's first cooperative banks—a precursor of the credit-union movement—was founded here; it is now a national historic site and museum.

★ ⑭ Continue along the shore road. As you gaze toward the sea, think of the hundreds of ships that sank in these waters, including the famed *Marco Polo*, which ran aground off Cavendish. Follow the signs to **Green Gables House** in PEI National Park, the green-and-white farmhouse that is the setting for Lucy Maud Montgomery's first and most famous novel, *Anne of Green Gables*. The book was published in 1908, and it became one of the most popular children's books ever written. It's about a young orphan girl adopted by a strict but kindly brother and sister who live on a Prince Edward Island farm. The story has so caught the imagination of readers that hundreds of thousands of visitors from around the world visit Green Gables every summer. The house, once owned by Montgomery's cousins, is organized to reflect the story. *Near Cavendish, in PEI National Park,* ☏ *902/673–6350.* ☞ *Admission charged.* ⊙ *Mid-May–late June, daily 9–5; late June–Aug., daily 9–8; Sept. and Oct., daily 9–5.*

⑮ In **New London,** west of Cavendish on Route 6, is the modest white house where Lucy Maud Montgomery was born in 1874. Among memorabilia on display are the author's wedding dress and personal scrapbooks. *In New London, on Rte. 6,* ☏ *902/886–2596.* ☞ *$1 adults, 50¢ children.* ⊙ *June and early Sept.–mid-Sept., daily 9–5; July and Aug., daily 9–7; mid-Sept.–mid-Oct., daily 9–5.*

⑯ The Blue Heron Drive follows the coastline south to the other side of the island through rolling farmland by the shores of Malpeque Bay, almost into Summerside. Across Malpeque Bay is **Lennox Island,** the largest Micmac Indian reserve in the province. The head of Malpeque Bay almost meets Bedeque Bay, nearly cutting the island in two. At Carleton, Blue Heron Drive intersects with Route 1, the main highway between Charlottetown and Borden and the terminus for the New Brunswick ferries. At the waterfront you'll see the ongoing construction of the bridge, which is to span the 14½ kilometers (9 miles) of the Northumberland Straight. When the bridge is completed in the summer of 1997 it will replace the car ferry. Prior to the late 1800s (when ferry service began) passengers and mail were taken across the straight in iceboats, which were alternately pushed, pulled, and rowed, even in horrendous winter weather. A memorial pays tribute to the crews of those ships.

⑰ Paralleling the coast, the drive continues past a fine Harris church at Crapaud to **Victoria,** a picturesque fishing village with antiques, art galleries, handicraft shops, and live summer theater in the historic **Victoria Playhouse** (☏ 902/658–2025 for ticket information and reservations).

⑱ The drive winds on through Argyle Shore to **Fort Amherst Port-La-Joye National Historic Site,** at the mouth of Charlottetown Harbour. This pretty spot, with its lighthouse, is the location of the first European settlement on the island, established in 1720 during French rule. You can picnic on the site while watching boats and cruise ships sail into the harbor. *32 km (20 mi) south of Charlottetown on Rte. 19 at Rocky Point,* ☏ *902/675–2220.* ⊙ *Mid-June–Labor Day, daily 10–6.*

Tour 3: Kings Byway

The Kings Byway follows the coastline of Kings County for 375 kilometers (225 miles) on the eastern end of the island. The route passes woodlots, patchwork-quilt farms, fishing villages, and historic sites in this green and tranquil section of the province. Starting at Charlottetown, take Route 1 east and follow Kings Byway counter-clockwise.

★ ⑲ **The Orwell Corner Historic Village** re-creates a 19th-century rural settlement in the form of a living farm museum, employing methods used by Scottish settlers in the 1800s, including the use of handsome draft horses. The village contains a beautifully restored 1864 farmhouse, school, church, community hall, smithy, and barns. On Wednesdays in the summer the village hosts musical evenings (*ceilidhs*) featuring traditional Scottish fiddle music by local musicians. Other special events occur year-round. *Rte. 1, ☎ 902/651–2013. ☛ $3 adults, children under 12 free. ☉ Late June–Labor Day, Tues.–Sun. 9–5; mid-May–late June and Labor Day–late Oct., Tues.–Fri. 10–3.*

Continue north from Orwell Village for about a mile, to where the road turns to gravel. Stop off at the **Sir Andrew MacPhail Homestead,** with an interpretive center and gardens that explain and reflect life in the early 20th century. This 140-acre property with walking trails commemorates the life of MacPhail, a local author and historian. *Off Rte. 1, Orwell, ☎ 902/651–2789 in summer; 902/659–2735 in winter. ☛ Admission charged. ☉ June and Sept., Tues.–Sun. 10–5; July and Aug., extended hrs.*

Continue up the gravel road to Route 24 and turn right to **Ben's Lake Trout Farm,** in Bellevue. This is an enjoyable attraction for the whole family, but especially loved by aspiring young anglers. Not only are you almost guaranteed a fish, but the staff will clean it and supply the barbecue and picnic table for a great meal. To get back to our tour, reverse the route. *Rte. 24, ☎ 902/838–2706. ☛ Free. ☉ Apr.–Oct.*

⑳ One of the island's most historic churches, **St. John's Presbyterian,** in Belfast, is just off Route 1 on Route 207. This pretty white church, on a hill against a backdrop of trees, was built by settlers from the Isle of Skye who were brought to the island in 1803 by Lord Selkirk.

㉑ Route 1 passes **Wood Islands,** the terminus for the Northumberland Ferries service to Nova Scotia, which operates while Northumberland Strait is free of ice, generally from May through December. The island-

㉒ dotted waters of **Murray Harbour** drain five rivers, and empty through the narrow gut between Poverty Beach and Beach Point. This favorite refuge for island yachtsmen supports a large fishing fleet.

TIME OUT Brehaut's Restaurant (☎ 902/962–3141) in Murray Harbour village, right by the fishermen's wharf, has a take-out and café downstairs and a pleasant dining room upstairs. Tasty, wholesome food in a rustic ambience, with very pleasant service, is what you'll get here.

The eastern coastline is dotted with fishing villages and long uncrowded beaches. Seal-watching and bird-watching boat tours are
㉓ available at Murray River and Montague; **St. Mary's Bay,** inside Panmure Island, offers excellent windsurfing behind a long protected
㉔ beach. Three rivers enter into Cardigan Bay. Seductive **Montague,** on
㉕ the Montague River, is the business hub of eastern PEI, while **Georgetown,** on a point between the Cardigan and Brudenell rivers, is a ship-
㉖ building town with a lively summer theater. **Bay Fortune,** a little-known scenic spot, has been a secret refuge of well-heeled Americans for two generations, and is home to the wonderful Inn at Bay Fortune (*see* Lodging, *below*) with old-time style and panache.

In early summer, you can see whole fields of blue, white, pink, and purple wild lupines sloping down to red cliffs and blue sea. The view from
★ ㉗ the hill overlooking the town of **Souris,** on the northeastern coast, is especially lovely. At Souris, a car-ferry links PEI with the Québec–owned Magdalen Islands. The Souris area is noted for its fine traditional mu-

sicians. An outdoor Scottish concert at Rollo Bay in July, featuring fiddling and step-dancing, attracts thousands every year.

TIME OUT   The **Uptown Restaurant** (☎ 902/687–4123), on the main street in Souris, is a Chinese restaurant with a difference. Ask about the silver aliwana fish—a Chinese species—in an aquarium on the wall, and try the "bumbleberry." pie.

㉘ About 8 miles north of Souris, off Route 16, is the **Basin Head Fisheries Museum,** spectacularly located on a bluff overlooking Northumberland Straight. Boats, gear, and photographs depict the life of an inshore fisherman. Displays include dioramas illustrating industry methods and materials, boat and fishermen's sheds, an aquarium, a smokehouse, a fish-box factory, a cannery, and coastal-ecology exhibits. On the property is a fine beach with changing rooms, locker rentals, and a canteen. *Off Rte. 16, north of Souris (Box 248),* ☎ *and* FAX *902/357–2966; off-season 902/368–6600.* ☞ *$3 adults, children under 12 free.* ☉ *June and Sept., Wed.–Fri. 10–3; July–Aug., daily 10–5.*

Walk over the cast-iron bridge by the museum. The exquisite, silvery beach stretches northeast for miles, backed by high, grassy dunes. Scuff your feet in the sand: it will squeak, squawk, and purr at you. These are known locally as the "singing sands," a phenomenon found in only a few locations worldwide.

㉙ Drive east on Route 16 for almost 16 kilometers (10 miles), to the **Elmira Railway Museum,** which recounts the development and history of the 19th- and early 20th-century PEI railway. Artifacts, maps, and photos are on display, as well as station telegraph equipment that's in excellent condition. There's also a gift shop in the museum. *Rte. 16A,* ☎ *902/357–2481.* ☞ *$1.50 adults, children under 13 free.* ☉ *Mid-June–Labor Day, Tues.–Sun. 9–5.*

Follow the shore road (Route 16) and visit **East Point Lighthouse**; ships from many nations have wrecked on the reef running north east from the lighthouse. Numerous detailed books depicting the mysteries and tales of life at sea are available in the gift shop in this lighthouse. An especially good stop for photographers and those interested in fish-
㉚ ing communities is **North Lake,** several kilometers (a few miles) from Basin Head.

For even more extensive dune scenery, follow Route 2 to St. Peter's
㉛ Bay, and Route 313 to **Greenwich.** The road ends among sand hills, but from here you can take a half-hour walk through beige dunes to reach the superb beach. These dunes are moving, gradually burying the nearby woods; here and there the bleached skeletons of trees thrust up through the sand like wooden ghosts. This area is also home of one of the island's finest golf courses, **The Links at Crowbush Cove, Lakeside** (Rte. 350, off Rte. 2 near Morell, ☎ 902/961–2800, 902/961–3100, or 800/377–8337).

Tour 4: Lady Slipper Drive

This drive—named for the delicate lady's slipper orchid, the province's official flower—winds along the coast of the narrow, indented western end of the island through very old and very small villages, which still adhere to a traditional way of life. Many of these hamlets are inhabited by Acadians, descendants of the original French settlers. The area is known for its oysters and Irish moss, but most famously for its potato farms: The province is a major exporter of seed potatoes worldwide, and half the crop is grown here.

③ From Charlottetown, take Route 2 to **Summerside,** the second-largest community on the island. A self-guided walking tour of Summerside, arranged by the Summerside Tourism Office, is a pleasant excursion through the leafy streets, with their spacious houses. Some of these homes are known as "fox houses"; silver foxes were first bred in captivity in western PEI, and for several decades Summerside was the headquarters of a virtual gold rush based on fox ranching. For more history and walking-tour brochures, stop in at the **International Fox Museum and Hall of Fame.** *286 Fitzroy St.,* ☎ *902/436–2400 or 902/436–1589.* ☛ *Free; $1 donation accepted.* ⊙ *May–Sept., Mon.–Sat. 9–6.*

A visit to Summerside should include a stop at both the **Eptek National Exhibition Centre,** located on the waterfront. This contemporary structure is named for the Micmac word for "warm spot". The spacious main gallery features changing history and fine arts exhibits from all parts of Canada. In the adjacent gallery is the **PEI Sports Hall of Fame,** where well-known island athletes are honored. *130 Water St.,* ☎ *902/888–8373,* 🖷 *902/888–8375.* ☛ *$1.50 adults, children under 12 free.*

The eight-day **Summerside Lobster Carnival,** held every July, includes livestock exhibitions, harness racing, fiddling contests, and lobster suppers. Midsummer **Grand Prix hydroplane races** take place in the harbor. The boats are powered by 1,500-horsepower engines and attain speeds of 240 kilometers (150 miles) per hour.

③ On Route 2, just west of Summerside, you will find the **Acadian Museum of Prince Edward Island,** located in **Miscouche.** The museum has a permanent exhibition on Acadian life as well as an audio-visual presentation depicting the history and culture of island Acadian people from the first settlement of 1720 to the present. Access to 30,000 genealogical cards listing Acadian descent is available. *Rte. 2, Miscouche,* ☎ *902/436–6237.* ☛ *$2.75 adults, $1.50 students, under 6 free, $7 families.* ⊙ *Weekdays 9:30–5; late June–Labor Day, Sat. 9:30–5, Sun. 1–5.*

③ Relatively few visitors travel west of Summerside, which is unfortunate for them and fortunate for you. Route 2 goes straight as an arrow through the drab plain of the Miscouche Swamp. Avoid this route by following the Lady Slipper signs from Miscouche to **Port Hill,** about 35 kilometers (22 miles) northwest of Summerside. The **Green Park Shipbuilding Museum and Historic House** was originally the home of shipbuilder James Yeo, Jr. This 19th-century mansion, restored and open to visitors, is topped by a cupola, from which Yeo observed his nearby shipyard through a spyglass. The modern museum building, located in what has become a provincial park, details the history of the shipbuilder's craft, which is brought to life at a re-created shipyard with carpenter and blacksmith shops. The park also provides an opportunity for some welcome R&R, with picnic tables and camping facilities, as well as swimming in the river (there may not be a lifeguard on duty). *Rte. 12, Port Hill,* ☎ *902/831–2206.* ☛ *$2.50 adults, children under 12 free.* ⊙ *Mid-June–Labor Day, Tues.–Sun. 9–5.*

③ Lady Slipper Drive leads to the tiny community of **Tyne Valley,** reputed to offer some of the finest food on PEI, as well as an annual summer Oyster Festival. The **Doctor's Inn,** in the village, offers free tours of its organic gardens. Lady Slipper Drive continues around Foxley Bay and Cascumpec Bay to **Alberton,** where Jacques Cartier made his first landing on the island. Oulton Island, just offshore, was the first place foxes were bred successfully in captivity and claims to be the world's first fur ranch.

③⑥ Follow the shore north to **Tignish,** another Acadian community. Everything in Tignish seems to be co-operative, including the supermarket, insurance company, fish plant, service station, and credit union. The imposing **parish church of St. Simon and St. Jude Parish House** (315 School St., ☎ 902/882–2049), across from Dalton Square, has a superb Tracker pipe organ, one of the finest such instruments in eastern Canada, and is often used for recitals by world-renowned musicians.

The **Dalton Centre,** on Church Street, was built by the first fox-breeder, Sir Charles Dalton, a Tignish native; it now includes a museum. *Church St.,* ☎ *902/882–2488.* ☛ *$1.50 adults, 75¢ children.* ☉ *Mid-June–Aug., Sun.–Fri. 10–5.*

★ ③⑦ Drive on to **North Cape,** where the island fades to a narrow north-pointing arrow of land with an imposing lighthouse. At low tide you can walk out onto one of the longest reefs in the world, a great spot to find tidal pools teeming with marine life. If you feel you are being watched, you probably are: Look offshore to where the seals gather for some prime people-watching! The curious structures nearby are wind turbines at the **Atlantic Wind Test Site,** set up on this breezy promontory to evaluate the feasibility of electrical generation by wind power. The **Interpretive Centre and Aquarium** offer information about marine life, local history, and turbines and windmills of the future. ☎ *902/882–2991.* ☛ *$2 adults, $1 senior citizens and students, children under 10 free.* ☉ *July and Aug., daily 9–9; mid-May–June and Sept.–late Oct., daily 10–6.*

TIME OUT   Wind & Reef (☎ 902/882–3535) is a licensed restaurant that serves good seafood meals and has a breathtaking view of the Gulf of St. Lawrence and Northumberland Strait.

From the cape, Lady Slipper Drive turns almost due south along the island's western shore. Near North Cape, just off the Drive, is the very popular natural rock formation called "Elephant Rock." You may see draft horses in the fields or working in the surf. They are "moss horses," used in harvesting a versatile and valuable sea plant known
③⑧ as Irish moss. At **Miminegash,** visit the **Irish Moss Interpretive Centre** and find out how much Irish moss was in your last ice-cream cone. Then take time for some Seaweed Pie (also from Irish moss) made at the adjacent Seaweed Pie Cafe. *Rte. 14, Miminegash,* ☎ *902/882–4313.* ☛ *Admission charged.* ☉ *Late June–Sept., weekdays 9–5.*

③⑨ At the southern tip of the western shore is **West Point,** with a tiny, manmade fishing harbor, provincial campsite, supervised beach, and what one recent visitor called an "insanely friendly" community. Above all, there is the **West Point Lighthouse,** 120 years old and the tallest on the island. When the lighthouse was automated, the community took over the building and converted it into an inn (you can book a room here) and museum, with a gift shop and an excellent, moderately priced restaurant attached. The area is steeped in ghostly tales and legends; ask about the Phantom Ship and the treasure that's supposed to be buried nearby. *Rte. 14,* ☎ *902/859–3605.* ☛ *$1.65 adults, $1.40 senior citizens, 85¢ children.* ☉ *Mid-May–mid-Oct., daily 8–9:30.*

④⓪ Lady Slipper Drive meanders back to Summerside through Région Evangeline, the main Acadian district of the island. At **Cape Egmont,** stop for a look at the **Bottle Houses,** the work of a retired carpenter: two tiny houses and a chapel built entirely out of glass bottles mortared together
④① like bricks. In **Mont-Carmel,** an adjoining community, are a magnificent brick church overlooking Northumberland Strait and an **Acadian Pio-**

neer **Village** with a church, school, blacksmith shop, store, restaurant (where you can sample authentic Acadian dishes), and modern accommodations. *Rte. 11,* ☎ *902/854–2227.* ☛ *Village: $2 adults, 75¢ children, 50¢ children under 6.* ◷ *Mid-June–mid-Sept., daily 10–7.*

SHOPPING

Prince Edward Islanders have been making beautiful homemade items since colonial days, when crafts were necessities of life. Island craftspeople excel at quilting, rug-hooking, weaving, woodworking, knitting, and pottery. Full information on outlets and types of crafts is provided by the **PEI Crafts Council** (156 Richmond St., Charlottetown C1A 1H9, ☎ 902/892–5152). There are more than 100 crafts outlets throughout the island.

The **Island Crafts Shop** has a wide selection of weaving, pottery, woodwork, and other items. Here you'll find the best variety and quality goods made by local artisans. *156 Richmond St., Charlottetown,* ☎ *902/892–5152.* ◷ *July and Aug., Mon.–Sat. 9–8, Sun. 11–4; Sept.–June, Mon.–Sat. 9:30–5.*

The **Wood Islands Handcraft Co-op Association Ltd.,** in southeastern Kings County, sells a large number of knitted and crocheted items and other crafts. *Murray River, Kings County,* ☎ *902/962–3539.* ◷ *Daily 9–5; July and Aug., daily 9–6.*

Along Lady Slipper Drive look for hand-turned bird's-eye maple products at the **Leavitts' Wood Craft** in Alberton. *Alberton,* ☎ *902/853–2504.* ◷ *Mon.–Sat. 8–5.*

The Dunes Studio and Gallery, on Rte 15, near Brackley Beach, is the island's most visually stunning shop and museum, featuring the work of leading local artists, as well as craftspeople from around the world. The production pottery studio is open for viewing, as is a rooftop water garden. *Brackley Beach,* ☎ *902/672–2586.* ◷ *May–Oct., daily 10–6; July and Aug., daily 9–9; off-season by appointment.*

Shoreline Sweaters, sometimes known as Tyne Valley Studio, in Tyne Valley, is where Lesley Dubey produces sweaters with a unique Fair Isle–style lobster pattern, and sells local crafts. *Lady Slipper Dr., Tyne Valley,* ☎ *902/831–2950.* ◷ *Mid-May–Sept., daily 9:30–5:30.*

You can buy fresh, canned, or frozen lobster and other seafood at numerous processing plants and retail stores throughout the island. Some, such as **Crabby's Seafood** in Wood Islands, will pack your purchases for travel. *Wood Islands, next to ferry,* ☎ *902/962–3228.* ◷ *Daily 7–7.*

SPORTS AND THE OUTDOORS
Bicycling
Prince Edward Island is popular with bike-touring companies for its moderately hilly roads and stunning scenery. Level areas can be found over most of the island, especially east of Charlottetown to Montague and along the north shore. However, shoulderless, narrow, secondary roads in some areas and summer's car traffic can be challenging for cyclists. An 8.7-kilometer (5.4-mile) path near Cavendish campground loops around marsh, woodland, and farmland. Cycling trips are organized throughout the province, and Prince Edward Island's Visitor Information Centres (*see* Important Addresses and Numbers *in* Prince

Edward Island Essentials, *below*) can recommend tour operators. Also, bicycles can be rented in Charlottetown and Cavendish.

Fishing
PEI offers some of the best brook-trout fishing in eastern Canada, as well as excellent deep-sea fishing off the island's northeast coast. Charter boats leave daily in summer from the fishing ports of Cove Head, North Lake, and North Rustico, for very elusive tuna and rich mackerel fishing; there are more than 20 boat charters to choose from.

Clam digging is possible in many less-populated coastal areas around the island. Ask at the Visitor Information Centres (VIC) (*see* Important Addresses and Numbers *in* Prince Edward Island Essentials, *below*) about open areas.

Golf
Popular with tourists, golfing in PEI is virtually hassle free: Tee-off times are easily booked any day of the week. the course at **Stanhope Golf and Country Club** (☎ 902/672–2842) is one of the most challenging on the island. In the western end, **Mill River Provincial Golf Course** (☎ 902/859–2238) in Mill River Provincial Park, 57 kilometers (35 miles) west of Summerside, is among the most scenic and challenging courses in eastern Canada. **Brudenell River Provincial Golf Course** (☎ 902/652–2332) at the east end of the island has hosted four national championships and three CPGA tournaments. The latter two courses are within major resort complexes. **Green Gables Course** (☎ 902/963–2488) in Cavendish is a scenic Scottish-style "links" course. The island's newest course, **The Links at Crowbush Cove** (☎ 902/961–3274), near Morell, is expected to be rated among the top five courses in Canada, and many say it is PEI's best.

Hiking
Hiking within the lush scenic areas of Prince Edward Island National Park and provincial parks is encouraged with marked trails. Some of the abandoned railway lines on the island are being upgraded to walking trails that lead to previously inaccessible areas. Many country roads are now protected as heritage roads, and provide a smooth walking surface for an uncomplicated hike. Or, pull over near a beach, take off your shoes, wiggle your toes in the sand, and listen to the sound of the surf and the cry of the gulls as you explore miles of coastal nature.

DINING

On Prince Edward Island, plain, wholesome, home-cooked fare is a matter of course. The service is friendly—though a little laid back at times—and the setting is informal everywhere but in a few restaurants in Charlottetown. Seafood is generally good anywhere on the island, with top honors being given to lobster and any dish using local produce.

Look for lobster suppers, offered both commercially and by church and civic groups. These meals feature lobster, rolls, salad, and mountains of sweet, home-baked goodies, and are usually presented at New London, New Glasgow, St. Ann's Church in Hope River, and Fisherman's Wharf in North Rustico. Check the local papers or the bulletin boards at local grocery stores.

What to Wear
Prince Edward Island is a casual place, as are most places throughout the Atlantic Provinces. Unless otherwise noted there is no need to wear a jacket and tie.

CATEGORY	COST*
$$$$	over $35
$$$	$25–$35
$$	$15–$25
$	under $15

per person, excluding drinks, service, 10% sales tax, and 7% GST

Bay Fortune

$$$$ ★ Inn at Bay Fortune. Superb local fresh-caught and -harvested ingredients are served in an ambience reminiscent of a by-gone era. Dine amid antiques, many pieces collected by actress Colleen Dewhurst when she owned the inn. This is where the movers and shakers take those they wish to impress. ✕ *Rte. 310, ☎ 902/687–3745. Reservations advised. MC, V. Closed late Oct.–mid-May. No lunch.*

Brackley Beach

$$$ ★ Shaw's Hotel and Cottages. This family-oriented hotel dating from the 1860s offers fine home cooking in an elegant, country setting. Lobster is served twice weekly, and the grand Sunday-night buffets draw people from near and far to sample fresh salmon, seafood casserole, home-baked breads, and a variety of popular desserts, such as cheesecake and fresh berries in season. Lunch is served in the tea room. ✕ *Rte. 15, Brackley Beach C1E 1Z3 ☎ 902/672–2022. Reservations advised. AE, MC, V. Closed Oct.–May.*

$$–$$$ ★ Dunes Cafe. This stunning café is an integral part of a pottery studio, art gallery, artisans outlet, and outdoor gardens. Elegant, soaring, wood ceilings add to a spacious setting that seats more than 80 people on two levels, as well as on an outside deck overlooking the dunes and marshlands of Covehead Bay. The chef specializes in local seafood and island lamb, and dishes use locally-grown, fresh produce, much of which comes from the café's own gardens. ✕ *Rte. 15, ☎ 902/672–2586. Reservations advised. AE, MC, V. Closed Nov.–May. No dinner weekdays in June, Sept., and Oct.*

Cavendish

$$ Fiddles 'n Vittles. Lively, friendly, and decorated in rustic marine, with fishnets hanging in the dining room, the restaurant is true to its theme: House specialties are fresh and fried seafood. ✕ *Bay Vista Motor Inn, R.R. 1, Breadalbane, ☎ 902/963–3003. AE, DC, MC, V. Closed mid-Sept.–mid-June.*

Charlottetown

$$$$ Lord Selkirk. The island's most sophisticated dining room offers an extensive, imaginative menu and has special theme nights. Service and ambience match the chefs' excellence, and a wine steward tops off a fine meal with an appropriate vintage. The soothing stylings of a pianist are heard throughout the restaurant, which has several seating selections, from open spaces to intimate dining areas. Few other island eateries can compete with the expertly presented gourmet delights served here. Local fare is the house specialty, with imaginative and exciting preparation by a fine team of chefs. ✕ *Prince Edward Hotel, 18 Queen St., ☎ 902/566–2222 or 800/441–1414. Reservations advised. AE, DC, MC, V.*

$$$ Culinary Institute of Canada. Students at this internationally acclaimed school cook and present lunch and dinner during the school year as part of their training. Here's an opportunity to enjoy excellent food and top service at reasonable prices. Call for schedule and reservations. ✕ *Kent St., ☎ 902/566–9550. Reservations required. MC, V. Closed May–Sept.*

$$$ **Griffin Room.** This cozy dining room of the Dundee Arms inn has a work-
★ ing fireplace and is filled with antiques, copper, and brass. The French
Continental cuisine uses only fresh, natural ingredients. Fresh seafood
is served year-round, and salmon, scallops, and crab are available all
winter. Specialties include rack of lamb, chateaubriand, and poached
or grilled fillet of salmon in a light lime-dill sauce. ✕ *Dundee Arms,
200 Pownal St.,* ☎ *902/892–2496. Reservations advised. MC, V.*

$$–$$$ **Claddagh Room Restaurant.** You'll find some of the best seafood in
★ Charlottetown here. The "Galway Bay Delight," one of the Irish
owner's specialties, is a savory combination of fresh scallops and
shrimp sautéed with onions and mushrooms, flambéed in Irish Mist,
and doused with fresh cream. A pub upstairs features live Irish enter-
tainment every night in summer and on weekends in winter. ✕ *131
Sydney St.,* ☎ *902/892–9661. Reservations advised. AE, DC, MC, V.*

$$ **Off Broadway.** Popular with Charlottetown's young professional set
is this attractive, cozy spot located near the Confederation Centre of
the Arts. It began modestly as a crepe-and-soup joint, and indeed, you
can still make a meal of the lobster or chicken crepe and the spinach
or Caesar salad that's served with it. But the restaurant also has a fairly
inventive menu of such Continental entrées as the hearty mussel chowder, fillets, and salmon. The old-fashioned private booths won't reveal
your indiscretions—including your penchant for one of the many
desserts. ✕ *125 Sydney St.,* ☎ *902/566–4620. Reservations advised.
AE, MC, V.*

$ **Sam's Family Restaurant.** This 50s-style diner has vinyl booths and good,
basic food with all the requisite dishes, including great burgers and tasty
fish-and-chips. Try their fries-with-the-works for a filling chow-down.
Go early or late since locals fill the place during prime dining hours!
✕ *121 St. Peter's Rd.,* ☎ *902/628–6565. No credit cards.*

Grand Tracadie

$$$$ **Dalvay-by-the-Sea.** Choose a table by the stone fireplace or dine with
a lake view on the enclosed terrace. The menu at this Victorian dining
room, located in the Dalvay-by-the-Sea Hotel in PEI National Park,
can best be described as contemporary cuisine. The menu changes
monthly to take advantage of local produce, seafood, and seasonal island specialties. Desserts, rolls, and breads are baked on the premises.
✕ *Rte. 6, near Dalvay Beach,* ☎ *902/672–2048. Reservations advised.
AE, MC, V. Closed late Sept.–early June.*

LODGING

Prince Edward Island offers a variety of accommodations at a variety
of prices, from full-service resorts and luxury hotels to moderately priced
motels, cottages, and lodges, to farms that take guests. Lodgings on
the north coast in summer should be booked early, especially if you're
planning a long stay.

CATEGORY	COST*
$$$$	over $75
$$$	$55–$75
$$	$40–$55
$	under $40

**All prices are for a standard double room, excluding 10% provincial
sales tax and 7% GST.*

Bay Fortune

$$$$ **Inn at Bay Fortune.** The regularity with which this facility is on "most
★ recommended" lists confirms its reputation as an enticing, unforget-

table get-away. The former summer home of a Broadway playwright, and more recently of actress Colleen Dewhurst (Marilla in *Anne of Green Gables*), it's now a charming inn overlooking Fortune Harbour and Northumberland Straight, offering superb dining (*see* Dining, *above*), cooking classes from a top chef, and a taste of genteel living. A full breakfast is included in room rates. ⊞ *Rte. 310, Souris, R.R. 4, C0A 2B0,* ☎ *902/687–3745 or 203/633–4930 (off-season). 11 rooms with bath, 8 with fireplace sitting areas. Closed late Oct.–mid-May.*

Blooming Point

$–$$$ **Blue Heron Hideaways.** The MacAndrews, the owners, are a film producer and a journalist who run these executive-style cottages, a luxury beach-house, and a honeymoon cottage located just 15 minutes from downtown Charlottetown. The safe, private beach offers access to sand dunes and much wildlife and it's a great place for windsurfing. An outboard motorboat and gas barbecues are available for guest use. Weekly rentals only are available from early June through mid-October. ⊞ *Meadowbank, R.R. 2, Cornwall, C0A 1H0,* ☎ *902/566–2427,* ℻ *902/368–3798. 1 2-bedroom cottage, 2 3-bedroom cottages, 1 waterfront cottage with bunkhouse, 1 6-bedroom oceanfront house with guest house. Pool, windsurfing, boating. No credit cards.*

Brackley Beach

$$$–$$$$ **Shaw's Hotel and Cottages.** Each room is unique in this 1860s hotel,
★ with antique furnishings, floral-print wallpapers, and hardwood floors. Half the cottages have fireplaces. This country elegance doesn't come cheap; Shaw's is one of the most expensive hotels on the island, but guests are welcome to many extra facilities including sailing (on small vessels) and windsurfing. If you'd like, choose to include in your room rate a home-cooked breakfast and dinner in the Shaw's dining room (*see* Dining, *above*). ⊞ *Rte. 15, C1E 1Z3,* ☎ *902/672–2022,* ℻ *902/672–6000. 40 units, including 18 cottages and 2 suites. Restaurant, bar, beach, boating, playground. AE, MC, V. Closed late Sept.–May except for 6 cottages open year-round.*

Cavendish

$$$ **Bay Vista Motor Inn.** This clean, friendly motel caters to families. Parents can sit on the outdoor deck and admire the New London Bay panorama while keeping an eye on their children in the motel's large playground. Almost all of the rooms have views of the bay. Fiddles 'n Vittles (*see* Dining, *above*) is a great place to eat with the family. ⊞ *R.R. 1, Breadalbane, C0A 1E0; in winter, R.R. 1, North Wiltshire C0A 1Y0,* ☎ *902/963–2225. 30 units, including 2 motel efficiencies. Restaurant, pool, golf, boating, fishing, playground. AE, MC, V. Closed late Sept.–mid-June.*

Charlottetown

$$$$ **Best Western MacLauchlans.** One of the many good hotels in the Best Western chain, this one is convenient to downtown and contains 17 apartment suites with bedroom, living room, kitchen, and bathroom. A senior-citizens' program is available. ⊞ *238 Grafton St., C1A 1L5,* ☎ *902/892–2461,* ℻ *902/566–2979. 143 units. Restaurant, bar, pool, hot tub, sauna, exercise room. AE, DC, MC, V.*

$$$$ **The Charlottetown.** This five-story, redbrick hotel with white pillars and
★ a circular driveway is just two blocks from the center of Charlottetown. The rooms and public areas offer the latest amenities but retain the hotel's old-fashioned flavor, with well-detailed, antique-reproduction furnishings. The grandeur and charm of the Confederation Dining Room will take you back to the elegance of a previous era. ⊞ *Kent and Pownal Sts., Box 159, C1A 7K4,* ☎ *902/894–7371,* ℻ *902/368–2178.*

107 rooms, 2 suites. Dining room, bar, indoor pool, sauna. AE, DC, MC, V.

$$$$ **Dundee Arms.** Depending on your mood, you can choose to stay in either a 1960s motel or a 1904 inn. The motel is simple, modern, and neat; the inn is homey and furnished with brass and antiques. The Griffin Room (*see* Dining, *above*), the inn's dining room, serves fine French cuisine. Continental breakfast is included in motel and inn rates. ⌸ *200 Pownal St., C1A 3W8,* ☎ *902/892–2496,* ℻ *902/368–8532. 18 rooms, including 2 suites. Restaurant, pub. MC, V.*

$$$$ **Prince Edward Hotel.** This hotel has received numerous prestigious in-
★ dustry awards, and for good reason. A member of the Canadian Pacific chain of hotels and resorts, the Prince Edward has all the comforts and luxuries of its first-rate counterparts—from Jacuzzis in some suites to a grand ballroom and conference center. Guest rooms are modern and decorated in warm pastels, and two-thirds of the units in this 10-story hotel overlook the developed Charlottetown waterfront. The lobby is a bright, open, two-story atrium complete with a waterfall above the front desk. ⌸ *18 Queen St., Box 2170, C1A 8B9,* ☎ *902/566–2222 or 800/441–1414,* ℻ *902/566–2282. 211 rooms, including 33 suites. 2 restaurants, bar, indoor pool, sauna, exercise room. AE, DC, MC, V.*

$$–$$$ **Duchess of Kent Inn.** This turreted Victorian bed-and-breakfast is packed with antiques, even in the bedrooms. It's within walking distance of Charlottetown's major sites, including the Confederation Centre. ⌸ *218 Kent St., C1A 1P2,* ☎ *902/566–5826 or 800/665–5826. 7 rooms share 5 baths. Closed Dec.–Apr.*

$$ **Sherwood Motel.** This is a small, clean, family-oriented motel about 5 kilometers (3 miles) north of downtown Charlottetown on Route 15. The friendly owners offer help in reserving tickets for events and planning day trips. Don't be daunted by the Sherwood's proximity to the airport—the motel sees very little traffic. ⌸ *R.R. 9, Winsloe, C1E 1Z3,* ☎ *902/892–1622 or 800/567–1622. 30 rooms with bath; 22 with kitchenettes; pets permitted. Kitchenettes. MC, V.*

$ **Court Bed and Breakfast.** In a residential area 2 kilometers (a little over a mile) from downtown, this two-story bed-and-breakfast with a welcoming red door offers large, simple, comfortable rooms and a full, hearty breakfast, including ham, eggs, bacon, muffins, and fresh fruits in season. ⌸ *68 Hutchinson Ct., C1A 8H7,* ☎ *902/894–5871. 2 rooms with shared bath. No credit cards. Closed Sept.–Apr.*

Grand Tracadie

$$$$ **Dalvay-by-the-Sea.** Just within the borders of the Prince Edward Island
★ National Park is this Victorian house, built in 1896 as a private summer home. Now a popular inn and restaurant, Dalvay-by-the-Sea offers Victorian-style rooms furnished with original antiques and reproductions. Guests can sip drinks or tea on the porch while admiring the inn's gardens, Dalvay Lake, or the nearby beach. If you want a little more action take a rowboat or canoe out on the lake. Breakfasts and dinners in the dining room, included in the room rates, are exceptional (*see* Dining, *above*). ⌸ *Rte. 6, near Dalvay Beach. Box 8, York, C0A 1P0,* ☎ *902/672–2048, or 902/672–2546 in winter. 31 rooms in main house and 2 cottages. Restaurant, bar, driving range, 2 tennis courts, windsurfing, boating. AE, MC, V. Closed mid-Sept.–mid-June.*

Montague

$$ **Lobster Shanty.** Roses growing outside the windows of its weathered-
wood facade, lovely vistas regardless of the weather, and the barn-
board–walled dining room contribute to the charming style of this motel. All rooms have picture windows and open onto a deck that overlooks the Montague River. A favorite pastime of guests is to go clam-digging

on the nearby beach. ☎ *102 Main St. S, C0A 1R0,* ☎ *902/838–2463,* FAX *902/838–5110. 10 rooms. Restaurant, bar. AE, MC, V.* ☉ *Year–round.*

O'Leary

$$$$ **Rodd's Mill River Resort and Conference Centre.** With activities ranging from night skiing and tobogganing to golfing, this is truly an all-season resort. An international dog-sled racing weekend is a popular winter event. Ask about year-round family-weekend packages. ☎ *Box 399, C0B 1V0,* ☎ *902/859–3555 or 800/565–RODD,* FAX *902/859–2486. 90 rooms including 3 suites. Dining room, 2 bars, 2 indoor pools, sauna, golf course, tennis court, squash, exercise room, windsurfing, boating, bicycles, ice-skating, cross-country skiing, tobogganing, pro shop. AE, MC, V. Closed Nov.–early Dec., Apr.*

Roseneath

$$$$ **Rodd's Brudenell River Resort.** A distinctive facility which opened in 1992, this is a great spot for the sports-minded, with it's indoor and outdoor swimming pools, 18-hole championship golf course, tennis courts, horseback riding, lawn bowling, canoeing, and two marinas. ☎ *Off Rte. 3 to Georgetown, Box 67, Cardigan, C0A 1G0,* ☎ *902/652–2332 or 800/565–0207, winter 902/892–7448,* FAX *902/652–2886. 50 rooms, 38 riverside chalets. Dining room, bar, sauna, exercise room. AE, MC, V. Closed Nov.–Apr.*

Summerside

$$$ **Loyalist Country Inn.** Located at the waterfront, this traditional inn with Victorian decor is close to the Eptek National Exhibition Centre and PEI Sports Hall of Fame, a marina, shopping mall, and outdoor summer entertainment. ☎ *195 Harbour Dr., Summerside, C1N 5B2,* ☎ *902/436–3333, 800/361–2668,* FAX *902/436–4304. 50 rooms, 10 with whirlpool. Dining room, bar, indoor pool, sauna, tennis court. AE, DC, MC, V.*

$$–$$$ **Quality Inn Garden of the Gulf.** Close to downtown Summerside, this clean motel is a convenient place to stay. The nine-hole golf course on the property slopes to Bedeque Bay. ☎ *618 Water St. E, C1N 2V5,* ☎ *902/436–2295 or 800/265–5551,* FAX *902/436–6277. 83 rooms, including 6 suites. Restaurant, bar, coffee shop, indoor and outdoor pools, 9-hole golf course. AE, DC, MC, V.*

$$ **Glade Motor Inn and Cottages.** Conveniently located 10 minutes from the Borden Ferry Terminal, this property has comfortable if generic motel rooms as well as cottages. What's different about the place is that it is set on a 300-acre farm, with horseback riding and nature trails. Kids get free rides in the corral. ☎ *Box 1387, C1N 4K2,* ☎ *902/436–5564. 33 units. Restaurant, bar, pool. AE, MC, V. Closed late-Sept.–mid-June.*

Tyne Valley

$$ **The Doctor's Inn Bed & Breakfast.** This charming, beautifully landscaped village home is a joy in summer, with its beds of herbs and flowers. The inn caters to cross-country skiers on winter weekends. There's plenty of opportunity to gather 'round the woodstove or fireplace and share good conversation over a warm drink. One dining room table seats up to eight, where you can experience fine meals based on what is available from local fishermen and farmers and from the inn's own organic gardens. ☎ *1 Rte. 167, C0B 2C0,* ☎ *902/831–2164. 2 rooms with shared bath. V.*

West Point

$$$ **West Point Lighthouse.** This unique property is still a functioning lighthouse (though automated), situated adjacent to a provincial park.

Nearby are nature trails and opportunities to dig clams, fish, and bike. Within the lighthouse is a museum and licensed dining room and patio; outside is the beach. Two rooms have a whirlpool tub. Bicycles available for guests. ⌂ *R.R. 2, O'Leary, C0B 1V0,* ☎ *902/859–3605 or 800/764–6854. 9 rooms. AE, MC, V. Closed Oct.–early May.*

THE ARTS

The highlights of the island's theater season are the productions of the **Charlottetown Festival,** which takes place from June through mid-September at the Confederation Centre of the Arts.

Special art exhibitions are offered in the Confederation Centre Art Gallery and Muse, one of Canada's premier museums. The permanent collection features the country's largest assemblage of paintings by Robert Harris (1848–1919), Canada's foremost portrait artist. For information and tickets to the festival, contact the **Confederation Centre of the Arts** (145 Richmond St., Charlottetown C1A 1J1, ☎ 902/628–1864; box office, 902/566–1267).

Eptek National Exhibition Centre and PEI Sports Hall of Fame, on the waterfront properties in Summerside, displays changing history and fine arts exhibits from all parts of Canada. *Harbour Dr., Summerside, C1N 1A9,* ☎ *902/888–8873.* ☞ *Admission charged.* ☉ *June–Sept., daily; Oct.–May, Tues.–Sun.*

The **King's Playhouse** (☎ 902/652–2053) in Georgetown, 50 kilometers (30 miles) east of Charlottetown, offers varied entertainment from June through early September. The **Victoria Playhouse** (☎ 902/658–2025) in Victoria, a half-hour's drive west of Charlottetown, features professional repertory theater. **The Feast** (☎ 902/436–7674) dinner-theater provides rollicking entertainment and a satisfying meal, hosting productions at Brothers Two Water Street Station restaurant in Summerside, as well as at various hotels in Charlottetown. **La Cuisine a Mémé** (☎ 902/854–2227), a French dinner-theater, offers typical Acadian entertainment, such as step-dancing and fiddle music, and a buffet in Mont-Carmel.

Concerts and musical festivals abound on the island, especially in summer. Live traditional Celtic music, with fiddling and step-dancing, can be heard almost any day of the week. Best bets: the outdoor fiddle festival (☎ 902/368–5555) at Rollo Bay in late July; the **College of Piping and Celtic Performing Arts of Canada** (☎ 902/436–5377) summer concerts and highland games in Summerside; Friday night ceilidhs at the **Benevolent Irish Hall** (☎ 902/892–2367) in Charlottetown; and the Sunday concerts of classical, sacred, and traditional music at **St. Mary's Church** (☎ 902/836–3733) in Indian River, between Charlottetown and Summerside.

PRINCE EDWARD ISLAND ESSENTIALS

Arriving and Departing

By Ferry
Two car-ferry services serve Prince Edward Island. **Marine Atlantic** (☎ 902/794–5700 or 902/855–2030) sails between Cape Tormentine, New Brunswick, and Borden, year-round, crossing daily between 6:30 AM and 1 AM. The crossing takes about 45 minutes and costs approximately $20 per car round-trip plus $8.50 per adult. The second service, **Northumberland Ferries** (☎ 902/566–3838; in the Maritimes, 800/565–

0201), sails between Caribou, Nova Scotia, and Wood Islands, from May to mid-December. The crossing takes about 75 minutes, and the round-trip costs approximately $27.25 per automobile and $7.75 per adult (reduced rates for senior citizens and children). No fares are collected inbound; you pay only on leaving the island. Neither service takes reservations.

By Plane

Charlottetown Airport is 5 kilometers (3 miles) north of town. **Air Canada** (☎ 902/892–1007 or 800/776–3000) and **Canadian Airlines International** (☎ 902/892–4581 or 800/665–1177) offer daily service to major cities in eastern Canada and the United States via Halifax. **Prince Edward Air** (☎ 902/892–5816) offers nonstop service to Moncton and Halifax from Summerside and Charlottetown. **Northwest Airlink** (☎ 902/628–6665 or 800/225–2525) operates a regular daily flight schedule between PEI and Boston.

Getting Around by Car

There are more than 3,700 kilometers (2,294 miles) of paved road in the province, including the three scenic coastal drives called Lady Slipper Drive, Blue Heron Drive, and Kings Byway. The adventurous will enjoy exploring the designated "Heritage Roads," which consist of red clay, the native soil base. These unpaved roads meander through undeveloped areas of rural PEI, where you're likely to see lots of wildflowers and birds. A four-wheel-drive vehicle is not necessary, but in spring and when the weather is bad the mud can get very deep.

Guided Tours

The island offers about 20 sightseeing tours, including double-decker bus tours, cycling tours, harbor cruises, and walking tours. Most tour companies are located in Charlottetown and offer excursions around the city and to the beaches.

Important Addresses and Numbers

Emergencies
Police and **fire,** dial 0.

Hospital
Queen Elizabeth Hospital (Riverside Dr., ☎ 902/566–6200).

Visitor Information
For prices and information before your trip, contact the **Prince Edward Island Department of Economic Development & Tourism,** Quality Service Division (Box 940, Charlottetown, PEI C1A 7M5, ☎ 902/368–4444 or 800/463–4PEI, FAX 902/368–4438). The department offers an excellent annual "Visitor's Guide," and maintains eight **Visitor Information Centres (VICs)** on the island. The main VIC is in Charlottetown (Oak Tree Pl., University Ave., ☎ 902/368–4444 or 902/463–4PEI, FAX 902/368–4438), and is open mid-May–October, daily; November–mid-May, weekdays.

6 Newfoundland and Labrador

Canada's easternmost province, Newfoundland, was a center of the world's cod fishing industry for 400 years until the supply ran out in 1992. In summer, Newfoundland's stark cliffs, bogs, and meadows become a riot of wildflowers and greenery, and the sea is dotted with boats and buoys. St. John's, the capital, is a classic harbor city.

By Margaret
M. Kearney

Updated by
Ana Watts

NEWFOUNDLAND WAS THE FIRST PLACE explorers John Cabot (1497) and Gaspar Corte-Real (1500) touched down in the New World. Exactly where they went no one knows, for neither survived a second voyage. But while he was here, Cabot reported that he saw fish in the water so thick you could dip your line in anywhere and catch as much as you wanted. Within a decade of the explorers' discovery, St. John's had become a crowded harbor. Fishing boats from France, England, Spain, and Portugal vied for a chance to catch Newfoundland's lucrative cod, which was to subsequently shape the province's history and geography.

At one time there were 700 hard-working settlements or "outports" dotting Newfoundland's coast, each devoted to catching, salting, and drying the world's most plentiful fish. Today, only about 600 of these settlements survive. Newfoundland's most famous resource has become so scarce that a partial fishing moratorium was declared in 1992 and extended in 1993. While the province waits for the cod to return, some 25,000 fishers and processors are going to school instead of going fishing.

Newfoundland and Labrador became part of Canada in 1949. For almost 400 years previous, however, the government had survived perfectly well on its own, until the Great Depression forced its economy to go belly-up. After 40-some years of confederation with Canada, the economy of the province has improved considerably, but the people are still of independent mind: Newfoundlanders regard themselves as North America's first separatists and maintain a unique language and lifestyle as well as their own customs.

Visitors to Newfoundland find themselves straddling the centuries. Old accents and customs are common in small towns and outports, yet the major cities of St. John's on the east coast and Corner Brook on the west coast are very much part of the 20th century. Regardless of where you visit—an isolated outport or lively Water Street—you're sure to interact with some of the warmest, wittiest people in North America. Strangers have always been welcome in Newfoundland, since the days when locals brought visitors in from out of the cold, warmed them by the fire, and charmingly interrogated them for news of events outside the province.

Before you can shoot the breeze, though, you'll have to acclimate yourself to the language: It's English all right, but provincial dialects are strong and vary from place to place. Newfoundland is one of two provinces in Canada with their own dictionaries. Prince Edward Island is the other, but its book has only 873 entries. The Newfoundland Dictionary has more than 5,000 words, mostly having to do with fishery, weather, and scenery. To get started, you can practice with the name of the province—it's *New'fun'l'nd,* with the accent on "land." However, only "livyers" ever get the pronunciation exactly right.

Depending on the time of year you visit, your experiences will be dramatically different. In spring icebergs float down from the north, and fin, pilot, minke, and humpback whales hunt for food along the coast. Their preferred cuisine? Caplin, a small, smeltlike fish that moves in schools and spawns on Newfoundland's many pebble beaches. During the summer, temperate days turn Newfoundland's stark cliffs, bogs, and meadows into a riot of wildflowers and greenery; and the sea is dotted with boats and buoys marking traps and nets. Fall is a favored season: The weather is usually fine; cliffs and meadows are loaded with berries; and the woods are alive with moose, elk, partridges, and rabbits, to name just a few residents. In the winter, the forest trails hum with the sound of snowmobiles and ATVs hauling wood home or taking the fishermen to their favorite lodges and lakes.

The tourist season runs from June through September, when the province is awash with festivals, fairs, concerts, plays, and crafts shows. A popular vacation plan for locals is to go gravel-pit camping: It's the tradition of parking a trailer in a handy place near a brook or pond and setting up camp. There's usually no view, but free campsites and sociable company make up for most inconveniences. Not only is camping—in a bare site or one with amenities—an inexpensive way for the family to vacation together, but it's a good way to take advantage of Newfoundland's pollution-free environment: Nice days are just that, with bright, intense sunshine, free of smog or haze. The temperature in late June through early September hovers between 75 and 85 degrees, and gently cools off in the evening, providing a good night's sleep.

EXPLORING

Tours in this chapter divide the province into the island of Newfoundland, beginning with St. John's and the Avalon Peninsula, and move west. Labrador is considered as a whole, with suggested driving and train excursions.

Tour 1: St. John's and the Avalon Peninsula

Numbers in the margin correspond to points of interest on the Newfoundland and Labrador map.

When Sir Humphrey Gilbert sailed into St. John's to establish British colonial rule for Queen Elizabeth in 1583, he found Spanish, French, and Portuguese fishermen actively working the harbor. As early as 1627, the merchants of Water Street—then known as "the lower path"—were doing a thriving business buying fish, selling goods, and supplying booze to soldiers and sailors. Today the city still encircles the snug, punchbowl harbor that helped establish its reputation.

St. John's

True early birds can begin their tour of the area at daybreak by filling up a thermos of coffee, getting some muffins, and driving on Route ★ ❶ 11 to **Cape Spear,** so they can be among the first to watch the sun come up over North America. Song birds begin their chirping in the dim light of dawn and whales feed directly below the cliffs, providing an unforgettable start to the day. **Cape Spear Lighthouse** (☎ 709/772–5367), Newfoundland's oldest such beacon, has been lovingly restored to its original form and furnishings and is open to visitors, daily 10–6 from early June through Labor Day.

❷ Those who are less ambitious may wish to begin exploring **St. John's** a little later in the day, when the Tourist Chalet on the waterfront is open. This is an old converted railway caboose, staffed from May through October. *Harbor Dr.,* ☎ *709/576–8514.* ☉ *May–Oct., daily 9–7.*

Whichever way you look—left or right—you'll see the always-fascinating array of ships that tie up along **Harbour Drive.** Walk the harbor front, a favorite route in St. John's, to the **Battery,** a tiny, still-active fishing village perched precariously on the steep cliffs between hill and harbor. A well-maintained 5-kilometer (3-mile) walking path leads ★ along the cliff edge, through the narrows, and zigzags through **Signal**

Hill National Historic Park. Alternatively, you can drive on the road that also leads to the park.

In spite of its height, Signal Hill was difficult to defend: Throughout the 1600s and 1700s it changed hands with every attacking French, English, and Dutch force. A wooden palisade encircles the summit of the hill, indicating the boundaries of the old fortifications. En route to the hill is the **Park Interpretation Centre,** with exhibits describing St. John's history. ☎ 709/772–5367. ☾ *Labor Day–May, daily 8:30–4:30; June–Labor Day, daily 8:30–8.*

Gibbet Hill, the rocky knob immediately to the west of the Interpretation Centre, was at one time used by local "authorities" as a place to hang miscreants. These dangling unfortunates were meant to send the message to anyone entering the harbor that misconduct would not be tolerated by the ruling fishing admiral. From the top of the hill it's a 500-foot drop to the narrow harbor entrance below.

Cabot Tower, at the summit of Signal Hill, was constructed in 1897 to commemorate the 400th anniversary of Cabot's discovery of Newfoundland. In 1901, in the shadow of the tower, Guglielmo Marconi received the first transatlantic wireless message, from Cornwall, England—the opening salvo in a communication revolution that would change the world. The tower is open to the public and contains a display on communications history. ☎ 709/772–5367. ☛ *Free.* ☾ *Labor Day–early June, daily 9–5; mid-June–Labor Day, daily 8:30–8, guides available on weekends in summer.*

If you are driving, come down from Signal Hill, make a right turn at Quidi Vidi Road, and continue to the right, down Forest Road, to **Quidi Vidi Village,** an authentic fishing community whose history goes back to the beginning of St. John's. If you are walking, paths lead from the summit and the Interpretation Centre to the village. **Quidi Vidi Battery,** near the entrance to the village harbor, is a small redoubt which has been restored to the way it appeared in 1812 and is staffed by costumed interpreters who will tell you about the hard, unromantic life of a soldier of the empire. *Quidi Vidi Village,* ☎ 709/729–2460 *or* 709/729–2977. ☛ *Free.* ☾ *July–early Sept., daily 10–5:30; winter by appointment.*

Quidi Vidi Lake, to the west of the village, is encircled by a leisurely path, popular with walkers and joggers. It's the site of the **St. John's Annual Regatta,** the oldest continuing sporting event in North America, which first took place in 1826. Weather permitting, the regatta begins on the first Wednesday in August: If you're in town you shouldn't miss it.

From the lake, follow the **Rennies River Trail** (4½ kilometers, or 3 miles) that cuts through the city along a wooded stream and ends at the only public fluvarium in North America, where you can observe spawning brown and brook trout in their natural habitat through underwater windows. Feeding time for the fish, frogs, and eels is 4 PM daily. *Newfoundland Freshwater Resource Center, Pippy Park,* ☎ 709/754–3474. ☛ *$2.75 adults, $2.25 students and senior citizens, $1.50 children.* ☾ *July–Aug., daily 9–5, guided tours at 11 AM, 1 and 3 PM; Sept.–June, closed Wed., open Sun. noon–4:30, every other day 9–4:30.*

To get back downtown, retrace your steps along the Rennies River Trail by foot, or drive down Prince Phillip's Drive and turn right onto Portugal Cove Road. This runs into New Cove Road—follow this and turn right onto King's Bridge Road which intersects with Water Street. As you walk around St. John's, you'll notice the diversity of architectural

QUEBEC

L'Anse
Loup
L'Anse au Clair
Blanc Sablon
Forreau
**L'Anse
Amour**
51 **Red Bay**
Cooks Har.
Raleigh
Cape
Onion
**L'Anse aux A
National His**
43
(510)
(436)
49 **50**
Strait of Belle
Isle
Flowers
Cove
(430)
Brig Bay
St. Barbe
Hare Bay
St. Julien's
Groais I.
44 **St.
Anthony**

Bartletts Har.
Port au Choix
Roddickton
Bell I.

Hawke Bay
(430)
Bellburns
Harbour Deep

Portland Creek
The Arches Provincial Park **42**
Fleur de Lys

Cow Head
St. Pauls
Jackson Arm
Baie Verte
La Scie

Rocky Harbour **41**
Bonne Bay
Woody Point **39**
Trout River **40**
**Gros Morne
Nat'l Park** **38**
Rattling
Brook
Nippers
Har.
Twillingate
Notre Dame
Bay
Fo
(410)
Springdale

**Richard
Squires
Memorial
Park** **37**
Sandy
Lake
South
Brook
(1)

Cox
Cove
36 **Deer
Lake**
Millertown
Junction
Badger
Botwood
Lew

York Harbour
Voys Beach
Corner Brook **45**
Lewis Hills
Humbermouth
Grand
Lake
Buchans
Red
Indian
Lake
(370)
(360)
**Grand Falls-
Windsor** **32**
G

Black Duck
Brook
Mainland
Port Au
Port
Peninsula
**Point au Mal
Prov. Park** **46**
47
Stephenville

St. Teresa
St. George's Bay
Jeffery's
(404)
Meelpaeg
Lake
Round
Lake
NEWFOUNDLAND
Po

Codroy R.
Cape
Anguille
(405)
N. Branch
St. Albans
(406)
(1)
Mountains
Long
Range
Hardy Cove
Terrence
(360)
(407)
**Port-
aux-Basques** **48**
Rose
Blanche
Burgeo
Harbour
Breton
Marystown **25**
Burin
Peninsula
Salt
Pond
**Grand
Bank**
26
Fortune
27
30
Buri
Gr. Miquelon I.
**Miquelon
(France)**
Lit. Miquelon I.
28
(220)
29
St. Lawren

TO NORTH SYDNEY
(Nova Scotia)
**St. Pierre
(France)**

Gulf of St. Lawrence
Long Range Mountains
White Bay
TO GOOSE BAY
(Labrador)
Marble Mountain
Buchans

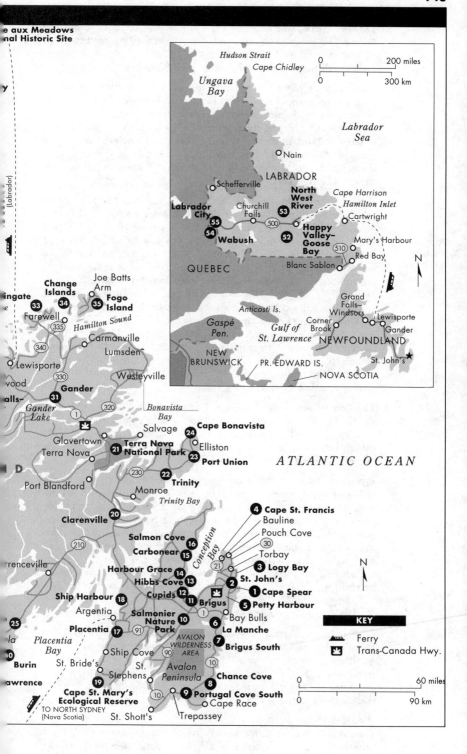

e aux Meadows
nal Historic Site

(Labrador)

Hudson Strait
Cape Chidley

0   200 miles
0   300 km

Ungava
Bay

Labrador
Sea

Nain

LABRADOR

Scheffferville

North
West
River

Cape Harrison
Hamilton Inlet

Labrador
City   **55**

Churchill
Falls   **53**

Cartwright

54

Wabush

500   **52**

Happy
Valley-
Goose
Bay

Mary's Harbour

510   Red Bay

QUEBEC

Blanc Sablon

N

Anticosti Is.

Grand
Falls–
Windsors

Gaspé
Pen.

Gulf of
St. Lawrence

Corner
Brook

Lewisporte

Gander

NEW
BRUNSWICK

PR. EDWARD IS.

NOVA SCOTIA

NEWFOUNDLAND

St. John's

ingate

**Change
Islands**

Joe Batts
Arm

33   **34**

35   **Fogo
Island**

Farewell

335

Hamilton Sound

340

Carmanville

Lumsden

Lewisporte

330

Wesleyville

wood

Gander

Gander
Lake

320

31

1

Salvage

Bonavista
Bay

Cape Bonavista

24

alls–

Glovertown

Terra Nova

**Terra Nova
National Park**

21

Elliston

23   **Port Union**

Port Blandford

230

22   **Trinity**

Monroe

Trinity Bay

ATLANTIC OCEAN

Clarenville

20

210

4 **Cape St. Francis**
Bauline
Pouch Cove

Salmon Cove

16

30

renceville

Carbonear

15

Conception
Bay

Torbay

Harbour Grace

14

3 **Logy Bay**

Hibbs Cove

13

21

Cupids

12

2   **St. John's**

Ship Harbour

18

11   **Brigus**

1 **Cape Spear**

Argentia

1

5 **Petty Harbour**

**Salmonier
Nature
Park**

10

6   Bay Bulls

Placentia

17

91

La Manche

25

Placentia
Bay

Ship Cove

**AVALON
WILDERNESS
AREA**

90

7   **Brigus South**

la

10

Burin

St. Bride's

St.
Stephens

Avalon
Peninsula

10

Chance Cove

awrence

**Cape St. Mary's
Ecological Reserve**

19

10

9 **Portugal Cove South**

Cape Race

TO NORTH SYDNEY
(Nova Scotia)

St. Shott's

Trepassey

8

KEY

Ferry

Trans-Canada Hwy.

0   60 miles
0   90 km

N

styles due to two major fires: one in 1846 and another in 1892. The 1892 fire stopped where George and Water streets intersect, at **Yellowbelly Corner.** This junction was so-named because in the 19th century it was a gathering spot for Irish immigrants from Wexford who wore yellow sashes to distinguish themselves from their Waterford rivals.

Look west on Water Street, where the block still resembles a typical Irish market town of the 1840s. To the east, however, Victorian-style architecture predominates, with curved mansard roofs typical of the popular Second Empire style. After the 1892 fire the city's elite moved to **Circular Road,** in the center of the city, out of reach of future fires, and built a string of impressive and highly ornamented Victorian mansions, which bear witness to the sizable fortunes made in the old days from the humble cod.

While you're downtown, take a look at the churches of St. John's, rich in architectural history. The **Basilica of St. John the Baptist** (Military Rd., ☎ 709/754–2170), with a commanding position above Military Road, overlooks the older section of the city and the harbor. The land was granted to the church by young Queen Victoria, and the edifice was built with stones from both Ireland and Newfoundland. From here you can also see the **Anglican Cathedral of St. John the Baptist** (22 Church Hill, ☎ 709/726–5677) on Church Hill, one of the finest examples of Gothic Revival architecture in North America. Nearby is the imposing **Gower Street United Church** (Gower St., ☎ 709/753–7286), with its redbrick facade and green turrets. At the bottom of Military Road, adjacent to Hotel Newfoundland, is the **St. Thomas Old Garrison Church** (Military Rd., ☎ 709/576–6632), where the English soldiers used to worship during the early and mid-1800s. All these churches usually schedule summer tours.

The **Commissariat House** (Kings Bridge Rd., ☎ 709/729–2460 or 709/729–6730), just around the corner from the Anglican church, has been restored to the way it appeared when it served as residence and office of the British garrison's supply officer in the 1830s. The interpreters—dressed in period costume—will show you around.

If you have time, set aside a morning or an afternoon to visit the **Memorial University Botanical Garden** in Pippy Park. This 110-acre garden and natural area at Oxen Pond has four pleasant walking trails and many gardens, including rock gardens and scree, a Newfoundland heritage-plants bed, ericaceous borders, peat and woodland beds, a wildlife garden, an alpine house, wildfire cottage and vegetable gardens, an herb wall, and native plant collections. The environmental education programs include seasonal indoor exhibits, introductory garden tours, wildflower and bird-watching walks, and many other special events. *306 Mt. Scio Rd., Pippy Park,* ☎ *709/737–8590.* ☛ *Fee is nominal.* ✆ *May–Nov., Wed.–Sun. 10–5; July and Aug., daily 10–5, till 8 Tues. and Thurs.*

Another beautiful spot in St. John's is **Bowring Park,** on Waterford Bridge Road. The expansive Victorian park was donated to the city by the wealthy Bowring family in 1911, and resembles the famous-inner city parks of London, England, after which it was modeled. Dotting the grounds are artfully designed ponds, ducks to feed, and rustic bridges; there's also a statue of Peter Pan.

Avalon Peninsula

Several half-day, full-day, and two-day excursions are possible from St. John's, and in each direction a different personality of the region unfolds. On the southern half of the peninsula are small Irish hamlets separated by large tracts of wilderness. The population of the northern half is more dense and still reflects its origin in Dorset and Devon, England. Here, homes are perched on narrow spits of land or tucked into the lee of cliffs.

COAST NORTH OF ST. JOHN'S

You can take a leisurely half-day trip to explore the scenic coastline north of St. John's. Take Route 30 (Logy Bay Road) to Marine Drive, ❸ which winds along the coastline, passing through **Logy Bay** and its remarkable cliffs. Along the way is **Ocean Sciences Centre,** with its outdoor seal tank where you can watch the animals frolic. Large aquariums in the Discovery Room are filled with local marine life, and a Touch Tank gives everyone a chance to meet and examine many marine animals face-to-face. *Marine Lab Rd.,* ☎ *709/737–3243.* ☛ *$2.50 adults, $1.50 senior citizens and children.* ⊘ *Victoria Day–Labor Day, daily 10–5, tours every ½-hr.*

Follow Route 30 to **Torbay** and turn west onto Route 21 to **Bauline,** an unspoiled fishing village that overlooks Conception Bay. Continue on Route 21 to **Pouch Cove,** one of the province's oldest communities, where the adventurous should follow the unpaved road that leads to ❹ **Cape St. Francis.** On the way to the cape, there's a short coastal walk. A local legend centers around the wreck of the *Waterwitch,* which capsized in 1875 in the water at the northern edge of Pouch Cove. Alfred Moores rescued 11 people from the floundering vessel by lowering himself by rope down the cliff. A sign marks the site along the coastal walk, but you can't see the wreck.

Leave Pouch Cove on Route 20 and head straight back, or connect to Route 30, which loops around toward Logy Bay, on your return to St. John's. For one more scenic pleasure en route, take in some views at the village of **Flat Rock,** on Route 20 just past Pouch Cove.

COAST SOUTH OF ST. JOHN'S

You can travel part of the peninsula's coast for a one- or two-day excursion, depending on how much time you have. Quaint coastal towns line the road, and the natural sites are beautiful.

Just south of St. John's pick up Route 10 and follow it along the southern coast toward Trepassey. Locals call this trip "going up the shore," even though it looks like you're traveling down on a map. The wildness of this coast is usually what's most striking to visitors, and La Manche and Chance Cove—both now-abandoned communities turned provincial parks—attest to the bounty of natural resources of the region.

Although a visit to many of the hamlets along the way will fulfill any ❺ search for prettiness, a few favorites are exceptional. **Petty Harbour,** ❻ ❼ **La Manche,** and **Brigus South,** have especially attractive settings and strong traditional flavors.

❽ ❾ In springtime, between **Chance Cove** and **Portugal Cove South,** in a stretch of land about 58 kilometers (36 miles) long, hundreds of caribou and their calves gather on the wide barrens near the road. Although the graceful animals are there during other times of the year, their numbers are few and it's difficult to spot them because they blend in so well with the scenery.

Route 10 loops around the peninsula and becomes Route 90, just past **St. Stephens.**

At the intersection of Routes 90 and 91, in Salmonier, you need to decide whether to continue north toward Salmonier Nature Park and on to Conception Bay, or to head west then south to Route 100 to Cape St. Mary's Ecological Reserve (*see* Route 100: The Cape Shore, *below*). Each option takes about three hours.

10 If you've decided to go north, travel to **Salmonier Nature Park,** 9 miles along, where visitors can see many of the animal species that are indigenous to the province. The park is a 1,214-hectare wilderness reserve area and has an enclosed 40.5 hectare exhibit that allows up-close viewing. *Salmonier Line, Rte. 90,* ☎ *709/729–6974 or 709/229–7888.* ☛ *Free.* ⊘ *Early June–Labor Day, Thurs.–Mon., noon–7; other times by appointment.*

Farther along Route 90 the road passes through the scenic Hawkes Hills, before meeting up with the Trans-Canada Highway (Route 1). Turn off at the Holyrood Junction (Route 62) and follow Route 70, which
11 skirts **Conception Bay,** to **Brigus.** Meander through this beautifully restored village with winding lanes, a teahouse, a floral park, and a museum set in a stone barn, where you can pick up a walking-tour brochure. *Ye Olde Stone Barn Museum, 4 Magistrate's Hill,* ☎ *709/528–3298.* ☛ *$1 adults, 50¢ children.* ⊘ *June–Labor Day, daily 1–5; Sept. and Oct., weekends 1–5.*

Brigus was the home of many sealing captains, including Captain Bob Bartlett, who in 1909 guided Commodore Perry to within 161 kilometers (100 miles) of the North Pole. Perry abandoned Bartlett before going on the last leg so he could claim full honors for himself. The move backfired, however, for without Bartlett's testimony Perry couldn't prove that he actually made the journey.

12 Continue on Route 70 to **Cupids,** founded in 1610 by the Bristol merchant John Guy and the site of the first permanent colony in Newfoundland.

Just beyond Brigus, Route 70 passes by Clarke's Beach, where you should turn right and follow Route 72 along a narrow sliver of land to **Port**
13 **de Grave** and **Hibbs Cove.** The **Port de Grave Fishermen's Museum, Porter House,** and **Old School House Community Museum** are actually in Hibbs Cove. Here you can learn about Newfoundland fisherman life-styles from the 1600s until the present. *Hibbs Cove, off Rte. 72,* ☎ *709/786–3912 or 709/786–3900.* ☛ *$1 adults, 50¢ students.* ⊘ *Mid-June–late June, daily 1–5; July–Labor Day, Mon.–Sat. 10–noon and 1–5, Sun. 1–5.*

14 About 10 miles farther on Route 70 is **Harbour Grace,** which was once the headquarters of Peter Easton, a 17th-century pirate. Beginning in 1919, Harbour Grace was the departure point for many attempts to fly the Atlantic. Amelia Earhart left Harbour Grace in 1932 to become the first woman to fly solo across the Atlantic. Several handsome stone churches and buildings remain as evidence of the town's pride.

15 Continue along Route 70 to **Carbonear,** another town with a fascinating history. In 1696 it was burned to the ground by the French, but the inhabitants retreated to a small fortified island in the harbor and successfully defended it against capture. Carbonear Island has been designated a National Historic Site to mark its colorful military past.

16 Farther along Route 70 is picturesque **Salmon Cove,** a sheltered bay with a grassy picnic area. The road is narrow and partly unpaved, but you'll be rewarded with the finest views of Conception Bay, especially as you drive up and over Blow Me Down Head. If you plan to travel on to **Bay de Verde,** at the northern tip of the peninsula, and down the other side of the peninsula on Route 80 along Trinity Bay, consider turning in for the night at one of the several hotels or bed-and-break-fasts (*see* Lodging, *below*) in the Harbour Grace–Carbonear area. Otherwise turn around and follow the same route back.

ROUTE 100: THE CAPE SHORE

If you opted for the Cape Shore route, from Salmonier west on Route 91 and south on Route 100, you're headed to Avalon's Cape St. Mary's Ecological Reserve.

⓱ Placentia, at the end of Route 91, was the French capital of New-foundland in the 1600s. Trust the French to select a beautiful place for a capital! **Castle Hill National Historic Park,** just north of town, is lo-cated on what remains of the French fortifications. The visitor's cen-ter has a "life at Plaisance" exhibit that shows the life and hardships endured by early English and French settlers. *Off Rte. 100,* ☎ *709/227–2401.* ☛ *Free.* ☉ *June–Labor Day, daily 8:30–8; Labor Day–May, daily 8:30–4:30.*

⓲ A worthwhile and nearby diversion from Placentia is **Ship Harbour,** an isolated, edge-of-the-world place that has the curious distinction of being the home of the free world. Off Route 102, amidst the splendor of Placentia Bay, an unpaved road leads to a monument marking the historic Atlantic Charter. It was on a ship in these waters where, in 1941, Roosevelt and Churchill signed the charter and formally announced the "Four Freedoms," which still shape the politics of the world's most successful democracies: freedom of speech, freedom of worship, freedom from want, and freedom from fear.

★ **⓳** To continue on the Cape Shore tour, double back to Route 100 and travel 24 miles to the **Cape St. Mary's Ecological Reserve** (☎ 709/729–2424), the most southerly nesting site in the world for gannets and com-mon and thick-billed murres. A newly paved road takes you within a mile of the seabird colony. Visit the interpretation center—interpretive guides are on site during the summer—then walk to within 100 feet of the colony of nesting gannets, murres, black-billed kittiwakes, and razorbills. You'll also be able to enjoy some of the most dramatic coastal scenery in Newfoundland.

Tour 2: Clarenville and the Bonavista and Burin Peninsulas

⓴ Clarenville is about two hours from St. John's via the Trans-Canada Highway (Route 1) and is the departure point for two different ex-cursions: the Discovery Trail and Terra Nova National Park. If you're interested in rugged terrain, golf, fishing, and camping, head 15 miles

㉑ west along the Trans-Canada Highway to **Terra Nova National Park,** on the exposed coastline that adjoins Bonavista Bay. If you are a golfer, you can play on one of the most beautiful courses in Canada, and the only one where a salmon river cuts through the 18-hole course. Call 709/543–2525 for a reservation; fees run between $24 and $30 per person, depending on the season. The park also offers attractive camp-sites, whale-watching tours, and nature walks. ☎ *709/533–2801 or 709/533–2802,* ℻ *709/533–2706.* ☛ *Park and vehicle permit $6 daily, $18 for 4 days, $30 seasonal (buy season pass before June 22 for $20); seniors $4.50 daily, $13.50 for 4 days, $22.50 seasonal (buy season pass before June 22 for $15).* ☉ *Daily.*

★ If history and quaint towns interest you, begin the tour in Clarenville, the starting point for Route 230—the **"Discovery Trail."** The route goes as far as the town of Bonavista, one of John Cabot's reputed landing

㉒ spots in 1497. On your way visit the historic village of **Trinity,** known as one of the jewels of Newfoundland. The village's picturesque views, winding lanes, and snug houses are the main attraction, and several homes have been turned into museums and inns. In the 1700s Trinity competed with St. John's as a center of culture and wealth. Its more contemporary claim to fame, however, is that its intricate harbor was a favorite anchorage for the British navy, and it was here that the smallpox vaccine was introduced to North America, by a local rector. An information center with costumed interpreters is open daily from July to September.

㉓ Port Union, just north of Trinity on Route 230, was built as a model fishing community a century ago by the pioneer unionist Sir William Coaker. **The Port Union Museum** (contact Linda Clarke, ☎ 709/464–3315) in the old railway station traces his career.

㉔ Still farther north along Route 230 is **Cape Bonavista,** a popular destination because of its association with Cabot's landing. The lighthouse on the point has been restored to the 1870 period. While here, visit the **Mockbeggar Property** to learn about the life of a well-to-do outport merchant in the years immediately before Confederation. *Off Rte. 230,* ☎ *709/729–2460 or 709/468–7300.* ☛ *Free.* ☺ *Late June–early Sept., daily 10–5:30.*

BURIN PENINSULA
The journey down to the Burin Peninsula is a three- to four-hour drive from the intersection of Routes 230 and 1 through the sometimes incredible landscapes along Route 210. The peninsula's history is tied to the rich fishing grounds of the Grand Banks, which established this area as a center for European fishery as early as the 1500s. By the early 1900s, one of the world's largest fishing fleets was based on the Burin Peninsula. Today its inhabitants still operate the fishery in the modern trawlers that harvest the Grand Banks.

㉕ Marystown is the largest town on the peninsula and is its major commercial center. The town's name was changed from Mortier to Marystown by a priest during World War I, and to keep the faith a 15-foot statue of the Virgin Mary watches the town and harbor. West from here **㉖** the road meets with Route 220 which runs south through **Grand Bank,** an attractive community with a fascinating fishing history. This town is famous in the area as one of the most beautiful communities on the Atlantic seaboard. For details about the town's past visit the **Southern Newfoundland Seamen's Museum,** housed in a sail-shape building that was the Yugoslavian Pavilion in Expo '67. *Marine Dr.,* ☎ *709/832–1484.* ☛ *Free.* ☺ *Weekdays 9–5; weekends 2–5.*

㉗ Just south of Grand Bank is **Fortune,** where you can catch the ferry to **㉘** France's only colony in North America—the islands of **St. Pierre** and **Miquelon.** These islands are the place to go if you crave French cuisine or a bottle of perfume. Shopping and eating are both popular pastimes, and if you plan to stay overnight, consider the Hotel Robert on St. Pierre. Visitors traveling to the islands should carry proof of citizenship; people from outside the United States and Canada will have to show valid visas and passports. A passenger ferry operated by **Lloyd G. Lake Ltd.** (☎ 709/832–2006) leaves Fortune daily at 2:15 PM from mid-June to late September. The crossing takes 55 minutes. The ferry leaves St. Pierre at 1 PM daily, and the round trip costs $55; children 2–18 are half price.

㉙ Back on Route 220, you may wish to stop at **St. Lawrence,** where in 1942 one of the worst disasters in military history befell the U.S. Navy. It was here that warships *Pollux* and *Truxton* ran aground during a February storm. Two hundred sailors perished, but the people of the area heroically pulled another 182 over the cliffs to safety. In gratitude the U.S. Navy built a hospital for the community. In the summer of 1992, some survivors of the disaster returned to renew their friendships with the people of St. Lawrence and to unveil the "Echoes of Valour" monument on the cliff overlooking the spot where the ships sank.

30 Following Route 220 will take you around the peninsula to the old town of **Burin,** a community built amidst intricate cliffs and coves. This was an ideal setting for pirates and privateers who used to lure ships into the rocky, dead-end areas in order to plunder them. Captain Cook was among those who watched for smugglers from "Cook's Lookout" on a hill that still bears his name. Also in Burin is the **Heritage House** museum (☎ 709/891–2217, ☛ Free. ☯ Mon. and Tues. 9–5, Wed.–Sun. 9–9), considered one of the best community museums in Newfoundland, which gives you a sense of what life was like in the past.

Tour 3: Gander, Grand Falls–Windsor, and Notre Dame Bay

31 The interior of Newfoundland is unpopulated beyond the main roads, with the towns of Gander and Grand Falls–Windsor the focal points for the region. **Gander,** a busy center with 12,000 people, is the home of Gander International Airport. During World War II it was chosen by the Canadian and U.S. Air Forces as a major strategic air base because of its favorable weather and secure location. After the war, the airport became an international hub, and young islanders would hang around to see the stars come and go, among them Zsa Zsa Gabor and Tyrone Power. Now, like all modern airports, it's tightly secured. Gander has many hotels and still makes a good base for your travels. The **Aviation Exhibition** in the airport's Domestic Passenger's Lounge (☎ 709/729–2460; open daily) traces Newfoundland's role in the history of air travel.

32 **Grand Falls–Windsor,** 50 minutes west of Gander along the Trans-Canada Highway (Route 1), was a paper-milling settlement founded by Lord Northcliffe in the early 1900s to supply newsprint for his growing newspaper empire. Within Grand Falls is the **Mary March Regional Museum,** which depicts the lives of the Beothuk Indians before they fell victim to disease and competition from early settlers. The museum is named for 23-year-old Demasduit (who was also known as Mary March, for the month in which she was captured), one of the last Beothuks, who was captured in 1819 during a brutal encounter that resulted in the death of her husband and child. *St. Catherine St., off Rte. 1,* ☎ *709/292-4522.* ☛ *Free.* ☯ *Weekdays 9–4:45 year-round, summer weekends and holidays 10–5:45, winter weekends and holidays 2–5.*

33 Using either Route 330 from Gander (Route 1) or Route 340 via the Trans-Canada Highway from Grand Falls–Windsor, wander north through wooded countryside and small villages to **Twillingate.** The inhabitants of this charming old fishing village make their living from the sea and have been doing so for nearly two centuries. Every year on the last weekend in July, the town hosts the **Fish, Fun and Folk Festival,** where all different kinds of fish are cooked every kind of way. Twillingate is also one of the best places on the island to see icebergs, and is known to the locals as "Iceberg Alley." These majestic and dangerous mountains of ice are awe-inspiring to see while they're grounded in early summer.

34
35 You might also be interested in taking a ferry ride to either **Change Islands** or **Fogo Island.** Branch off Route 340 to Route 335, which takes

you through scenic coastal communities on the way to the ferry to either of the islands, located in Farewell. These islands give one the impression of a place frozen in time. Clapboard homes are precariously perched on rocks or built on small lots surrounded by vegetable gardens. As you walk the roads, look for moose and herds of wild Newfoundland ponies who spend their summers grazing and enjoying the warm breeze off the ocean.

Tour 4: Deer Lake and the Great Northern Peninsula to St. Anthony

㊱ **Deer Lake** was once just another small town on the Trans-Canada Highway, but the opening of Gros Morne National Park in the early '70s and a first-class paved highway passing right through to St. Anthony changed all that. Today, with an airport and car rentals available, Deer Lake is a good starting point for a fly-drive vacation.

㊲ Head north out of Deer Lake on Route 430 to Route 422 and **Sir Richard Squires Memorial Park.** The park is natural and unspoiled, and it contains one of the most interesting salmon fishing areas in Newfoundland. This drive will also take you through **Cormack,** which is one of the best farming regions in the island.

★ **㊳** Return to Route 430, continue north, and in a short while you'll be on the **Viking Trail** leading into **Gros Morne National Park** (☎ 709/458–2417). Because of its geological uniqueness and immense splendor, this park has been named a UNESCO World Heritage Site. Among the more breathtaking visions are the expanses of wild orchids in springtime. There is an excellent **interpretation center** (☎ 709/458–2417), which has displays and videos about the park. Camping and hiking are popular recreations in the park, and boat tours are available. It takes at least two days to see Gros Morne properly.

Scenic **Bonne Bay,** a deep, mountainous fjord, divides the park in two. You can drive around the perimeter of the fjord on Route 430 going north.

㊴ In the south of the park is **Woody Point,** a charming community of old houses and imported Lombardy poplars. Until it was bypassed by the now-defunct railway, the community was the commercial capital of the west coast. Rising behind Woody Point are the **Tablelands,** a unique rock massif that was once an ancient seabed. Its rocks are toxic to most plant life, and Ice Age conditions linger in the form of persistent snow and moving rock glaciers.

㊵ Follow Route 431 to scenic **Trout River Pond** and the once isolated and still unusual community of **Trout River.** The **Green Gardens Trail,** a four-to-five-hour hike, is along the way and it's one you'll remember for your lifetime, but be prepared to do a bit of climbing on your return journey. The trail passes through the Tablelands barrens and descends sharply down to a fairy-tale coastline of eroded cliffs, sea stacks, and lush green meadows.

㊶ On the northern side of the park, situated along coastal Route 430, is **Rocky Harbour,** with a wide range of services and a luxurious indoor public pool—the perfect thing to soothe tired limbs after a strenuous day.

The most popular attraction in the northern portion of Gros Morne is the boat tour of **Western Brook Pond,** which is reached by a leisurely 45-minute walk from the main highway through an interesting mix of bog and woods. Cliffs rise 2,000 feet on both sides of the gorge and high waterfalls tumble over ancient rocks. If you have strong legs and are in good shape, another natural attraction is the 10-mile hike up

Gros Morne Mountain, at 2,644 feet the second-highest peak in Newfoundland. Weather permitting, your labor will be rewarded by a unique arctic landscape and spectacular views. The park's coast in the north offers visitors an unusual mix of sand beaches, rock pools, and trails through tangled dwarf forests known locally as "tuckamore." Sunsets, seen from Lobster Point Lighthouse, are spectacular. Keep an eye out for whales and visit the lighthouse museum, devoted to the history of the area.

42 Just a short distance north of the park, on Route 430, is the **Arches Provincial Park,** a geological curiosity where the pounding sea has cut a succession of caves through a bed of dolomite.

Continuing north, parallel to the Gulf of St. Lawrence, you'll find yourself refreshingly close to the ocean and the wave-tossed beaches: Stop to breathe the fresh sea air and listen to the breakers. The Long Range Mountains to your right reminded Jacques Cartier, who saw them in 1534, of the long, rectangular-shape farm buildings of his home village in France. Small villages are interspersed with rivers where salmon and trout grow to be "liar-size." The remains of the Maritime Archaic Indians and Dorset Eskimos have been found in abundance along this coast, and there's an interesting interpretation center (☎ 709/623–2601 or 709/623–2608) at Port au Choix.

★ **43** Proceed about 130 miles on Route 430, then turn onto Route 436 to **L'Anse aux Meadows National Historic Site.** This UNESCO World Heritage Site was discovered in 1960 by a Norwegian team, Helge and Anne Stine Ingstad. Most believe the remains of the long sod houses here were built around 1000 as the site of Norseman Lief Erikson's colony in the New World. The Canadian Parks Service has established a marvelous **interpretation center** (☎ 709/623–2601) and has meticulously reconstructed some of the sod huts. With fires burning inside and sheepskins about, one does get a sense of centuries past. *Rte. 436,* ☎ *709/623–2601 or 709/623–2608.* ☛ *Free.* ☉ *Visitor center: mid-June–Labor Day, daily 9–8.*

44 Return to Route 430 and head south about 10 miles to **St. Anthony,** a beautiful town settled around a natural harbor at the tip of the Great Northern Peninsula. Take a trip out to the lighthouse—you may see an iceberg or two floating by.

St. Anthony is also the home of the **Grenfell Mission.** The huge hospital, adjacent to Charles S. Curtis Memorial Hospital on the west side of town on a hill overlooking the harbor, attests to the work done by Sir Wilfred Grenfell, a British medical missionary, who established nursing stations and cooperatives and provided medical services to the scattered villages of northern Newfoundland and the south coast of Labrador in the early 1900s. The main foyer of the hospital has a decorative tile mural that's worth a visit. **Grenfell House,** the home of Sir Wilfred and Lady Grenfell, has been restored to period condition and can also be visited. ☎ *709/454–3333, ext. 263.* ☛ *$2 adults, $1 senior citizens, students and children.* ☉ *Mid-May–mid-Oct., daily 10–8; winter by appointment.*

Don't leave without visiting the **Grenfell Handcraft** store (☎ 709/454–3576). Importing craftspeople to train the villagers to become self-sufficient in a harsh environment was one of Grenfell's aims. A windproof cloth that villagers turned into well-made parkas came to be known as Grenfell cloth. Beautiful clothes fashioned out of Grenfell cloth have quality and style not found anywhere else and they are available for sale here. Return to Deer Lake along Route 430.

Tour 5: Corner Brook and the West Coast

㊺ **Corner Brook** is Newfoundland's second-largest city and the hub of the west coast of the island. Mountains fringe three sides of the city and there are beautiful views of the harbor and the Bay of Islands. Corner Brook is also home to one of the largest paper mills in the world. Every July the city hosts the **Hangashore Folk Festival,** where you can go to hear some great traditional Canadian and Newfoundland music.

If you plan to explore the west coast, Corner Brook is a convenient hub and point of departure. It is only three hours from the Port-aux-Basques ferry and is an attractive and active city. The town enjoys more clearly defined seasons than most of the rest of the island, and in summer there are many pretty gardens to enjoy. The **Marble Mountain Ski Resort** (☎ 709/639–8531 on the slopes or 709/634–2160 for the office), just east of the city, has the highest slopes and the most snowfall in eastern North America and is growing rapidly as a ski center.

The north and south shores of the **Bay of Islands** have fine paved roads—Route 440 on the north shore and Route 450 on the south—and both offer a scenic half-day drive. On both roads, farming and fishing communities exist side by side. Take a camera with you—the scenery is breathtaking, with farms, mountains, and pockets of brilliant wildflowers.

㊻ **㊼** On another day, drive farther west on the Trans-Canada Highway and turn off at Route 460. Spend some time at the **Point au Mal Provincial Park** and stop in **Stephenville,** home of the old Harmon Air Force Base and now home to the annual Stephenville Arts Festival (mid-July to early August). The peninsula itself was largely settled by the French, who brought their way of life and language to this small corner of Newfoundland.

㊽ As you move farther down the Trans-Canada Highway toward **Port-aux-Basques,** Routes 404, 405, 406, and 407 will bring you into the small Scottish communities of the **Codroy Valley.** Nestled in the valley are some of the finest salmon rivers and most productive farms in the province, all of this against the backdrop of the Long Range Mountains and the Lewis Hills, from which gales strong enough to stop traffic hurl off the plateau and down to the coast.

Tour 6: Labrador

Isolated from the rest of the continent, Labrador has remained one of the world's truly wild places, and yet its two main centers of Labrador City–Wabush and Happy Valley–Goose Bay offer all the amenities available in larger, urban centers. Labrador is steeped in history, a place where the past invades the present and life evolves as it did many years ago, a composite of natural phenomena, wilderness adventure, history, and culture.

Labrador's vast landscape—294,330 square kilometers (113,204 square miles) of land and 8,000 kilometers (5,000 miles) of coastline—is home to a small but richly diverse population with a history that in some cases stretches back thousands of years; in other cases, the mining towns of Labrador West for example, the history goes back less than four decades.

Straits

The trip from Blanc Sablon to Red Bay on Route 510 will take you through the small fishing communities of L'Anse au Clair, Forteau, and **㊾** L'Anse au Loup. In **L'Anse au Clair,** you can walk the "Doctor's Path," where long ago Dr. Marcoux searched out herbs and medicinal plants

in the days when hospitals and nursing stations were few and far between. Anglers can try their luck for trout and salmon on the scenic
Forteau and Pinware rivers. The Straits were a rich hunting-and-gath-
ering ground for the continent's earliest peoples.

The elaborate Maritime Archaic Indian burial site discovered near
⑤ **L'Anse Amour,** about 12 miles from L'Anse au Clair, is 9,000 years old.
A plaque marks the site. The L'Anse Amour lighthouse was constructed
in 1857 and is the second-tallest lighthouse in Canada. During the
month of August, the annual **Labrador Bakeapple Festival** in **Forteau**
draws people from miles around for music, feasting, and celebration.

The **Labrador Straits Museum** provides an interesting glimpse into the
history and lifestyle of the area. *Rte. 510 between Forteau and L'Anse
au Loup,* ☎ *709/927–5659.* ✏ *$1.50.* ◷ *Summer, daily.*

You must drive to the very end of Route 510 to visit the area's main
★ **⑤** attraction: **Red Bay,** the site of a 16th-century Basque whaling station
and the province's newest UNESCO World Heritage Site. Basque
whalers began harpooning migrating whales from flimsy boats in frigid
waters a few years after Cabot's discovery of the coast in 1497. Between 1550 and 1600 Red Bay was the world's whaling capital. A visitor center (☎ 709/920–2197, ◷ Mid-June–early Oct., Mon.–Sat.
8–8, Sun. noon–8) interprets the Basque heritage through film and ar-
tifact. Between June and October, a boat will take you on a short journey over to the actual site of excavations on Saddle Island.

Coastal Labrador

You can tour coastal Labrador aboard Marine Atlantic's car ferry (*see*
Arriving and Departing *in* Newfoundland and Labrador Essentials,
below) from Lewisporte, Newfoundland. The trip takes 33 hours one-
way, and two regularly scheduled return trips are made weekly. A second ferry travels from Happy Valley–Goose Bay to Nain, Labrador's
northernmost settlement. This trip takes two weeks to complete. As
both ferries are supply boats, carrying all sorts of food and goods for
people living along the coast, you'll stop at a number of summer fishing stations and coastal communities. Reservations are required (☎
709/695–7081).

⑤ **Happy Valley–Goose Bay** is the chief service center for coastal Labrador.
The town was founded in the 1940s as a top-secret air base used to
ferry fleets of North American–manufactured aircraft to Europe. It is
still used as a low-level flying training base by the British, Dutch, and
German air forces.

⑤ **North West River** is a pleasant, half-hour drive to the east on Route
520, and on the way you'll pass the **Snow Goose Mountain Ski Club**
(☎ 709/896–5923). North West River was founded as a Hudson's Bay
trading post and is the former Labrador headquarters of the International Grenfell Association. It retains its frontier charm. Nearby **She-
shatshit** is the home of the Montagnais Innu Indians of Labrador. The
spirit in which the Innu (Naskapi-Montagnais) people inhabited the
interior for centuries can still be felt the moment you step outside the
region's modern mining communities.

Labrador West

Labrador West's subarctic landscape is challenging and unforgettable.
The terrain offers some of the world's best angling and wilderness adventure opportunities.

The best way to see this area is to ride the **Québec North Shore and
Labrador Railway** (☎ 418/962–9411), which leaves Sept Isles, Québec,

three times a week in summer and twice a week in the winter. The 7–8 hour trip through to Schefferville takes you through nearly 600 kilometers (350 miles) of virgin forest, spectacular waterfalls, and majestic mountains.

54 **55** The modern towns of **Wabush** and **Labrador City** have all the amenities of larger, urban centers, including accommodations, sports and recreational facilities, good shopping, live theater, and some of the finest hospitality you will find anywhere. Nearby is the **Smokey Mountain Alpine Skiing Center** (open mid-November–late April, ☎ 709/944–3505), with trails and slopes for both beginners and advanced skiers.

SHOPPING

The main centers of Newfoundland and Labrador—St. John's, Clarenville, Gander, Grand Falls, Corner Brook, Labrador West—all have modern shopping centers. However, the smaller communities often offer interesting crafts and native wares. Wander about—each town and village has its own country store and crafts store or general store. There are even some stores where packages are still wrapped in brown paper and tied with string.

St. John's
BOOKS
Most bookstores have a prominent section devoted to local history, fiction, and memoirs. **Word Play** (221 Duckworth St., ☎ 709/726–9193 or 800/563–9100) also carries a wide selection of magazines and books of general interest to visitors.

HANDICRAFTS
St. John's has more than its fair share of fine craft shops. **NONIA** (Newfoundland Outport Nurses Industrial Association, 286 Water St., ☎ 709/753–8062) was founded in 1920 to give Newfoundland women in the outports an opportunity to earn money to support nursing services in these remote communities. Their reputation for fierce independence was as colorful as their reputation for turning homespun wool into exquisite clothing. Today the shop continues to sell these fine homespun articles as well as lighter and more modern hand-made items. **The Salt Box** (194 Duckworth St., ☎ 709/753–0622) sells local crafts and specializes in pottery. **The Cod Jigger** (245 Duckworth St., ☎ 709/726–7422) carries handmade wool sweaters, socks, and mitts as well as Newfoundland's unique Grenfell coats. **The Devon House Craft Gallery** (59 Duckworth St., ☎ 709/753–2749) is owned by the Newfoundland and Labrador Crafts Development Association and carries only juried crafts. **The Newfoundland Weavery** (177 Water St., ☎ 709/753–0496) carries rugs, prints, lamps, books, crafts, and other gifts. Newfoundlanders are also very proud of their antiques, and two St. John's shops are worth a visit: **Murray's Antiques** (414 Blackmarsh Rd., ☎ 709/579–7344) is renowned for silver, china, and fine mahogany and walnut furniture; **Livyers** (202 Duckworth St., ☎ 709/726–5650) carries locally crafted furniture and is a great spot for digging through books, prints, and maps.

MUSIC
Fred's Records (198 Duckworth St., ☎ 709/753–9191) has the best selection of local tapes and CDs, as well as other music.

St. Anthony
At St. Anthony, on the northern tip of Newfoundland, browse in the **Grenfell Handcraft Store** (*see* Exploring, *above*).

SPORTS AND THE OUTDOORS

Many provincial and all national parks in Newfoundland have hiking and nature trails. The west coast offers opportunities for mountain climbing in the summer and skiing in the winter.

Hiking

Coastal and woods trails radiate from most small communities. However, you can never be sure how far the trail will go unless you ask a local. Be careful: Landmarks are few, the weather is changeable, and it is surprisingly easy to get lost. Many small communities now also have formal walking trails.

Fishing

Newfoundland has 105 salmon rivers and trout streams. Angling in these unpolluted waters is a fisherman's dream. Seasonal and regulatory information can be obtained from the **Department of Tourism and Culture** (☎ 800/729–2830).

Skiing

There are ski resorts near Clarenville, Labrador City, and Happy Valley–Goose Bay; and groomed cross-country ski trail systems in St. John's, Clarenville, Terra Nova National Park, Gros Morne National Park, Labrador City, and Happy Valley–Goose Bay, among other places.

DINING AND LODGING

Dining

John Cabot and Sir Humphrey Gilbert raved about "waters teeming with fish." Today, despite the fishing moratorium, seafood is still an excellent value in Newfoundland and Labrador. Many restaurants offer seasonal specialties featuring a wide variety of traditional wild and cultured species. While cod may still be available it may not be locally harvested. It will still, however, be traditionally prepared—pan-fried, baked, or poached. Try cod tongues, salt cod, fish and brewis (it is cod of course!). Aquaculture species like steelhead trout, salmon, mussels, and sea scallops are available in better restaurants. Cold-water shrimp, snow crab, lobster, redfish, grenadier, halibut, and turbot are also good seafood choices.

Two other foods you shouldn't leave without trying are partridgeberries and bakeapples. Partridgeberries are a small, lush-tasting relative of the cranberry and locally they are used for just about everything—pies, jams, cakes, pancakes, and even as a sauce for turkey and game. Bakeapples in the wild are a low-growing berry that looks like a yellow raspberry—you'll see them ripening in bogs in August throughout Newfoundland and Labrador. Enterprising youngsters sell them by the side of the road in jars. If the ones you buy are hard, wait a few days and they'll ripen into rich-tasting fruit. They're popular on ice cream or spread on fresh homemade bread. In Scandinavia they're known as cloudberries and are made into a liqueur.

You may also hear Newfoundlanders talk about the herb they call summer savory. Newfoundlanders are so partial to this peppery herb that they slip it into most stuffings and stews. Growers in the province ship the product all over the world, and Newfoundlanders visiting relatives living outside the province are usually asked to "bring the savory."

Only the large urban centers across the province, especially St. John's and Corner Brook, have gourmet restaurants. Fish is a safe dish to order just about everywhere—even in the lowliest take-out. You'll be agreeably surprised by the quality of the meals along the Trans-Canada Highway: Restaurants in the Irving Gas Station chain, for example, offer thick homemade soups with dumplings, and Sunday dinners that draw in local customers for miles around. Don't be shy about trying some of the excellent meals offered in the province's expanding network of "hospitality homes," where home cooking goes hand in hand with the warm welcome for which Newfoundlanders are famous.

WHAT TO WEAR
Dress is casual everywhere except at the very expensive ($$$$) listings.

CATEGORY	COST*
$$$$	over $50
$$$	$35–$50
$$	$20–$35
$	under $20

per person, excluding drinks, service, and 12% sales tax

Lodging

Newfoundland and Labrador offer lodgings that range from modestly priced "hospitality homes" to luxury accommodations. In between, visitors can choose from affordable, basic lodging and mid-priced hotels. In remote areas, visitors should be prepared to find very basic lodgings. However, the lack of amenities is usually made up for by the home-cooked meals and the great hospitality that you'll encounter. Life is definitely more relaxed here: If you're expected at a "hospitality home" and you're running late, your host or hostess will leave your room key with a welcome note in the mailbox!

CATEGORY	COST*
$$$	over $100
$$	$60–$90
$	under $60

All prices are for a standard double room, excluding service charge.

Cape Onion
LODGING

$ Tickle Inn at Cape Onion. This refurbished, century-old fisherman's house on the beach is probably the most northerly residence on the island of Newfoundland. Guests often gather round the Franklin stove in the parlor after a day of exploring the area meadows, hills, and coast, or taking a trip to the Viking settlement at L'Anse aux Meadows (about 45 kilometers [73 miles] away). Continental breakfast is included in the room rate and other meals are available. There are just four rooms and they share baths. ☎ *R.R. 1, Box 62, Cape Onion, A0K 4J0,* ☎ *709/452–4321 June–Sept.; 709/739–5503 Oct.–May. 4 rooms. Dining room. MC, V.*

Clarenville
DINING AND LODGING

$$ Holiday Inn. There are no surprises at this chain member; rooms are standard Holiday Inn fare. ☎ *Box 967, Clarenville, A0E 1J0,* ☎ *709/466–7911,* FAX *709/466–3854. 64 rooms. Restaurant, bar. AE, DC, MC, V.*

Corner Brook
DINING AND LODGING

$$ Best Western Mamateek Inn. Rooms are more modern than at the Glyn-
★ mill Inn (*see below*). The dining room, which serves good Newfoundland home-cooked food, is known for its exquisite view of the whole city. Sunsets seen from the restaurant are remarkable. ☎ *Rte.*

1, Box 787, A2H 6G7, ☎ 709/639–8901, FAX 709/639–7567. 55 rooms. Restaurant. AE, MC, V.

$$ Glynmill Inn. This charming inn has the feel of old England. It was once
★ the staff house for the visiting top brass of the mill. Rooms are cozy and the dining room serves basic and well-prepared Newfoundland seafood, soups, and specialty desserts made with partridgeberries. There's also a popular steak house in the basement. ⌕ *Cobb's La., Box 455, A2H 6E6, ☎ 709/634–5106 or 800/563–4400 (Canada), FAX 709/634–5181. 90 rooms. 2 restaurants. AE, MC, V.*

$$ Holiday Inn. Again, there's nothing extraordinary here, aside from the convenience of being located right in town. You'll be pleased to know that the outdoor pool is heated. Some of the rooms have minibars. The restaurant is average, aside from good seasonal fish dishes. ⌕ *48 West St., A2H 2Z2, ☎ 709/634–5381, FAX 709/634–1723. 103 rooms. Restaurant, lounge, minibars, pool. AE, DC, MC, V.*

$–$$ Comfort Inn by Journey's End Motel. This is a comfortable, modern motel with an attractive interior (the dominating colors are dusty rose and blue) and beautiful views of either the city or the Bay of Islands. ⌕ *41 Maple Valley Rd., Box 1142, A2H 6T2, ☎ 709/639–1980, FAX 709/639–1549. 80 rooms. Restaurant. AE, MC, DC, V.*

Deer Lake
DINING AND LODGING

$$ Deer Lake Motel. The guest rooms here are clean and comfortable, and the food in the café is basic, home-cooked fare. You'll find the seafood dishes exceptionally well prepared. ⌕ *Box 820, A0K 2E0, ☎ 709/635–2108, FAX 709/635–3842. 54 rooms, 2 suites. Café. AE, DC MC, V.*

Gander
DINING AND LODGING

$$ Albatross Motel. This motel has a deserved reputation as an attractive
★ place to stop off for a meal. Try the cod au gratin—you won't find it this good anywhere else. Rooms are basic and clean. ⌕ *Box 450, A1V 1W8, ☎ 709/256–3956, FAX 709/489–6365. 104 rooms, 4 suites. Restaurant. AE, DC, MC, V.*

Grand Falls
DINING AND LODGING

$$ Mount Peyton Hotel. The rooms aren't soundproof here, but they are clean and comfortable. The excellent Newfoundland menu makes this a great place to break up your journey across the island. ⌕ *214 Lincoln Rd., A2A 1P8, ☎ 709/489–2251, FAX 709/489–6365. 150 rooms. Restaurant. AE, DC, MC, V.*

L'Anse aux Meadows
LODGING

$ Valhalla Lodge Bed & Breakfast. Located adjacent to the Viking site at L'Anse aux Meadows, this is the only game in town, but that doesn't make it any less comfortable and inviting. Note the interesting fossils in the rock fireplace in the dining room. Hot breakfasts are available, and other meals can be had on request. ⌕ *Gunner's Cove, Griquet A0K 2X0, ☎ 709/623–2018 in summer; 709/896–5476 in winter. 6 rooms. V.*

Port-aux-Basques
DINING AND LODGING

$$ St. Christopher's Hotel. This clean, comfortable hotel is a recent addition in Port-aux-Basques that offers quiet, air-conditioned rooms and good food. Rooms also have satellite TV. ⌕ *Caribou Rd., Box 2049,*

A0M 1C0, ☎ *709/695–7034,* ℻ *709/695–9841. 58 rooms. Restaurant, meeting room. AE, DC, MC, V.*

St. John's

DINING

$$$ **The Cellar.** This restaurant, situated in a historic building on the wa-
★ terfront, gets rave reviews for its innovative Continental cuisine fea-
turing the best local ingredients. Menu selections include blackened fish
dishes and tiramisù for dessert. ✕ *Baird's Cove, between Harbour and
Water Sts.,* ☎ *709/579–8900. Reservations advised. AE, MC, V.*

$$$ **Stone House.** Situated in one of St. John's most historic buildings—a
★ restored 19th-century stone cottage—this dining room features imported
game and Newfoundland specialties. ✕ *8 Kennas Hill,* ☎ *709/753–
2380. Reservations advised. AE, DC, MC, V.*

$$–$$$ **Flake House.** A five-minute cab ride from the major hotels is Quidi Vidi
Village, a vibrant, oceanfront historic site with a faithfully reproduced
flake house (where fishermen dried their fish and ate lunch). A little
more formal than it sounds, it specializes in seafood including some
blackened fish dishes and lots of lobster and clams. You'll also find
rack of lamb, Cajun-spiced alligator, veal, and duck entrées. ✕ *16 Bor-
rows Rd., Quidi Vidi Village,* ☎ *709/576–7772. Reservations advised. AE, DC, MC, V.*

DINING AND LODGING

$$$ **Hotel Newfoundland.** This hotel replaces an old hotel that stood on
★ this site for many years. St. John's residents gather here for special oc-
casions, and it's noted for its Sunday and evening buffets, its charm-
ing rooms that overlook St. John's harbor, its atrium, and the fine cuisine
of the Cabot Club. ▣ *Box 5637, A1C 5W8,* ☎ *709/726–4980,* ℻
709/726–2025. 288 rooms, 14 suites. Restaurant. AE, DC, MC, V.

$$–$$$ **Delta St. John's.** In this convention hotel in downtown St. John's,
★ rooms overlook the harbor and the city. The restaurant, Brazil Square,
is noted for its breakfast and noon buffets. ▣ *120 New Gower St.,
A1C 6K4,* ☎ *709/739–6404,* ℻ *709/570–1622. 276 rooms, 9 suites.
Restaurant. AE, DC, MC, V.*

$$ **Quality Hotel by Journey's End Motel.** This hotel overlooks St. John's
harbor. Like other Journey's Ends, it offers clean, comfortable rooms
at a reasonable price. The hotel's restaurant, Rumplestiltskins, has a
splendid view and an unpretentious, attractive menu. ▣ *Hill O'Chips,
A1C 6B1,* ☎ *709/754–7788,* ℻ *709/754–5209. 161 rooms. Restaurant. AE, DC, MC, V.*

LODGING

$$ **Compton House Bed & Breakfast.** Housed in a charming, restored his-
★ toric St. John's residence in the west end of the city, this inn is profes-
sionally run and beautifully decorated. Twelve-foot ceilings and wide
halls give the place a majestic feeling, and rooms done in pastels and
chintzes add an air of coziness. The location, within easy walking dis-
tance of downtown St. John's, is ideal. ▣ *26 Waterford Bridge Rd.,
A1E 1C6,* ☎ *709/739–5789. 4 rooms, 2 suites. AE, MC, V.*

$$ **Prescott House Inn.** Local art decorates the walls of this house, which
★ has received a Heritage Award. The city's most popular bed-and-
breakfast, it has been made even better by a modernization that tastefully blended the new and the old. Located downtown, it's central to
shopping and attractions. ▣ *17–21 Military Rd., A1C 2C3,* ☎ *709/
753–7733,* ℻ *709/753–6036. 15 rooms, 7 suites. MC, V.*

$ **Gower Street House Bed & Breakfast.** This gracious former home of
the late photographer Elsie Holloway has been designated by the Newfoundland Historic Trust as a point of interest. It's also an ideal set-

ting for paintings by prominent local artists. The downtown location is within walking distance of all the city's main attractions. Room rates include a full, hot breakfast with traditional dishes as well as standard contemporary fare. ⌨ *180 Gower St., A1C 1P9,* ☎ *709/754–0047 or 800/563–3959,* ☏ *709/754–5721. 4 rooms. Lounge, access to laundry. MC, V.*

THE ARTS AND NIGHTLIFE

It has been a long-standing claim (since at least the 1700s) that St. John's has more bars per mile than any city in North America. Each establishment has its own personality and a couple are famous for their Irish music: **Erin's Pub** (186 Water St., ☎ 709/722–1916) and the **Blarney Stone** (342 Water St., 2nd Floor, ☎ 709/754–1798). George Street, in downtown St. John's, is a beautifully restored street of pubs and restaurants. Open-air concerts can be heard there during the annual **George Street Festival** and on many other occasions.

Newfoundlanders love a party, and from the cities to the smallest towns they celebrate their history and unique culture throughout the summer with festivals and events. The **Newfoundland and Labrador Folk Arts Festival,** held in St. John's in early August, is the province's best-known traditional music festival. **The Newfoundland International Irish Festival** held in St. John's each July features international performers and lots of locals, too. It even includes a Leprechaun Festival for the kids. Local folk music festivals occur in every part of the province during the summer. You'll also encounter a host of community celebrations, community dinners, and church teas.

The province has an unusually active arts community. Most major towns have an arts and culture center, which offers live theater presentations, ballet, and concerts by local, national, and international artists. The **Resource Centre for the Arts** (LSPU Hall), on Victoria Street in St. John's (☎ 709/753–4531), is one of the country's oldest and most innovative experimental theaters. In addition to a busy fall and winter season, the center enjoys a busy summer, with cabarets, outdoor concerts, plays for children and adults, and alternative concerts. The **Stephenville Festival** (☎ 709/643–4982) is held throughout July and into August in Stephenville, an hour's drive south of Corner Brook. The festival is the province's major annual summer theatrical event and features a well-produced mix of light musicals and serious drama.

St. John's has a dozen commercial and public art galleries, nearly all of which feature local artists. Newfoundland's unique landscape, portrayed realistically or more experimentally, is a favorite subject.

The Art Gallery of Newfoundland and Labrador, (formerly the Memorial University Art Gallery) is the province's largest public gallery and exhibits historical and contemporary Canadian arts and crafts with an emphasis on Newfoundland and Labrador artists and artisans. *Allandale Rd. and Prince Philip Dr.,* ☎ *709/737–8209.* ☛ *Free.* ☉ *Tues.–Sun., noon–5.; Fri. 7 PM–10 PM; closed Mon.*

The **Emma Butler Gallery** (111 George St., ☎ 709/739–7111) features a large selection of Newfoundland art including works by David Blackwood and Christopher Pratt. **Christina Parker Fine Art** (7 Plank Rd., ☎ 709/753–0580) represents local and national artists in all mediums, including painting, sculpture, drawing, and fine art prints. Several galleries specialize in reasonably priced work aimed at the visitor market.

NEWFOUNDLAND AND LABRADOR ESSENTIALS

Arriving and Departing

By Car Ferry

Marine Atlantic (Box 250, North Sydney, NS B2A 3M3, ☎ 902/794–5700 or 709/772–7701, TDD 902/794–8109, FAX 902/564–7480) operates a car ferry from North Sydney, Nova Scotia, to Port-aux-Basques, Newfoundland (crossing time is six hours); and, from June through October, from North Sydney to Argentia, twice a week (crossing time 12–14 hours). In all cases, reservations are required. For information about getting to Labrador, *see* Tour 6 *in* Exploring, *above.*

By Plane

The province's main airport for connections from all major North American and European destinations is **St. John's. Canadian Airlines International** (☎ 800/426–7000 in the U.S., 800/665–1177 in Canada) and **Air Canada** (☎ 800/776–3000 in the U.S., 709/726–7880 in Canada) fly into Newfoundland. **Air Nova** (☎ 800/776–3000 in the U.S., 800/563–5151 in Newfoundland), **Provincial Airlines** (☎ 709/576–1666), **Labrador Airways** (☎ 709/896–3387 in U.S., 800/563–3042 in Newfoundland), and **Air Atlantic** (☎ 800/563–8359 in the U.S., 709/576–0274 in Newfoundland) are regional connectors. Airports in Newfoundland are at Stephenville, Deer Lake, St. Anthony, Gander, and St. John's; airports in Labrador are located in Happy Valley–Goose Bay, Wabush, and Churchill Falls.

By Train

Rail service (☎ 418/962–9411) is provided between Sept Isles, Québec, and Labrador City and Schefferville in Labrador by Iron Ore Canada's Québec North Shore and Labrador Railway. For more information about this train, *see* Tour 6 *in* Exploring, *above.* There is no train on the island.

Getting Around

Newfoundland

BY BUS

CN Roadcruiser (☎ 709/737–5912) runs a trans-island bus service. Buses leave at 8 AM from St. John's and Port-aux-Basques. Small buses known as outport taxis connect the major centers with surrounding communities.

BY CAR

Newfoundland has an excellent highway system, and all but a handful of secondary roads are paved. The province's roads are generally uncrowded, adding to the pleasure of driving. Traveling time along the Trans-Canada Highway from Port-aux-Basques to St. John's is about 13 hours, with time out for a meal in either Gander or Grand Falls. The trip from Corner Brook to St. Anthony at the northernmost tip of the island is about five hours. The drive from St. John's to Grand Bank on the Burin Peninsula takes about four hours.

In winter some highways may close during and after severe snowstorms. For winter road conditions on the west coast and in Labrador, call the **Department of Works, Services, and Transportation** (in Deer Lake, ☎ 709/635–2162; in Grand Falls and Central Newfoundland, ☎ 709/292–4300; in Clarenville, ☎ 709/466–7953; in St. John's, ☎ 709/729–2391).

Labrador
From the island of Newfoundland, you can fly to Labrador via St. John's, Gander, Deer Lake, or Stephenville. Route 500 links Labrador City with Happy Valley–Goose Bay via Churchill Falls. If you plan on doing any extensive driving in any part of Labrador, you should contact the Department of Tourism and Culture (☎ 709/729–2830 or 800/563–6353) for advice on the best routes and road conditions.

To explore the south coast of Labrador, catch the ferry at St. Barbe on Route 430 in Newfoundland to Blanc Sablon, Québec. From here you can drive to Red Bay along Route 510. Conditions on this 439-kilometer (300-mile) unpaved wilderness road are best between June and October.

At publication, summer travel was still possible by car ferry through **Marine Atlantic** (Lewisporte, Newfoundland, ☎ 709/535–6876; Happy Valley–Goose Bay, Labrador, ☎ 709/896–0041; in the U. S., 800/341–7981). The ship travels from Lewisporte in Newfoundland to Cartwright, on the coast of Labrador, and then through the Hamilton inlet to Happy Valley–Goose Bay. Reservations are required. Roads are gradually being built into these areas and demand for the ferry service is dwindling, so check to be sure it is still available before you make plans.

Guided Tours
Adventure Tours
Adventure touring in Newfoundland and Labrador is experiencing a period of rapid growth. Local adventure tour operators offer sea-kayaking, ocean-diving, canoeing, wildlife viewing, mountain biking, white-water rafting, heli-hiking, and interpretive walks in the summer. In winter, snowmobiling, heli-skiing, and caribou- and seal-watching expeditions are popular. Before choosing an operator it's advisable to contact the Department of Tourism and Culture to make sure you're calling a reputable outfit. **Eastern Edge Outfitters** (☎ 709/782–1465) offers east-coast sea-kayaking tours and white-water kayaking instruction. **Gros Morne Adventure Guides** (☎ 709/458–2722 or 709/686–2241) offers sea-kayaking up the fjords and land-locked ponds of Gros Morne National Park, as well as a variety of hikes and adventures in the area. **Tuckamore Lodge** (☎ 709/865–6361) in Main Brook uses its luxurious lodge on the Great Northern Peninsula as a base for viewing caribou, seabird colonies, whales, and icebergs. **Labrador Scenic Ltd.** (☎ 709/497–8326) in North West River organizes tours through central and northern Labrador with an emphasis on wildlife and Labrador's spectacular coast.

Boat Tours
The number of boat tours has increased in recent years. South of St. John's, in Bay Bulls, **O'Brien's Bird Island Charters** (☎ 709/753–4850 or 709/334–2355) and **Gatherall's Sanctuary Boat Charters** (☎ 709/334–2887) offer popular two-hour excursions featuring whale-, iceberg-, and seabird-watching as well as cod jigging. Great Island Tours (☎ 709/432–2272 or 706/432–2781) charters a 10.7-meter boat on an hourly basis, accommodating up to 18 people.

The number of boat tours has increased in recent years. South of St. John's, in Bay Bulls, **O'Brien's Bird Island Charters** (☎ 709/753–4850 or 709/334–2355) and **Gatherall's Sanctuary Boat Charters** (☎ 709/334–2887) offer popular two-hour excursions featuring whale-, iceberg-, and seabird-watching as well as cod jigging. **Great Island Tours** (☎ 709/432–2272 or 706/432–2781) charters a 10.7-meter boat on an hourly basis, accommodating up to 18 people.

On the Trinity–Bonavista Peninsula, **Ocean Contact Limited** (☎ 709/464–3269) is an established specialist in whale-watching and whale research. Dr. Peter Beamish's book, *Dancing with Whales,* documents their interesting findings. **Island Rendezvous** (☎ 709/747–7253) offers two days of boating and an overnight stay on Woody Island, Placentia Bay. **Island View Boat Tours** (☎ 709/535–2258) promises a mussel and lobster boil-up on the beach, an island treasure hunt, and a chance to visit abandoned settlements and Indian sites in the Lewisporte area. **Twillingate Island Boat Tours** (☎ 709/884–2242) specializes in iceberg photography in the iceberg-rich waters around Twillingate. There is an iceberg interpretation center right on the dock.

On the west coast, 2,000-foot-high cliffs and spectacular landlocked fjords are the main attraction. **Bontours** (☎ 709/458–2730 or 709/458–2256) runs the best-known of the sightseeing trips—up Western Brook Pond in Gros Morne National Park. **Tableland Boat Tours** (☎ 709/451–2101) runs tours up Trout River Pond near the southern boundary of the park. **Seal Island Boat Tours** (☎ 709/243–2376 or 709/243–2278) explores St. Paul's Inlet, an area of the park rich in seals, terns, and other marine and shore life.

Bus Tours

McCarthy's Party (☎ 709/781–2244) in St. John's offers guided bus tours across Newfoundland (May–Oct.) in addition to a variety of charter services. **Fleetline Motorcoach Tours** (☎ 709/722–2608) in Holyrood and **K.P. Motorcoach Tours** (☎ 709/632–5808) in Corner Brook also offer island-wide tours. Local tours are available for Port-aux-Basques, the Codroy Valley, Corner Brook, the Bay of Islands, Gros Morne National Park, the Great Northern Peninsula, and St. John's.

Important Addresses and Numbers

Emergencies

Dial 911 for medical emergencies and police.

HOSPITALS

St. Clare's Mercy Hospital (154 Le Marchant Rd., ☎ 709/778–3111), **Grace Hospital** (241 Le Marchant Rd., ☎ 709/778–6222), and **General Hospital** (300 Prince Philip Dr., ☎ 709/737–6300) in St. John's; **George B. Cross Hospital** (Manitoba Dr., ☎ 709/466–3411) in Clarenville; **James Paton** (125 Trans-Canada Hwy., ☎ 709/651–2500) in Gander; **Western Memorial** (Brookfield Ave., ☎ 709/637–5000) in Corner Brook; **Charles S. Curtis Memorial Hospital** (West St., ☎ 709/454–3333) in St. Anthony; and **Captain William Jackman Hospital** (410 Booth Ave., ☎ 709/944–2632) in Labrador City.

Visitor Information

The Department of Tourism and Culture (Box 8730, St. John's, New Brunswick A1B 4K2, ☎ 709/729–2830) distributes brochures and maps from its offices in the Confederation Building, West Block, St. John's. The province also maintains a tourist information line (☎ 800/563–6353), which operates year-round, 24 hours a day.

From June until Labor Day, a network of **visitor information centers,** open 9–9, dots the province. These centers carry up-to-date information on events, accommodations, shopping, and crafts stores in their area. There are in-season visitor information booths at the airports in Gander and St. John's. The city of St. John's operates a complete information center in a restored railway carriage next to the harbor.

INDEX

FRENCH VOCABULARY

One of the trickiest French sounds to pronounce is the nasal final *n* sound (whether or not the *n* is actually the last letter of the word). You should try to pronounce it as a sort of nasal grunt—as in "huh." The vowel that precedes the *n* will govern the vowel sound of the word, and in this list we precede the final *n* with an *h* to remind you to be nasal.

Another problem sound is the ubiquitous but untransliterable *eu*, as in *bleu* (blue) or *deux* (two), and the very similar sound in *je* (I), *ce* (this), and *de* (of). The closest equivalent might be the vowel sound of "stood."

English	French	Pronunciation

Basics

Yes/no	Oui/non	wee/nohn
Please	S'il vous plaît	seel voo play
Thank you	Merci	mair-**see**
You're welcome	De rien	deh ree-**ehn**
That's all right	Il n'y a pas de quoi	eel nee ah pah de kwah
Excuse me, sorry	Pardon	pahr-**dohn**
Sorry!	Désolé(e)	day-zoh-**lay**
Good morning/ afternoon	Bonjour	bohn-**zhoor**
Good evening	Bonsoir	bohn-**swahr**
Goodbye	Au revoir	o ruh-**vwahr**
Mr. (Sir)	Monsieur	muh-**syuh**
Mrs. (Ma'am)	Madame	ma-**dam**
Miss	Mademoiselle	mad-mwa-**zel**
Pleased to meet you	Enchanté(e)	ohn-shahn-**tay**
How are you?	Comment allez-vous?	kuh-mahn-tahl-ay-**voo**
Very well, thanks	Très bien, merci	tray bee-ehn, mair-**see**
And you?	Et vous?	ay voo?

Numbers

one	un	uhn
two	deux	deuh
three	trois	twah
four	quatre	**kaht**-ruh
five	cinq	sank
six	six	seess
seven	sept	set
eight	huit	wheat
nine	neuf	nuf
ten	dix	deess

eleven	onze	ohnz
twelve	douze	dooz
thirteen	treize	trehz
fourteen	quatorze	kah-torz
fifteen	quinze	kanz
sixteen	seize	sez
seventeen	dix-sept	deez-**set**
eighteen	dix-huit	deez-**wheat**
nineteen	dix-neuf	deez-**nuf**
twenty	vingt	vehn
twenty-one	vingt-et-un	vehnt-ay-**uhn**
thirty	trente	trahnt
forty	quarante	ka-**rahnt**
fifty	cinquante	sang-**kahnt**
sixty	soixante	swa-**sahnt**
seventy	soixante-dix	swa-sahnt-**deess**
eighty	quatre-vingts	kaht-ruh-**vehn**
ninety	quatre-vingt-dix	kaht-ruh-vehn-**deess**
one-hundred	cent	sahn
one-thousand	mille	meel

Colors

black	noir	nwahr
blue	bleu	bleuh
brown	brun/marron	bruhn/mar-**rohn**
green	vert	vair
orange	orange	o-**rahnj**
pink	rose	rose
red	rouge	rouge
violet	violette	vee-o-**let**
white	blanc	blahnk
yellow	jaune	zhone

Days of the Week

Sunday	dimanche	dee-**mahnsh**
Monday	lundi	luhn-**dee**
Tuesday	mardi	mahr-**dee**
Wednesday	mercredi	mair-kruh-**dee**
Thursday	jeudi	zhuh-**dee**
Friday	vendredi	vawn-druh-**dee**
Saturday	samedi	sahm-**dee**

Months

January	janvier	zhahn-vee-**ay**
February	février	feh-vree-**ay**
March	mars	marce
April	avril	a-**vreel**
May	mai	meh
June	juin	zhwehn
July	juillet	zhwee-**ay**
August	août	ah-**oo**
September	septembre	sep-**tahm**-bruh

October	octobre	awk-**to**-bruh
November	novembre	no-**vahm**-bruh
December	décembre	day-**sahm**-bruh

Useful Phrases

Do you speak English?	Parlez-vous anglais?	par-lay **voo** ahn-**glay**
I don't speak French	Je ne parle pas français	zhuh nuh parl pah frahn-**say**
I don't understand	Je ne comprends pas	zhuh nuh kohm-**prahn** pah
I understand	Je comprends	zhuh kohm-**prahn**
I don't know	Je ne sais pas	zhuh nuh say **pah**
I'm American/ British	Je suis américain/ anglais	zhuh sweez a-may-ree-**kehn**/ahn-**glay**
What's your name?	Comment vous appelez-vous?	ko-mahn voo za-pell-ay-**voo**
My name is . . .	Je m'appelle . . .	zhuh ma-**pell** . . .
What time is it?	Quelle heure est-il?	kel air eh-**teel**
How?	Comment?	ko-**mahn**
When?	Quand?	kahn
Yesterday	Hier	yair
Today	Aujourd'hui	o-zhoor-**dwee**
Tomorrow	Demain	duh-**mehn**
This morning/ afternoon	Ce matin/cet après-midi	suh ma-**tehn**/set ah-pray-mee-**dee**
Tonight	Ce soir	suh **swahr**
What?	Quoi?	kwah
What is it?	Qu'est-ce que c'est?	kess-kuh-**say**
Why?	Pourquoi?	poor-**kwa**
Who?	Qui?	kee
Where is . . .	Où est . . .	oo ay
the train station?	la gare?	la gar
the subway station?	la station de métro?	la sta-**syon** duh may-**tro**
the bus stop?	l'arrêt de bus?	la-**ray** duh **booss**
the terminal (airport)?	l'aérogare?	lay-ro-**gar**
the post office?	la poste?	la post
the bank?	la banque?	la bahnk
the . . . hotel?	l'hôtel . . .?	lo-**tel**
the store?	le magasin?	luh ma-ga-**zehn**
the cashier?	la caisse?	la **kess**
the . . . museum?	le musée . . .?	luh mew-**zay**
the hospital?	l'hôpital?	lo-pee-**tahl**
the elevator?	l'ascenseur?	la-sahn-**seuhr**
the telephone?	le téléphone?	luh tay-lay-**phone**

Where are the restrooms?	Où sont les toilettes?	oo sohn lay twah-**let**
Here/there	Ici/là	ee-**see**/la
Left/right	A gauche/à droite	a goash/a drwaht
Straight ahead	Tout droit	too drwah
Is it near/far?	C'est près/loin?	say pray/lwehn
I'd like . . .	Je voudrais . . .	zhuh voo-**dray**
a room	une chambre	ewn **shahm**-bruh
the key	la clé	la clay
a newspaper	un journal	uhn zhoor-**nahl**
a stamp	un timbre	uhn **tam**-bruh
I'd like to buy . . .	Je voudrais acheter . . .	zhuh voo-**dray** ahsh-**tay**
a cigar	un cigare	uhn see-**gar**
cigarettes	des cigarettes	day see-ga-**ret**
matches	des allumettes	days a-loo-**met**
dictionary	un dictionnaire	uhn deek-see-oh-**nare**
soap	du savon	dew sah-**vohn**
city plan	un plan de ville	uhn plahn de **veel**
road map	une carte routière	ewn cart roo-tee-**air**
magazine	une revue	ewn reh-**vu**
envelopes	des enveloppes	dayz ahn-veh-**lope**
writing paper	du papier à lettres	dew pa-pee-**ay** a **let**-ruh
airmail writing paper	du papier avion	dew pa-pee-**ay** a-vee-**ohn**
postcard	une carte postale	ewn cart pos-**tal**
How much is it?	C'est combien?	say comb-bee-**ehn**
It's expensive/cheap	C'est cher/pas cher	say share/pa share
A little/a lot	Un peu/beaucoup	uhn peuh/bo-**koo**
More/less	Plus/moins	plu/mwehn
Enough/too (much)	Assez/trop	a-say/tro
I am ill/sick	Je suis malade	zhuh swee ma-**lahd**
Call a doctor	Appelez un docteur	a-play uhn dohk-**tehr**
Help!	Au secours!	o suh-**koor**
Stop!	Arrêtez!	a-reh-**tay**
Fire!	Au feu!	o fuh
Caution!/Look out!	Attention!	a-tahn-see-**ohn**

Dining Out

A bottle of . . .	une bouteille de . . .	ewn boo-**tay** duh
A cup of . . .	une tasse de . . .	ewn tass duh
A glass of . . .	un verre de . . .	uhn vair duh
Ashtray	un cendrier	uhn sahn-dree-**ay**
Bill/check	l'addition	la-dee-see-**ohn**

Bread	du pain	dew pan
Breakfast	le petit-déjeuner	luh puh-**tee** day-zhuh-**nay**
Butter	du beurre	dew burr
Cheers!	A votre santé!	ah vo-truh sahn-**tay**
Cocktail/aperitif	un apéritif	uhn ah-pay-ree-**teef**
Dinner	le dîner	luh dee-**nay**
Dish of the day	le plat du jour	luh plah dew **zhoor**
Enjoy!	Bon appétit!	bohn a-pay-**tee**
Fixed-price menu	le menu	luh may-**new**
Fork	une fourchette	ewn four-**shet**
I am diabetic	Je suis diabétique	zhuh swee dee-ah-bay-**teek**
I am on a diet	Je suis au régime	zhuh sweez o ray-**jeem**
I am vegetarian	Je suis végétarien(ne)	zhuh swee vay-zhay-ta-ree-**en**
I cannot eat . . .	Je ne peux pas manger de . . .	zhuh nuh **puh** pah mahn-**jay** deh
I'd like to order	Je voudrais commander	zhuh voo-**dray** ko-mahn-**day**
I'm hungry/thirsty	J'ai faim/soif	zhay fahm/swahf
Is service/the tip included?	Est-ce que le service est compris?	ess kuh luh sair-**veess** ay comb-**pree**
It's good/bad	C'est bon/mauvais	say bohn/mo-**vay**
It's hot/cold	C'est chaud/froid	say sho/frwah
Knife	un couteau	uhn koo-**toe**
Lunch	le déjeuner	luh day-zhuh-**nay**
Menu	la carte	la cart
Napkin	une serviette	ewn sair-vee-**et**
Pepper	du poivre	dew **pwah**-vruh
Plate	une assiette	ewn a-see-**et**
Please give me . . .	Donnez-moi . . .	doe-nay-**mwah**
Salt	du sel	dew sell
Spoon	une cuillère	ewn kwee-**air**
Sugar	du sucre	dew **sook**-ruh
Waiter!/Waitress!	Monsieur!/ Mademoiselle!	muh-**syuh**/ mad-mwa-**zel**
Wine list	la carte des vins	la cart day **van**

NOTES

Fodor's Travel Publications

Available at bookstores everywhere, or call 1–800–533–6478, 24 hours a day.

Gold Guides
U.S.

Alaska

Arizona

Boston

California

Cape Cod, Martha's
Vineyard, Nantucket

The Carolinas & the
Georgia Coast

Chicago

Colorado

Florida

Hawaii

Las Vegas, Reno,
Tahoe

Los Angeles

Maine, Vermont,
New Hampshire

Maui

Miami & the Keys

New England

New Orleans

New York City

Pacific North Coast

Philadelphia & the
Pennsylvania Dutch
Country

The Rockies

San Diego

San Francisco

Santa Fe, Taos,
Albuquerque

Seattle & Vancouver

The South

U.S. & British Virgin
Islands

USA

Virginia & Maryland

Waikiki

Washington, D.C.

Foreign

Australia &
New Zealand

Austria

The Bahamas

Bermuda

Budapest

Canada

Cancún, Cozumel,
Yucatán Peninsula

Caribbean

China

Costa Rica, Belize,
Guatemala

The Czech Republic
& Slovakia

Eastern Europe

Egypt

Europe

Florence, Tuscany
& Umbria

France

Germany

Great Britain

Greece

Hong Kong

India

Ireland

Israel

Italy

Japan

Kenya & Tanzania

Korea

London

Madrid & Barcelona

Mexico

Montréal &
Québec City

Moscow, St.
Petersburg, Kiev

The Netherlands,
Belgium &
Luxembourg

New Zealand

Norway

Nova Scotia, New
Brunswick, Prince
Edward Island

Paris

Portugal

Provence &
the Riviera

Scandinavia

Scotland

Singapore

South America

Southeast Asia

Spain

Sweden

Switzerland

Thailand

Tokyo

Toronto

Turkey

Vienna & the Danube

Fodor's Special-Interest Guides

Branson

Caribbean Ports
of Call

The Complete Guide
to America's
National Parks

Condé Nast Traveler
Caribbean Resort and
Cruise Ship Finder

Cruises and Ports
of Call

Fodor's London
Companion

France by Train

Halliday's New
England Food
Explorer

Healthy Escapes

Italy by Train

Kodak Guide to
Shooting Great
Travel Pictures

Shadow Traffic's
New York Shortcuts
and Traffic Tips

Sunday in New York

Sunday in
San Francisco

Walt Disney World,
Universal Studios
and Orlando

Walt Disney World
for Adults

Where Should We
Take the Kids?
California

Where Should We
Take the Kids?
Northeast

Special Series

Affordables
Caribbean
Europe
Florida
France
Germany
Great Britain
Italy
London
Paris

Fodor's Bed & Breakfasts and Country Inns
America's Best B&Bs
California's Best B&Bs
Canada's Great Country Inns
Cottages, B&Bs and Country Inns of England and Wales
The Mid-Atlantic's Best B&Bs
New England's Best B&Bs
The Pacific Northwest's Best B&Bs
The South's Best B&Bs
The Southwest's Best B&Bs
The Upper Great Lakes' Best B&Bs

The Berkeley Guides
California
Central America
Eastern Europe
Europe
France
Germany & Austria
Great Britain & Ireland
Italy
London
Mexico

Pacific Northwest & Alaska
Paris
San Francisco

Compass American Guides
Arizona
Chicago
Colorado
Hawaii
Hollywood
Las Vegas
Maine
Manhattan
Montana
New Mexico
New Orleans
Oregon
San Francisco
South Carolina
South Dakota
Texas
Utah
Virginia
Washington
Wine Country
Wisconsin
Wyoming

Fodor's Español
California
Caribe Occidental
Caribe Oriental
Gran Bretaña
Londres
Mexico
Nueva York
Paris

Fodor's Exploring Guides
Australia
Boston & New England
Britain

California
Caribbean
China
Florence & Tuscany
Florida
France
Germany
Ireland
Italy
London
Mexico
Moscow & St. Petersburg
New York City
Paris
Prague
Provence
Rome
San Francisco
Scotland
Singapore & Malaysia
Spain
Thailand
Turkey
Venice

Fodor's Flashmaps
Boston
New York
San Francisco
Washington, D.C.

Fodor's Pocket Guides
Acapulco
Atlanta
Barbados
Jamaica
London
New York City
Paris
Prague
Puerto Rico

Rome
San Francisco
Washington, D.C.

Rivages Guides
Bed and Breakfasts of Character and Charm in France
Hotels and Country Inns of Character and Charm in France
Hotels and Country Inns of Character and Charm in Italy

Short Escapes
Country Getaways in Britain
Country Getaways in France
Country Getaways Near New York City

Fodor's Sports
Golf Digest's Best Places to Play
Skiing USA
USA Today The Complete Four Sport Stadium Guide

Fodor's Vacation Planners
Great American Learning Vacations
Great American Sports & Adventure Vacations
Great American Vacations
National Parks and Seashores of the East
National Parks of the West

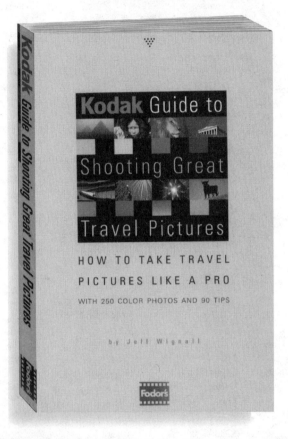